Additional praise for Jill Fredston's *Rowing to Latitude*

"A writer with a keen sense of poetry and style, [she] breathes life into the landscape by letting the land give her life."
—*Chicago Tribune*

"Beguiling." —Gail Caldwell, *The Boston Globe*

"Be it storm, bear, or iceberg, nothing is predictable in Fredston's account." —*Natural History*

"*Rowing to Latitude* would be just another human-conquers-nature thriller if it wasn't for Jill Fredston's writing. Where has she been all our lives? Erudite, heartfelt, eloquent, adventurous, witty, tragic, liberating, concerned, poetic, blunt—all this can happen on a single page, and very often does. Her entire book has the quality of the moods of the sea, vividly personalized by her ability to melt the descriptive into the spiritual. She writes rings around the mass-market travel scribblers." —Dana De Zoysa, *The Midwest Book Review*

"Fredston makes you see wilderness as a more precious commodity than you thought, and inspires you to stretch your limits physically and mentally." —Lynne McNeil, *The San Diego Union-Tribune*

"The book . . . is far more than an adventure travel narrative. It also is a deeply personal memoir and love story."
—Brian Maffly, *The Salt Lake Tribune*

"On the long list of new books devoted to explorations of what is left of the planet's wilderness, *Rowing* is among the best."
—Craig Medred, *Anchorage Daily News*

Rowing to Latitude

Rowing to

NORTH POINT PRESS

Latitude

Journeys Along the Arctic's Edge

JILL FREDSTON

A division of Farrar, Straus and Giroux New York

North Point Press
A division of Farrar, Straus and Giroux
19 Union Square West, New York 10003

Copyright © 2001 by Jill Fredston
Maps © 2001 by Jeffrey L. Ward
Distributed in Canada by Douglas & McIntyre Ltd.
Printed in the United States of America
Published in 2001 by North Point Press
First paperback edition, 2002

The Library of Congress has cataloged the hardcover edition as follows:
Fredston, Jill A.
    Rowing to latitude : journeys along the Arctic's edge / Jill Fredston.— 1st ed.
        p.   cm.
    ISBN 0-374-28180-7 (hard : alk. paper)
    1. Fredston, Jill A.—Journeys.   2. Canoes and canoeing—Alaska.   3. Women
canoeists—United States—Biography.   4. Canoeists—United States—Biography.
I. Title.

GV782.42.F74 A3 2001
797.1'22'092—dc21
[B]   2001030049

Paperback ISBN: 0-86547-655-1

Unless otherwise credited, all photographs are by the author

Designed by Abby Kagan

www.fsgbooks.com

9   10   8

For my parents,

Elinor and Arthur Fredston,

whose generosity and love long ago

exceeded my ability to thank them

Contents

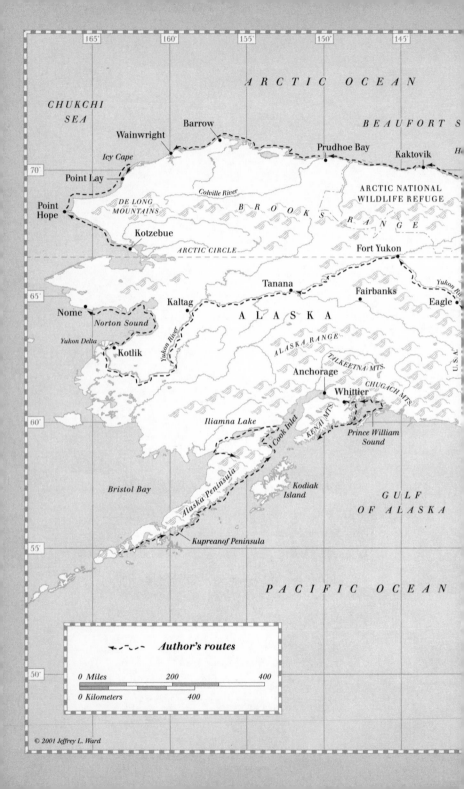

I wish to speak a word for nature, for absolute freedom and wildness.

—Henry David Thoreau, "Walking"

Preface

FOR YEARS my husband, Doug Fesler, and I have led a double life. In the winter, we work together as avalanche specialists. Then, with the lighter days of summer, we disappear (though my mother hates that word) on three-to-five-month-long wilderness rowing and kayaking trips. Somehow, more than twenty thousand miles have slid under our blades, a function of time and repetitive motion rather than undue strength or bravery.

Once, far down the Yukon River, which begins in western Canada and cleaves Alaska, an old Athabascan subsistence fisherman hailed us from his aluminum skiff. In keeping with local custom, he was in no hurry to talk, preferring to drift in silence while his eyes appraised us through a poker mask of wrinkles. In time he asked, "Where you come from?" And a minute or two later, "Where you go?" More silence, while he digested our answers. Eventually he pronounced, "You must be plenty rich to spend the summer paddling." Doug leaned back, grinned, and replied without a trace of the awkwardness I feared was lit in neon upon my face, "If we were rich, we'd have a boat with a motor like yours."

Though we are far from rich and occasionally prey to bouts of motor envy, paddling is our preferred mode of travel, at least until our joints completely disintegrate. It allows us to tickle the shoreline, and opens our senses to the rhythms around us. We are more attuned to our surroundings when we are moving at only five miles per hour, maybe six on a good day. With hours to think, it is also a little harder to escape from ourselves.

We always travel in two boats. This gives us an extra margin of safety and allows us to carry several months' worth of supplies. More important, such separation keeps us from hating each other. It would take better people than we are to share a small boat day after day and then to crawl into the same tent night after night, for weeks on end. Until 1994, there was also the practical consideration that we propelled our boats differently. I am firmly committed to rowing, which does not allow any part of my body to ride for free. My legs, when confined by the spray skirt of a kayak, instantly begin to twitch, and my arms feel cast in bronze. Doug favored kayaking for the first thirteen thousand of the miles we journeyed together; oddly, he thought it was important to see where he was going. But at last he converted, reluctantly acknowledging the greater efficiency and speed afforded by a sliding seat and long oars.

Onlookers frequently remark that they would love to do similar trips if only they had the time, or the necessary experience. No matter how often I've heard these comments, they still give me pause. As for time, we give it a high priority; if we wait too long, we will be unable to row. And we've gained the experience by doing, stroke by stroke.

Most often, though, people question why we undertake these trips at all. They might as well ask us why we breathe or eat. Our journeys are food for our spirits, clean air for our souls. We don't care if they are firsts or farthests; we don't seek sponsors. They are neither a vacation nor an escape, they are a way of life.

On a trip down the Yukon River in 1987, we made a habit of asking Native people who lived along its shores how far up- and downriver they had traveled. Usually they had ranged less than fifty miles in either direction—some a little farther in these days of snowmachines and skiffs with hefty outboard engines. Just over halfway down the river, however, at about the twelve-hundred-mile mark, we met Uncle Al, an Athabascan elder. He was slightly stooped with age but straightened when he answered, brown eyes aglow. As a young man, he said, he had traveled by canoe all the way to the headwater lakes, and had also followed the river a thousand miles from his home to the sea. When we asked why, he looked puzzled. "I had to know where the river came from and where it was going." We give a version of the same answer. We do these trips because we need to. The world of phones, computers, and deadlines cannot compare with singing birds, breaching whales, magnificent light shows, and crackling ice.

If, on the day I took possession of my first ocean shell from the canopy of a dusty truck, someone had informed me that I would row more than enough miles to take me to the far side of the world and back, I would have marveled at the notion. As with most burgeoning ventures, this book also began innocently, as a holiday letter sent annually to friends, family, and those who had helped us along the way. The letters were evidently passed along through a maze of unseen channels. Before long, we began to receive requests from people we'd never heard of to add their names to our mailing list. If laziness or a hectic avalanche season caused us to miss a year, we'd end up fielding phone calls from obscure corners of the world from people who were sure we had met one too many polar bears.

Still, I shared the skepticism of the round-faced Inupiaq man who, weary of passing visitors to the Arctic declaring themselves instant experts, invited us to his house for whale blubber only after I had assured him in good faith that I was not writing a book. It was not until our stories began to take on a life of their own—retold to us by people unaware of their origins and unlikely ever to find themselves experiencing the expanse of the Arctic firsthand—that the stirrings of the book within became much harder to ignore.

In the last few years, I've felt increasing urgency to give voice to the caribou that graze without fear along the Labrador shore, to the wide-shouldered brown bears of the Alaska Peninsula who depend upon the annual migration of salmon, to fjords uncut by roads or power lines. Doug and I are drawn to northern latitudes not out of sheer perversity, as our families claim, but because we seek wild country. The prevailing nasty weather of the sub-Arctic and Arctic can be a great deterrent to both dense settlement and tourism. But during our travels, we've witnessed the lengthening shadow of our civilization's influence over remote corners of the natural world. What finally galvanized me into writing, though, was an even more tangible reminder of the fragility of all that surrounds us. When my mother was diagnosed with advanced cancer, she said, "You have to write this book before I die." I responded, "All right, but you have to live a long time."

In the process of journeying, we seem to have become the journey, blurring the boundaries between the physical landscape outside of ourselves and the spiritual landscape within. Once, during a long crossing in Labrador, we found ourselves in fog so thick that it was impossible to see even the ends of our boats. Unable to distinguish gray water from gray air, I felt vertigo grab hold of my equilibrium, and the world began to spin. I needed a reference point—the sound of Doug's voice or the catch of my blades as they entered the water—to know which way was right side up. Rounding thousands of miles of ragged shoreline together, driven by the joys and fears of not knowing what lies around the next bend, has helped us to find an interior compass.

Doug and I have awoken many Alaska winter mornings inside cabins so fogged with the warm vapor of our dreams that we couldn't tell if the dark shape outside the window was a moose or a tree. To bring the object outside into clearer view, we had to start within, scraping a hole in the frost with our fingernails. This book begins much the same way.

Rowing to Latitude

And so in time the rowboat and I became one and the same—like the archer and his bow or the artist and his paint. What I learned wasn't mastery over the elements; it was mastery over myself, which is what conquest is ultimately all about.

—Richard Bode, *First You Have to Row a Little Boat*

1

The Pull of Rowing

WHEN I WAS TEN, my family moved to a house at water's edge in Larchmont, a well-heeled town on Long Island Sound north of New York City. Initially, I was anchored in the rose garden, with only a cheap marine air horn to engage in the bustle of my new backyard. I'd give three quick blasts, the local signal used by crews for pickup from their moored sailboats and motor cruisers, then duck behind the seawall, chortling as the launch from the yacht club circled aimlessly, looking for passengers. Though my distinguished lawyer father denies it, I'm quite sure the idea was originally his.

As a belated birthday present, my parents gave me a rowboat, on the condition that they could name it. I craved a boat so intensely that I would have sacrificed more than my pride. Promises to do dishes for a year or not to spy on my teenage sisters could have been extorted. But all my parents wanted was to choose a name. That seemed simple enough until I was marooned on the wrong side of a closed door, while the two people who theoretically loved me most in the world conferred, oblivious to the passage of time. Finally, the moment came when I was led to see my new boat. A five-foot fiberglass pram, almost as wide as it was long, with two unscratched wooden oars, a speckled blue interior, plank seat, and shiny oarlocks: it was perfect. Prominently emblazoned on its stern, in oversized black letters, were the words *Ikky Kid.* My eldest sister, Dale, insists that the name was her inspiration.

Being ten, I did not waste time pondering the message my family was trying to convey. I just launched my boat, clambered in, and rowed away to a new freedom. In hindsight, the name was a good fit. It accurately described a stick-figure brat with a tendency to whine. Dale remembers me as a nonconformist from an early age, but I think the label is a euphemism. I was stubborn, allergic to criticism, and loath to admit I was wrong. I'd back myself into corners and say things I didn't mean but was too proud to recant. "I'm not hungry," I'd assert, then wind up listening to my stomach growl through the night.

Ikky Kid provided an outlet for my frustrations. I spent most of my time in her, cruising all the crannies of Larchmont Harbor, slipping past large houses with their stone gazebos and private docks. I followed families of Canada geese as they swam sedately through rustling salt marsh grasses and surprised couples nestled in the smooth granite of a waterside park shaded by stout oak trees. I rowed to imaginary Olympic glories. Once, trying to execute one of my father's poorer plans, I towed a putrid, bloated swan that had washed up on our beach out beyond the harbor's breakwater to the main body of Long Island Sound, which stretches more than a hundred miles from open ocean off Rhode Island to New York City. I passed whole days inside that little boat, swigging warm orange juice from a carton, gobbling cookies, lying in the sun, reading, drifting. It was a world of its own, and I was the captain.

The next summer, accompanied by a friend in an equally undersized sailboat, I made the seven-mile crossing to Long Island. We swam gleefully, uninvited and unnoticed, in the outdoor pool of a stately Gatsby-type house with a sloping green lawn lined by bright beds of flowers. On our way home and scarcely a mile from Larchmont Harbor, we were stopped by the Coast Guard. A pockmarked, humorless man in an orange jumpsuit asked our ages, carefully logged our names and addresses onto a clipboard, and called our parents. It hadn't occurred to us to think about the distance or the danger. We were simply heading for another shore, propelled by a spirit that reminds me of Joseph Conrad's words: "I remember my youth and the feeling that will never come back any more—the feeling that I could last for ever, outlast the sea, the earth, and all men."

My family's turreted, slate-roofed house was one of only four on a small island. At low tide, it was close enough to the mainland so that a good long jumper might have been able to make the leap onto a thick bank of hold-your-nose muck. There was an arched stone bridge, but as far as I was concerned, living on an island meant rowing everywhere. I rowed to my junior high school, undeterred by the fact that if it was low tide when school let out, I had to walk home and return later when there was enough water in the channel to float the boat.

It is impossible to move a rowing boat across the surface of the water without leaving an imprint, a disappearing record of the boat's passage. I'll never know if *Ikky Kid* shaped the way I see the world or was simply the outlet for the person I already was. Certainly, I was given plenty of other opportunities. Regular piano lessons and long fingers didn't inspire me to be a pianist, and my mother's good cooking unfortunately did not encourage me to follow suit. I wouldn't have minded converting hundreds of hours on tennis courts into a career as a professional player, but I wasn't good enough. My tendency was to go for instant gratification, for the slam, rather than biding my time for an opening. I do know that from the moment I stepped into *Ikky Kid*, at some waterline level, I sensed the potential of using my own power to compose a life. *Ikky Kid* floated me into wider horizons, away from my circle of competitive, achievement-oriented friends, giving me room to find good company in myself and in nature.

I have a friend whose short, pudgy son was determined to play high school basketball. None of us wanted to discourage him, but the odds seemed starkly slim. Josh spent hours at the hoop in the driveway, challenging all comers to games of one-on-one. Then, seemingly overnight, he metamorphosed into two tall legs on a lean frame that almost had to stoop to enter a doorway. Everyone was surprised but him. It was as though he had known all along the possibilities within him. Rowing helped me to outgrow my Ikky Kid persona in the same way. I just bided my time and took a while to let others in on the secret.

Ikky Kid only whetted my appetite for the outdoors. Though confused by how they had ended up with a kid like me in suburban New York, my parents did everything they could to foster my interests, shipping me further and further west. In my early teens, they packed me off to a ranch camp in Wyoming, where I earned coveted status as a "roughrider" by guiding my horse through swamps and drinking, with eyes scrunched shut, snake blood that tasted suspiciously like lemon juice. With an unopened tin of snuff conspicuously stuck in the back pocket of my jeans, I came home saying *crik* instead of *creek*, and spent hours trying to lasso the dog. When I returned from a National Outdoor Leadership School (NOLS) wilderness skills course the following year, the same dog refused to eat a coffee cake I baked over a fire in the backyard but deigned to keep me company when I forsook my bed for a sleeping bag outside.

Under the misleading headline "She Practices What She Preaches," an article in the local newspaper featured a photograph of me at sixteen, looking like an orangutan with long arms and drooping shoulders. I was about to spend weeks hauling rocks with a Student Conservation Association trail crew in Yosemite National Park. In the article, I chirp, "I'm going to be involved with the wilderness for the rest of my life. If I don't do something about it now, there won't be any wilderness left later." I graduated early from high school and interned for an environmental education program in New Jersey, which wasn't as oxymoronic as it sounds. By eighteen, I was a National Park Service summer naturalist at the Grand Canyon. Photographs from that era show me looking as cool as I knew how—my left hip juts out at an angle, both hands are stuffed into the pockets of drab green pants, the trademark flat-brimmed hat is pulled firmly over my head, and the gold-colored badge over the pocket of my gray shirt appears excessively polished.

It was another small boat adventure, however, that probably deserves the credit for getting me into college. The summer before my senior year, while kayaking in Alaska's Prince William Sound on a second NOLS course, I'd been with five others when a pod of orcas surrounded our double kayaks. Orcas do not deserve the sinister reputation reflected by their common name. They are known as killer whales because they compensate for their relatively small size by hunting in packs, but they generally avoid people. In more than a month, we'd only seen their distinctive tall, triangular fins from afar. But on the second-to-last day of the trip, a group made up mostly of mothers and young materialized out of the mist. One pulled up so close that it looked as if a submarine had docked alongside our kayak. They nuzzled around us for maybe half a minute and then, with gentle exhalations, slid back beneath the sea.

None of the other group members we reunited with at trip's end believed our story of the orcas until they smelled us. Inured by days of continuous rain, we had been oblivious to the fallout of whale spout drizzling onto our clothes, hair, and hands, imbuing every surface with the essence of rotting fish. I took at least ten prolonged, peel-the-paper-off-the-walls showers in an Anchorage hotel room, then boarded a plane to head back to New York for my last semester of high school. Before the plane had even left the gate, all the passengers in my row, on both sides of the aisle, had changed their seats while I pretended I didn't know why. On the second morning of school, I received a summons from the health counselor. She said, "Jill, I don't understand it. You have always been a good student, and you've come to school dressed nicely, but your teachers are complaining that you seem to have an odor problem this year."

It is not encouraging to be seventeen years old and not know if you are going to smell like raw sewage for the rest of your life. Even my parents made me sit at the lonely end of the dining-room table. Determined to find a solution, Mom poured tomato juice over me in the bathtub because she'd heard that it neutralizes skunk odor, but I can definitively say that it does not work for whale spout. It does, however, leave deep, reddish stains that make the bathtub look like the preferred spot for nocturnal sacrifices. Desperate for ideas, I called the others in the group, including a middle-aged lawyer in California who had canceled all appointments and was conducting business by phone. A worrisome week went by before we were all restored to our fragrant selves. When the college applications asked for an essay on a recent memorable experience, I didn't have to think long.

I chose Dartmouth College in New Hampshire, where the air was clean and the mountains close. Gravitating toward courses in geography and environmental studies, I toyed with the idea of becoming an environmental lawyer, a career that struck me as a respectable compromise between a mainstream occupation and my environmental leanings. In the meantime, I rowed, not so much because I had an urge to compete as because rowing seemed an instinctive physical extension of the maturity and independence I felt in leaving home.

I was walking across the green in the center of campus when I saw my first racing shell, suspended on sawhorses, so thin it was translucent. The hull was more than sixty feet long, with eight sets of sliding seats, one right behind the other. I was no longer the scrawny kid given doughnuts at camp as part of a weight-gain program, but at five feet eight I was still made up mostly of sharp bones and right angles, with a strength born more of determination than of mass. Though team members attempting to recruit passersby of significant size overlooked me, I was hooked.

Crew boats were like nothing I'd ever rowed. The "eights" were waterborne rockets—capable of exhilarating speed that made *Ikky Kid* at her fastest look like a stunted wannabe. Learning to use my legs, arms, and back to drive a thirteen-foot oar through the water while rolling back and forth on a little wooden seat was like learning to walk again. The unified effort of my body had to be carefully synchronized with that of seven other women, while we were steered and encouraged by a small coxswain with a disproportionately large voice. When we matched each other perfectly, which didn't happen often enough to take for granted, we had "swing." Then the boat would surge forward, trailing a symmetrical signature of whirling pools from each oar.

Too frequently, swing eluded us. In our first race, we lacked the discipline to keep our hands steady, so we kept throwing the boat off balance, causing one unfortunate after another to "catch a crab"—get her oar stuck in the water. The veering boat would slow, sometimes to a stop, the coxswain would rage, and we'd thrash like dying fish before getting the boat back on course and up to speed. Only because the five other teams were similarly inexperienced did we eke out a win. In our post-race exuberance, we drifted past two sets of warning buoys and nearly went over a dam in our borrowed eight-thousand-dollar shell. It was an inauspicious start to a magnificent season in which we reigned undefeated until the final championships, when we faced corn-fed mesomorphs from Wisconsin.

My memories of that race are ragged. Someone crabbed at the start and we skidded backward, into water abandoned by the other boats. I remember the coxswain's disembodied howls coming through a speaker under my seat, exhorting us to pull as we never had before. And we did. It might be the only time in my life that I haven't held just a little bit of myself in reserve. "I HAVE THEIR SEVEN!" the voice shrieked as we drew up to the stern of the first boat ahead. "NOW GIVE ME THEIR FIVE!" Foot by foot, we clawed past the rower in the bow seat. One boat behind us, four still ahead. We became one long, gasping body with sixteen muscled arms and knotted calves. *Can't pull harder. Have to. No. Must.* Beyond logical thought, out of air, two boats behind now. Nothing but the voice, exploding waves of pain, and a rising roar of spectators. Spots in my eyes, dead legs, lungs sucked dry, heart splitting my chest, searing fire in my back. *Breathe. Can't. Must.* Only two more boats. The voice thundered. *Quit. Can't. Breathe. Can't. Must.* "LAST TEN STROKES!!" the voice promised, and counted them aloud like drumbeats. I emptied the last fragments of myself into my oar. *Die. Soon.* "FIVE MORE!" I had nothing left but a silent scream. We crossed the finish line and I slid into darkness, into a quiet that even the voice couldn't penetrate.

Consciousness came with the sound of my teammates vomiting into the water. The coxswain, a woman again, explained that it was a photo finish, a matter of inches being decided upon by officials. Eight bodies now instead of one, we lay back against one another's numb legs, swilling air, unable to ignore the pain, which was as excruciating as frozen fingers beginning to thaw. We managed a clumsy rag-doll-like row to the dock, but the world was a grainy television screen, a fuzz of speckled gray. Landing, I leaned in the wrong direction, fending off into harmless air rather than reaching for the wood float. The rest of our team poured onto the dock, knowing that we were too far gone to lift the boat out of the water and over our heads by ourselves. First place was awarded to the mesomorphs, but surprisingly, that was of little matter.

I didn't row all four years at Dartmouth, partly because foreign study kept me away during several semesters of racing, but mostly because I thought it demeaning to be in any boat other than the varsity and was afraid to take that chance. Accustomed to having most things come easily, I hadn't yet learned the discipline of total commitment. Rowing at very competitive levels means at least three hours of training every day. It means long hours in the weight room and on running trails in exchange for a few minutes of the purging euphemistically called racing. Despite the coach's constant reminders to have "fast hands" or a "quick catch," my rowing stroke never seemed to achieve the level of perfection I'd commended myself for in *Ikky Kid*. And my eyes were a problem. During practices especially, they kept wanting to drift out of the boat, and around each outside bend in the river rather than staying drilled into the back of the woman in front of me. I was discovering that at heart I am more of an endurance rower than a sprinter. For me, rowing is about more than moving fast. It is about going somewhere.

After college, a landlocked winter in Colorado's mountains, and a summer on Greenland's ice, I took rowing across the ocean with me to England, where I began graduate study in polar regions and glaciology at the University of Cambridge's Scott Polar Research Institute. I had given up on becoming an environmental lawyer when I realized that I'd seldom be outdoors. British rowing required some adaptation. For one thing, I needed to learn how to speak English, as I discovered after my first practice session, when an excited coach asked, "Can I come knock you up in the morning?" Only after an awkward pause did I understand that he wanted to round me up for an early-morning row. I enjoyed the more-than-century-old British rowing traditions, however, especially the pleasing barbarism of some of the races. The object of one series was to catch the boat that started ahead of us and literally "bump" it. Our women's four was good. We dodged dead cows floating in the narrow river channel and managed to beat the less select men's eights. With a sprig of bush in our bow to signify a win, we rowed back down the river to the genteel applause of spectators on both banks and sipped champagne from the silver cup presented to us.

It surprised me that the coaches were so enthusiastic about my rowing, but it was gratifying enough that I stifled the temptation to tell them about my bigger, more able teammates at home. I knew that while I might have become a slightly better rower, the main difference was that I was now surrounded by a pool of women who knew less about pushing themselves than I did. For the most part, female athletics in British schools were at a level and priority similar to that of the United States in the 1950s, well before Title IX mandated gender equity in sports.

The embryonic state of women's sports was just one example of entrenched British chauvinism that took me by surprise, especially in a country following its female prime minister into war over the Falkland Islands. For the first time in my sheltered life, I kept bumping up against assumptions about what I was supposed and not supposed to do because I was a woman. My face still bronzed from months of living on the Greenland Ice Sheet, I sat in mute astonishment through a private meeting with the former director of a prestigious British polar program as he railed that "gals" shouldn't be allowed to work on Arctic or Antarctic research projects. "It is very disruptive, you know," he said, as if he thought I really should know or, worse yet, agree. If I wanted to speak to a professor outside of my comparatively relaxed institute, I perceived after a few bad outings that it was best to wear a skirt.

I left England anxious to trade confined waters for open spaces, and to leave manicured greens, black academic gowns, prescribed manners, and overcooked brussels sprouts behind. Armed with a master's degree and one trophy oar, I arrived in Anchorage during the summer of 1982. It wasn't a question of whether I would explore Alaska's coastline, which beckoned with more miles than those of the lower forty-eight states combined, only of when and how. Sea kayaking was beginning to be popular, but the five weeks I'd spent as a seventeen-year-old in Prince William Sound spinning my arms like a pinwheel had convinced me that kayaks were not for me, at least not while I had legs and an understanding of leverage. The only wilderness rower I knew rowed a heavy wooden dory that made me feel like a galley slave. It surprised me that there were no rowing boats made for touring. There were recreational "ocean" shells that were sturdier and more stable than racing boats, but they were either undecked like canoes, inviting swamping in big water, or hatched over so that there wasn't room for much more than a water bottle and car keys.

Still, I had to start somewhere, so I ordered a recreational shell by phone. The sister of a friend drove it from Maine, across the country and up the Alaska Highway, while I waited impatiently, eyes flitting from the university desk where I worked to a map of Alaska on the wall. The boat, an Alden double, was eighteen feet long, with patriotic colors—a red deck, white trim, and blue hull. With its wide-open interior, it could be rowed as either a single or a double. Eventually, I would build watertight bulkheads and deck it over, making a vast storage space accessible through removable hatches and reducing the swampable area to a cockpit large enough to accommodate only the four-foot-long track for the sliding seat. Aluminum riggers extended from the track and over the gunwales of the boat, and on the end of each arm was a brass oarlock. Nine-foot-nine-inch oars, varnished to a gloss and disarmingly light, slid into these oarlocks and were held in place by a plastic collar, called a button in rowing terminology. The bottom of the boat was flat, which I gradually learned gave the boat a tendency to slide off the waves sideways in beam seas and cause me to smash my hands together. I would also discover that the lay-up of the fiberglass was relatively thin for the abuse to which it would be subjected.

On my boat's first full day in Alaska, I took her, by car and train, to Prince William Sound and headed into tidewater glacier country. No matter how far I'd come since *Ikky Kid*, for the third time in my life I needed to learn to row. I had never sculled before— that is, rowed a boat with a sliding seat and an oar in each hand.

A few years earlier I'd bought a brand-new car with a manual transmission before I knew how to shift and had to ask a friend to drive it off the lot. This time there was no one to help me steer my unscratched boat out of the harbor, so, like a drunk lurching through a sobriety test, I wove an incompetent course, praying I wouldn't ram one of the moored boats with a skipper aboard. Once safely beyond the bemused onlookers, I took stock. The sliding seat was familiar, but the oars were another story. My hands appeared to be locked in a catfight, the fingernails of the left one scraping the already bloody knuckles of the right. Out of mothballs came a college rowing drill. Ignoring the lower half of my body, I used only my arms, guiding them in the circular motion needed to drop the oars into the water and lift them back out. Now I was going somewhere, albeit slowly and with a very short stroke. Gradually, the harbor receded. When the truce between my hands appeared more than transitory, I added shoulder swing. Little by little, I began to introduce my legs, at first using just a few inches of the slide, then more and more, until I was bringing my knees all the way to my chest. Before long I had the boat moving in a more or less straight line, skimming past gravel beaches and silver skeletons of standing trees killed by the tidal wave from the 1964 Great Alaska Earthquake. It was the start of a learning curve that has carried me through progressively bigger waves, thicker ice, and stronger currents. Though the angle of the curve has gentled with experience, the fact that I'm unlikely ever to row to its end holds great appeal.

Sculling is the closest I'll ever come to being a ballerina, to creating visual music. A good rowing stroke is fluid, circular, continuous. It is unmarred by pauses, lurches, arm yanks, or back heaves. The end of one stroke is the beginning of the next, the movement so smooth and graceful that it is impossible to tell exactly where the power is coming from. It should look misleadingly easy, almost effortless. Most beginners are amazed when they fall off the seat, bang their hands together, and propel themselves in circles.

To describe rowing, I find myself closing my eyes and listening for the catch, the instant when both blades enter the water at precisely the same moment, and feeling the boat run underneath me. At the catch, my chest brushes against the steep bend of my knees, and my arms are fully extended toward the stern. People reach for my biceps when they hear I'm a rower, but really my legs and back do most of the work. Lifting my hands slightly to drop the oars into the water, I instantly lock on with my legs and thrust off the foot stretchers. The oars, with little more than the blades buried, begin to arc through the water. When my legs are about halfway down, my back starts to open up, leaning toward the bow, as though I'm sinking into a favorite soft chair with my arms outstretched. Only during the last part of the stroke do my arms bend and provide the pull to bring the oar handles to my chest. Throughout the stroke, my oar handles move in a straight plane; they do not loop upward, rowboat style, or the oar shafts would dive deep into the sea. At the finish, my hands drop down to my stomach and my knuckles rotate skyward, lifting the oars, feathering the blades so that they are parallel to the water, and pushing the oar handles aft. My legs and back follow my arms up the slide, as gently as possible, lest I push the boat in the wrong direction and lose hard-won inches. That's a complete stroke, repeated about twenty times per minute, sometimes for fourteen hours a day—the equivalent of a marathon or two—most days of the week, month after month. In rowing, rhythm is everything.

That first summer of rowing in Alaska, my college roommate, Carlie Geer, came to visit days after she had won a silver medal in single sculling at the 1984 Los Angeles Olympics and we ventured into Prince William Sound in two boats. As we planed our way around Decision Point on the return, a passing commercial fisherman cut his engine and yelled, "You guys look great. You should be in the Olympics!"

Carlie called my attention to the way my style of rowing was evolving, from reasonably finessed racing technique to pragmatic wilderness mode. I had slowed my strokes, especially the return of my hands at the end of each stroke, in order to get the most glide possible out of a loaded boat. In rough water, rather than always rowing left hand over right as is the protocol, I sometimes slid one hand in front of the other in order to keep skin on my knuckles. To help me navigate through ice and ensure that I could still rotate my neck at the end of the day, I looked alternately over each shoulder to steer rather than consistently glancing over the same one.

Doug asserts that rowing has made me dyslexic. I call the bow of the boat "the back" because it is behind me. Along the same logical lines, the stern is "the front." I steer off of a terrain feature "ahead" of me that I can see, like a notch on a ridge or a snow patch, despite the fact that it recedes as I row. In his kayaking days, Doug and I skirmished a few times when he instructed me to go left or right, causing me to turn toward the obstacle we were trying to avoid. Seeking harmony, we adopted a color-coded system based on the red and green plastic collars on the oars. Now it is "go green" or "go red."

Traveling backward, which most people think of as rowing's greatest liability, has trained me to enjoy looking at where I have been as well as to move toward objectives I can't see, ready to react to the unexpected, like a low-lying iceberg or an off-angle wave. I, of course, think this has had a beneficial influence upon my career, making me flexible, resourceful, and willing to shift in less conventional directions. My father would say that it accounts for my seasonal unemployment. With a few dramatic exceptions, though, I've rarely run into obstacles. If the shoreline is uncomplicated—that is, not cluttered with rocks or ice—I'll turn around and take a second to mentally map the next stretch of coast. I use my ears more than I ever would have guessed. They can pick up the lapping of the water against a fixed object like a rock or alert me to unexpected shallows. People walk, birds fly, I row backward to move forward.

Zen is a stroke without beginning or end. It is a sensation of being completely connected and disconnected in the same moment, a feeling of pure harmony and symmetry. It happens when my oars are just extensions of my arms and my legs seem to grow out of the boat. I am not consciously working or thinking in any disciplined way. The boat flows. I am a marionette, the boat is part of me, the water is air, the journey the ultimate magic carpet ride. Or maybe I am the boat—its heart, its motor, its spirit. My legs are pistons, I could row forever.

Any prolonged rowing causes a marked physical metamorphosis. Once, in Labrador, an urchin of a boy who could have been Oliver Twist clasped his thin fingers around my biceps and exclaimed in an almost incomprehensible 1800s Cockney accent frozen in time by the emigration of his ancestors, "Jeez, ye got lumps welded onto ye arms." I end a trip with my stomach muscles bunched in six neat compartments, hands as tough as walrus hide, sculpted shoulders, and a back that looks as if it has been implanted with bicycle tubes paralleling my spine. The bones of my buttocks are so thoroughly bruised by the rowing seat that, for months afterward, I squirm on unpadded chairs. Once, at a resort on the Alaska Peninsula, I was introduced to a florid-faced oil executive from Texas with initials for a name. He recoiled when we shook hands and looked at me as though I'd jetted in from Mars with the express purpose of horrifying him. "Honey," he said, "no woman deserves hands like that."

Doug and I try to break our bodies in slowly. We begin with five-to-eight-hour days and, over the course of about three weeks, work up to the double digits. After miles of rowing, my creaky knees may not let me leap tall buildings in a single bound, but I feel as if I could at least heft a skyscraper or two over my head. En route from Seattle, after weeks of battling headwinds, Doug rolled over in the sleeping bag one morning to inform me that he didn't think his heart was beating. On reflection, I decided I had the same problem. We took our resting pulses. They were only 37 beats per minute; during the winter, they are normally around 60. Our conditioning peak lasts until about the three-month mark. Then, led by overused joints, limited fresh food, and depleted body fat—despite calorie-laden snacks and a dollop of olive oil on almost everything—we begin to slide off the back side of the curve.

To my great regret, I never look as imposing as I feel. Inevitably, upon my return every fall, my friends exclaim, "You look terrible!" and compare my frame to that of an emaciated refugee. On a ferry south in 1995, after rowing twenty-five hundred miles from Sweden to Russia, we met a German tourist who said, "It must be a problem for a little woman like you to keep up with a big, strong man like Doug." While my brain flipped through a jukebox of responses, rejecting most of them as too scathing, Doug answered truthfully that, thanks to technique, I was faster than he.

As we've grown to better understand our needs and have taken on increasingly unforgiving coasts, the boats we row have undergone a physical transformation as well. It has been a long time since they resembled anything we could buy in a store. They are closer to extensions of ourselves, customized over the years to the point where they feel like a second skin. It seems appropriate that rowing boats are called shells. We are like turtles. Our boats are our homes, our safety dependent upon them.

Comparing a racing single to an oceangoing shell is like equating a toothpick with a log. The former is generally twenty-six feet long and weighs less than a pound per foot. Any rower forgetful enough to let go of the oars can flip like a pancake. Paddling in rough water or landing in surf is as unthinkable as driving a Ferrari on a road covered with deep snow. Wilderness rowing requires boats that are fast but stable and forgiving enough to let us stand in the cockpit to stretch or scout a route through ice. They must be light enough to allow us a hernia-free way of hauling them up the beach at night, sometimes hopping slimy boulders in the process. And they must have ample cargo capacity inside secure, watertight bulkheads. More room for food means greater range, more freedom to stay out longer and reach more remote, wilder country.

In British Columbia, at the dock of a fish-packing plant where several wayfaring yachts were moored, I met a rumpled man in his thirties who was very interested in our "canoes." I still remember my bewilderment that he could so differently perceive my boat, with its riggers and oars. But we kept chatting. I asked him in turn about his "canoe" and he invited me aboard. *Winter Hawk* was forty-eight feet long, with three queen-size beds, a washer/dryer, a dishwasher, a trash compactor, and a video intercom that reached into every corner of the boat. Doug later reported that the engine-room floor was clean enough to use as a plate, but I was preoccupied by the full-sized couch. It was luxuriously soft and I spent as much time as I could on it, tantalized by the idea that I could lie motionless while the boat traveled.

The man's mother graciously plied me with oranges and confessed, in a thick Oklahoma drawl, that she had thought they were "roughing it" before they met us. It was apparent to both his mother and me that though we had traveled the same coast, what we had seen and heard and felt had been shaped by our modes of travel. She knew the harbors, I looked for beaches. The distances between places seemed shorter to her—a mile was a matter of scant minutes and fuel. She saw green walls of forests while I, closer to shore, discerned individual trees. No locals along the way had taken one look at *Winter Hawk* and insisted that the owners come home with them for the night. This kind woman with a neat gray bun on top of her head couldn't fathom how we could feel comfortable moving so slowly, perched only inches above the waterline. I struggled for words to explain why, for me, that was precisely the draw. Our boats don't allow much insulation from the environment; they force us to be absorbed by it.

It's a reliable maxim that most boaters are convinced that their particular craft is the ultimate. On the Yukon, we met four Germans floating the river on a barge they'd built by lashing six rusty oil drums with fraying rope, piecing together a plywood platform from scraps, and scavenging a ratty green couch. This ragged approximation of something capable of floating didn't stop one of them from commenting on my shell, "God, that's a strange boat to find on the Yukon." Owners of big boats are especially skeptical of anything smaller. But at times our boats seem safer than their larger counterparts. When conditions get rough and the captains of forty-foot vessels are seeking anchorages and fretting about their exposure to the storm, we simply tie down our boats well above the tideline and go read in the tent.

On my first long rowing trip with Doug, a Canadian customs official asked for the name of my modified Alden double. I hesitated, embarrassed to admit that my boat was nameless, but Doug stepped in, confidently christening her *Ikky Kid II*. Later he renamed her *The Mother* (pronounced "muthuh") *Ship* because of her weight and impressive cargo capacity. She seemed always to have room for the rock or oversized bone he wanted to cart home.

Eventually, I moved on to other hull designs and sold *The Mother Ship* to a friend I'd taught to row by putting a rowing frame on top of our woodpile so that the oars would clear the ground. Seeing the distress in my eyes, Claire promised that *The Mother Ship* would write me regularly about her excursions with "the new gal." Her successor was *Princess*, so named to reinforce my reputation as a wicked stepmother after I'd dubbed a heavier, wider, slower boat Doug's daughter Sunna was rowing *Porky*. *Princess* was the product of a collaboration with Mike Neckar of Necky Kayaks near Vancouver, Canada.

Mike is a former Czechoslovakian national whitewater kayak champion who typically greets me by thrusting my body over his head and then bouncing me once or twice off his trampoline-like belly. Wielding a saw in one hand, he helped design the boat with a casualness that belied tremendous knowledge. If we thought the bow was too long, he chopped it off. Several times I flew to Seattle and drove north to the Canadian border with my oars and rowing frame to test his latest idea. Usually, I was just rowing a plug, basically the plywood-and-cedar-strip mold from which the boat would be made. It had sides that extended no more than a couple inches above the water. Mike would slap in a few horizontal supports for rigidity and brush on a little fiberglass resin to keep it afloat for a short, though unspecified, period of time. We'd drive it to a nearby pond with enough duck poop to fertilize all the cornfields in Iowa. Then Mike, and sometimes Doug, would wait impatiently while I pushed off in a paper-thin hull that wasn't even a boat, not knowing whether it would immediately dunk me into scum that was water in name only.

As a starting point, Mike used the hull of a double sea kayak called a Tofino that he already manufactured. He reconfigured the deck so that the only open area was the cockpit, which was rimmed by a raised mahogany-and-plastic coaming, or freeboard, built by Doug as a splash guard. *Princess* is twenty feet long, thirty-three inches at her widest point, and is made of Kevlar, a material that is stronger and lighter than fiberglass. With the frame for the sliding seat and oarlocks screwed into the cockpit, she weighs in at roughly 120 pounds. Her pointed, lifted bow resembles a shark's jaw and rides well in turbulent seas, keeping me relatively dry rather than drenching me with spray.

Princess is a cargo hog, with capacity for three months of food and Arctic gear inside her three watertight bulkheads. As with her predecessor, the bow and stern compartments are accessible through large removable hatches. We've also put small circular hatches at the far ends of the bow and stern decks to make it easier to pull gear in and out of the remoter recesses. The third hatch, a Plexiglas door, opens directly into the cockpit. This space is nicknamed "the refrigerator" and makes an ideal place to store cheese, which, for weight distribution, should be near the center of the boat. I also stow lunch here, comforted by its proximity.

I pushed off in *Princess* for the first time in northwestern Alaska, on a trip that began with a three-hour crossing of Kotzebue Sound. I had loaded the boat the same way I was used to loading *The Mother Ship,* with most of the weight in the bow. Just when we had paddled far enough away from the beach for it to be counterproductive to return, I realized that my boat wasn't capable of going in a straight line. It seemed to wander in a variety of wide arcs, depending on the initial direction it was knocked off course by a wave. While I worked my way into a tantrum, Doug kept studying the boat, asking annoyingly analytical, rational questions. By the time we finished the crossing, he had convinced me to repack the boat, putting more weight in the stern to help it track. The boat has gone in a straight line ever since.

Princess is like an old, comfortable shoe where every toe has a well-defined place. I trust her. She has kept me afloat in northwest, southwest, and southeast Alaska and carried me just about the full length of the Labrador coast twice. In all, I've rowed her over eight thousand miles. But in 1991, the summer we discovered why the Inuit invented kayaks instead of rowing boats, when we harnessed ourselves like mules and pulled our boats across a mostly frozen ocean and wet gravel beaches, I began to resent every one of her 120 pounds, especially as Doug's kayak weighed two-thirds less. We started to scheme about a boat that could handle the water as well as the Tofino but was lighter and smaller so that it might be more maneuverable in thick ice.

More visits with Mike Neckar ensued. We built one whole boat, a modification of a single kayak, before we discovered that she was too skittish for our purposes. By our next attempt, Mike was tired of customizing individual boats. He wanted to make a mold of the top deck and produce a number of rowing boats at a time. When he asked if I thought I could get ten orders, I called him back the next morning to give him the names of ten people whose deposits were in the mail.

The result was the Amarow, an adaptation of another Necky double kayak called an Amaruk. It is nineteen feet five inches long, also made of Kevlar, and weighs about sixty pounds empty. The hull is narrower than the Tofino's, but keeps its twenty-nine-inch beam for a comparatively long stretch, so that it is equally stable. Though the Amarow is slightly shorter, with a bow more like a pelican's mouth than a shark's jaw, it has just as much cargo capacity as the Tofino. Doug needs about four days to customize a boat into shape once it arrives by barge, including building a coaming, fiberglassing in blocks to hold the removable rowing frame, and reinforcing vulnerable parts of the hull.

As of this writing, there are twenty-four Amarows in the world. Some of the people who committed three thousand dollars to buying a boat, oars, and rowing frame were die-hard kayakers, attracted by the idea of using their whole body to row. The competitive kid in me misses being the captain of a one-of-a-kind boat. But there is a deep satisfaction in hearing Doug or another brainwashed convert rattle through the same well-worn explanations. Yes, the rowing boat is seaworthy. No, it isn't too hard to row backward. And so on.

Traveling with rigid boats longer than your average car is not an easy proposition. Our two Amarows made their way to Sweden via barge, truck, and freighter. We rowed to Russia and ferried the boats back to Tromsø, Norway. A supply boat carried them to Bjørnøya, a dot in the Arctic Ocean, and the following spring a coast guard vessel provided a lift to Spitsbergen, east of Greenland. They made their own way around the island, with us at the oars. At the end of the trip, we were unsure how to get them home, reluctant to keep asking favors of friends of friends. So, after anxious debate, we sawed the hulls in half. While I fretted uselessly nearby, Doug and our partner, John, borrowed an electric saw in exchange for a fifth of whiskey and sliced each boat in two, right through the middle of the cockpit. It seemed a blatant act of mutilation, like sawing off a foot. The boats, which had looked so perfect minutes before, now looked deformed and pitifully fragile. I was shaken by the reminder that the indomitable craft to which I entrusted my life on cold oceans was really a mere one-eighth inch of ragged Kevlar.

The Amarows might never float again, but at least they fit on the plane. We flew with them from Spitsbergen to Copenhagen. On the next plane to Seattle, the pilot switched on the intercom and, in a crisp Scandinavian accent, apologized for the half-hour delay at the gate, explaining, "There is something jammed on the loading dock." Doug and I, surmising correctly what was stuck, slunk down into our seats behind newspapers, willing ourselves invisible.

At home, we had extra-strong fiberglass bulkheads built so that the bow and stern sections could be reattached. I wanted to bolt the stern section of my red boat to Doug's yellow bow, but he wasn't interested. We now have break-apart boats, though the process of putting them together or taking them apart takes about half a day per boat. Once they are bolted together, they do not leak a drop.

After a second summer rowing in Greenland, we flew home with all our gear rather than leaving it for another season as planned. The hitch was that we had a stopover in New York and would then be transferring to a less cooperative airline. From my parents' house, I called the airline to put a note in our reservation that we'd be traveling to Alaska with "kayaks." The agent informed me curtly, "We absolutely don't take boats of any kind. You can ship them as cargo, in which case they can travel on the same plane." I called cargo, but they quoted an outrageous price.

What to do? In the middle of a toss-and-turn night, I decided that we didn't have boats, we had "yakboards." I knew that surfboards were allowed on board for an overweight charge of fifty dollars and was quite sure that yakboards wouldn't surface on a computer list as forbidden. Doug, dubious but humoring me, went to a hardware store and bought heavy black plastic, which he wrapped around each boat section. At the airport, he asked a skycap about the procedures for checking our shotgun, which was stowed inside one of the boat sections. "Oh, don't walk through that door," the skycap cautioned, pointing toward the security gate we'd have to pass through before reaching the ticket counter.

"If you do, they are going to have to call Port Authority and, Lord have mercy, you're going to wish you'd never been born. Let me get a ticket agent to come out here to check you in."

At the car, we had a conversation that could have convinced a sane man he was crazy. "We don't take canoes or kayaks," insisted the agent. "Oh," I responded in my friendliest tone, "these aren't boats, they are yakboards." After numerous iterations, the agent and her supervisor decided that our nine-foot-long, more than two-foot-thick boat sections were yakboards after all. Walking to the counter with Doug, the agent asked, "What exactly is a yakboard, anyway?" Without missing a beat, Doug described something that was a cross between a boogie board and a surfboard. The agent did not even look twice when attaching a baggage tag to the "poles," our bundled package of oars with obvious handles and blades.

At the Anchorage airport, as I was dragging one boat section across the floor toward our waiting truck, an agent of the same airline greeted me with a smile. "So, you've been kayaking? Good for you!"

The day is colorless and cold, fog shrouds the fjord, seaweed scents the air. It is early in the morning, sadistically early, but somehow Doug and I are up and moving. From inside my hood, my field of vision is limited to Doug, kayaking about twenty feet from me. Knowing that there is no floating ice, I steer off of him, not bothering to turn around. I row with my eyes half closed, over black water that feels like silk. The oars drop into the water with a sharp, clean bite at the beginning of each stroke. I am no longer obsessing about bed. In time, Doug notices that my boat is beginning to veer gently off course. He paddles a little harder to catch up and observes me carefully. My arms and legs are working in unison, my face is peaceful, my mouth is wide open. He watches me for another half mile before he decides that it is abnormal to sleep while rowing and wakes me. Doug reports that even when I sleep in the tent at night, my arms and legs spasm as though I am rowing. He flatteringly describes it as akin to sleeping with a frog.

In wilderness rowing, I found a synthesis of my love of nature and my passion for rowing, a balance point that felt like the perfect union of body and soul. There weren't seven other people to follow or a coxswain to steer and urge me on. I was the only rower, so I didn't have to worry about being the best. I didn't even know anyone who could tell me what I needed to know. At almost every turn, there was something to figure out—what shape hull would best grip the side of a mountainous swell, how to pack gear for a hundred days, how to do surf landings, how to keep mind and body going when terrified, bored, or bones-to-dust exhausted. Along the coast of Norway in 1995, we were often told, "You are very brave to live in the nature." The implication was that we needed courage to master the storms, the sudden winds, the torrential rains, and the big seas. But these are things that can never be mastered. If what we do has required any courage at all, it is in attempting to master ourselves. Wilderness rowing is far more than sport to me; it has been a conduit to knowing and trusting myself. It is my way of being, of thinking, of seeing. My rowing has taken me north and pushed me to explore my own horizons. In the process, rowing has evolved from something I do to some way that I am. Figuratively and literally, I have spent years rowing to latitude.

It is something—it can be everything—to have found a fellow bird with whom
you can sit among the rafters while the drinking and boasting and reciting and fighting
go on below; a fellow bird whom you can look after and find bugs and seeds for;
one who will patch your bruises and straighten your ruffled feathers and mourn
over your hurts when you accidentally fly into something you can't handle.

—Wallace Stegner, *The Spectator Bird*

2

Tufluk Kabloona

ANCHORAGE BEGAN as a tented railroad construction camp in 1915. Home to more than half the population of Alaska, it is now a generic sprawl of squat shopping malls, wedged between the Chugach Mountains and Cook Inlet, which extends more than two hundred miles inland from the ocean. The cars parked outside Kmart proclaim "The Last Frontier" on their license plates. Although the city is nicknamed "Los Anchorage," vestiges of frontier Alaska remain. Small planes, on floats, wheels, or skis, buzz continually overhead, coming from or going to "the bush." Chinked log cabins lean quietly into the shadows of oil company headquarters. Moose wander main streets, lynx cross the ski trails that weave through town, bears ransack garbage cans. The few business suits about are worn mostly by those who work in the tallest buildings. Pile-jacketed people are always heading out on wilderness trips and, in summer, exchanging tips about salmon runs or particularly prolific blueberry patches. Avalanches claim victims in places that are only a twenty-minute drive from downtown. New arrivals to the North are spoken of disparagingly as cheechakos, innocents who might not even know that the term "Outside" refers to the lower forty-eight states. The sun rises only 6° above the horizon on the darkest day of the year. Fiery March sunsets glow for over an hour, and in June it is possible to read outdoors at midnight. Probably the most commonly asked question is "How many years have you lived here?" In Alaska, long residence is a badge that buys more credibility than schools attended or jobs held.

En route to a summer of hiking in the Arctic in 1982, I passed through Anchorage and dropped in at the University of Alaska's Arctic Environmental Information and Data Center. I knew nothing about the place but its name, which seemed a perfect composite of most of my extracurricular and academic life to date. Delighting in the contrast to prim England, where letters of introduction were needed for virtually everything, I was immediately ushered through the low-slung concrete building to meet with the director of the center. In his late fifties, Dave Hickok looked like the captain of a ship, which, in a sense, he was. While his dog, Hey You!, lay underneath the round confer-ence table, Dave bounded from subject to subject—one minute describing Anchorage rent open in 1964 by an earthquake releas-ing ten million times the energy of the atomic bomb at Hiro-shima, the next explaining the politics of Native land claims. He might as well have leapt to a window, flung it wide, and cried, "Here it is—Alaska! The place for you!" The obvious reason for me to move to Alaska was that, given my specialty in snow and ice, there weren't too many other places where I could find a job. But the steely pragmatism for which I am known supplies only a

partial truth. My whole self, every fiber, craved Alaska's unique-
ness, its possibilities, its wildness.

The center had never had a position for a snow and ice specialist, but Dave was an investor in people. "I'll tell you what, honey,"
he said. "You go off to the Brooks Range and let me see what I
can do. And while you're in Anaktuvuk Pass"—a Nunamiut
Inupiat village of about three hundred people—"look up my
friend Riley." By the time I returned six weeks later, a job had
miraculously been advertised in the newspaper for someone with
credentials exactly like mine, and my résumé had been slipped
into the mill. Almost before my laundry dried, I was hired. No
references were called; in typical Alaskan style, Dave took me at
my word. Already I had an inkling that he would figure strongly
in my life, though neither of us could know that he was about to
launch me in the avalanche business, or that ten years later, long
after Dave had tried to set me up with his son Bruce, I would dig
Bruce's body out of an avalanche.

Exactly as I'd hoped, I now had the chance to meld my interests in applied science and wilderness, to work outdoors on projects that required me to think. Anything frozen was deemed my
purview—I studied the noisy chaos of river ice breaking up in
the spring and charted the seasonal movement of sea ice on
Alaska's oceans. Within a short time of my arrival, responsibility
for the Alaska Avalanche Forecast Center was shifted from the
federal government to the university, prompting Dave to float my
name as lead forecaster and potential director. "Jill knows something about snow," he said, with the confidence of a magician.
"She can learn whatever she needs to."

Doug Fesler was the state's reigning avalanche authority, so
widely respected and well known that in Alaska his name was
practically synonymous with the subject. When his opinion was
sought, he urged against my selection. Looking right through the

veneer of fancy colleges and credentials on my résumé, Doug said, "What does she know about avalanches?"

The truth was I knew nothing about them. However, as with the outdoors in general, my fascination with snow had started early. Photographs of me at age seven show me doing pretty much the same things I've ended up getting paid for—holding pieces of ice, falling on skis, and shoveling snow. Still, as far as I knew I had never even seen an avalanche, though years later, when Doug asked to see my photographs of a surging glacier on which I had worked in Canada, in the background were the remains of a huge slab avalanche.

Doug was right about me, but I was tapped for the job. I first laid eyes on him shortly after my hire, when I snuck into the back row of the museum auditorium where he was speaking about the avalanche history of Alaska. "Does Alaska have an avalanche problem?" he asked, then set about answering the question with photograph after photograph he'd taken of mangled trains, buried roads, shredded power lines, and houses jammed with snow. Doug explained that he had first become interested in avalanches as a park ranger when he'd had to recover the bodies of avalanche victims from places he wouldn't have hesitated to go himself. Subsequently, he had created a school to educate others. He looked the part of an avalanche expert, with a solid torso, eyes squeezed into a perpetual squint, and a huge beard that gave him the aura of a mountain sage. I knew myself for what I was—an imposter who'd become interested in avalanches because they had been assigned.

I made the rounds of most of the avalanche workers in the state, eagerly scribbling into a crisp stenographer's pad while they raged about everything that had been wrong with the federally administered forecast center. The list was long. Although the center was responsible for issuing avalanche and mountain weather forecasts, it had been run by meteorologists who had no familiarity with mountains or snow. One of them had arrived at the local ski resort to check out the location of several high-elevation weather stations clutching a brand-new pair of skis with no bindings. Incredulous ski patrollers asked him how he intended to fasten his boots to the skis. When he asked how this might be done, they answered flippantly, "We'll just drive a couple nails through the soles." "Okay," he said. The same meteorologist crawled awkwardly out of a helicopter at a ridge-top weather station four thousand feet above the Seward Highway near Anchorage. Six years of technical training in meteorology did not prevent him from asking, "Why is it so cold up here?"

Though such incompetence had disgusted him, Doug was the only avalanche specialist to spend much time giving me constructive advice. The first time I visited his office, a clutter of ski poles, shovels, and ropes strewn among stacks of paper, I prayed I wouldn't ask too stupid a question. With winter fast approaching, Doug had far too much to do to take me on as a project. He said in a friendly growl, "If you want to learn about avalanche dragons, you have to go to the den of the dragons. Put on your fat boy pants, rappel into the starting zones when the storms are howling, watch the slopes load, measure the slope angles, and see what it takes to make them slide." I nodded knowingly, though I didn't have a clue what fat boy pants were and the rest of the mission sounded like a death sentence.

After surreptitious research, I went out at lunchtime and purchased a pair of surplus olive-green insulated overalls, otherwise known as fat boy pants, at an Army/Navy store. I also bought three alarm clocks, which I placed six feet from my bed, halfway to the bathroom, and at the brink of the shower. Their cumulative jangle was barely enough to get me stumbling toward the office at the perversely necessary, bottomlessly black, frost-on-the-windshield hour of four-thirty in the morning.

When the office work was done, and on days off, I drove into one of the four mountain ranges within sight of Anchorage. If the weather was good, I'd stretch climbing skins over the bottoms of my cross-country skis and climb a couple thousand feet to the fracture lines of recently released slides, a bungling detective trying to piece together contributing factors. When it was bad, I'd take a deep breath, cinch my hood, lower my goggles, and force myself out of my car. I was the kid who always whined about her cold fingers. Nervous when confronted with heights, I flunked slides in nursery school. But I was also a good student, and this was how I had been told to learn. I lowered myself by rope onto a slope and sat for hours, making crabbed, cold notes about the anatomy of the storm and corresponding changes in the snow layers. The snowpack has various ways of announcing when it is ready to avalanche. It can make heart-stopping *whumphing* noises, indicating the collapse of a critical weak layer, or send cracks arcing across a slope, giving notice that the snow is humming with built-up elastic energy like a dangerously stretched rubber band. When the snow was in such a critical state, I'd try to tip the balance by jumping on small slopes from a safe spot. No sooner had one slope thrilled me by breaking into blocks, accelerating into a cloud of white, before I'd be looking for another candidate to make avalanche. At home, every surface was covered with drying gear or a jumble of books on meteorology and snow, cracked open and awash in yellow highlighting.

Doug's work and mine overlapped, so we saw each other frequently. Each occasion was an opportunity for me to ambush him with questions, for which he always seemed to have clear, detailed answers. When we helicoptered into the mountains, he was an encyclopedia of facts and lore. The names of fluted peaks and dates of memorable avalanches rolled off his tongue while I tried to memorize them all. Doug knew the lay of the ridges and alpine valleys so intimately that once, when I asked him to close his eyes in a helicopter, he was able to tell where we were just by the turns the pilot was making.

One season ticked into another, separated by only four green months of summer. I spent so much time lurking about avalanche dens that I began to think like an avalanche dragon. I knew where they lived and what fired them to life. Doug told me that I was the fastest learner he'd ever seen, which only fueled my desire to learn more. We often went together to test the stability of the snow, investigate accidents, or search for victims. By the time my third season melted away, the forecast center was thriving, and I'd begun to anticipate Doug's lines when we taught avalanche workshops. Together, we'd written a well-received avalanche book. He had become the kind of friend you have as a kid. We would romp around through snowy mountains tinted purple by midafternoon sunsets, then go home to separate lives. He was thirteen years older and lived with his wife and three daughters—Lahde, Sunna, and Turi— in a log cabin. I had a handsome, smart boyfriend, an apartment above a bingo parlor, and definite expectations of what my life would be like.

My friend Nan describes me during this period of my mid-twenties as "a walking chemistry experiment." I was very sure of myself, with opinions as absolute as pure elements. The best mates were close in age. Love was a matter of conscious choice. Divorce was failure. Fat people should work out more. Vulnerabilities were to be hidden. Aging was to be dreaded. I summed up people's assets and liabilities as I perceived them, making snap judgments based upon appearance, educational background, or career path. Nan says it was fascinating to watch the alchemy that occurred as I allowed more and more gray into the mix, forming fiercely loyal attachments to people who did not fit my strict formulas. She points to Doug as a prime example.

I grew up on the East Coast, where academic credentials are a good part of who you are. Doug flunked the second, ninth, and eleventh grades. *Sshhhh*, I would think every time he announced that he had liked those grades so much, he'd done them twice. I did not yet appreciate that it had taken decades, and the discovery that he was dyslexic, for Doug to be able to make such jokes. At fourteen, feeling unwanted and branded as a failure, Doug had run away from home for the first time, living under a tarp in a nearby woods for six days until defeated by teenage hunger. His self-esteem wasn't helped by the guidance counselor who advised him that since he would never make it through high school, his best bet was to drop out and join the Army.

Fortunately, Doug was self-reliant and adventurous. When he was four, living in rural Illinois, his mother would send him outside to amuse himself. He had a habit of expanding his allowed perimeter, wandering in mazes of tall cornstalks or to the small pond across the road to pick watercress and spy on ducks. Some days, he would flag down the driver of the county's big orange road grader. His face still lights up remembering the sense of power he had, squeezed into the sliver of lap space between the operator's potbelly and the oversized steering wheel.

When Doug and I were driving back to Alaska from Labrador in 1989, we saw an exit for Dundee on the interstate outside of Chicago. "Dundee!" Doug exclaimed. "That's my old stomping ground. Let's see if we can find my old house." I was intent on covering miles westward, and skeptical that, without an address, Doug could find a house he'd left when he was four. But Doug clearly recalled, even anticipated, specific clumps of trees and bends in the road. He directed me through town, intently studying shadows on the hills and gauging our position relative to a large red-brick smokestack. With almost no meandering, he led us to the house, which was, predictably, dramatically smaller than he recalled. We walked into the woods to find the pond but there was no water anywhere. Just as I was questioning the credibility of his memory, we noticed that a cluster of trees was growing in a slight depression. They were about a foot thick, smaller and younger than the surrounding trees. The pond of Doug's childhood was in the process of becoming a forest.

By the time Doug was six or seven, his greatest fear was that when he grew up, he would have to dress each day in a stiff gray business suit, wear slippery-soled leather shoes, and commute by crowded train, briefcase in hand, to a city of sirens. His father, a shoe company executive, followed this ritual unquestioningly, as did the other adult men Doug knew, leaving home early and returning late. To Doug, the idea of working in an office every day seemed like a life sentence, with no option for parole.

One day, Doug dragged home a very dead, very smelly woodchuck almost as big as he was. Thus began a lifelong passion for natural history and for collecting—rocks, bird nests, bones, butterflies, rusty horseshoes, and live bullfrogs were all fair game. Over time, he put together larger collections of fossils, arrowheads, shells, feathers, stamps, coins, menus, postcards, and photographs. By the time he was a teenager, his room, with its shelves of carefully catalogued and indexed artifacts, looked like a museum, and he had become the youngest member of the Massachusetts Archaeological Society. For Doug, the process of collecting is a way of figuring how the pieces of the puzzle fit together, a means of making sense of the world around him. Though he has lost most of his early collections, he still ends most trips with rocks in his pockets—and, if he is sufficiently stealthy, in mine.

In high school, the only subject in which Doug excelled was art. The clay sculptures, wood carvings, and drawings from his teenage years, with gnarled hands and twisted faces, reflect his pain. Still intensely personal, his art today is shaped by nature. A bird he carved from cottonwood bark conveys not only the flutter of wings but the character of the tree. A wolf mask made of whalebone, with caribou antler eyes, hangs in our kitchen, speaking of open spaces and long winters. Doug says that he feels like the "great white imposter" because his art so closely resembles that of Alaska Natives. But the common language can be explained by a powerful shared bond with nature.

Doug left home for good toward the end of the eleventh grade. A spark inside told him there must be something better out there, and his only chance of survival was to go look for it. By some means he can't remember or even justify since he was most comfortable in forests and hills, Doug found his way to New York City. He slept in alleys because he couldn't find any benches that weren't full, and used his last $1.50 to purchase entry to the New York World's Fair. Doug made the rounds of thirty-nine restaurants until he was hired at a cheap steak-house chain in the bowels of the Wisconsin Pavilion.

I was six that summer, with a pixie haircut, teeth that begged for braces, and the nickname Barnacle because of my propensity to climb on people. My family often visited the World's Fair, which was less than an hour's drive from home, but I'm sure we never ate a $1.99 steak dinner prepared by Doug. We were too busy trying foreign foods. I sampled my first Belgian waffle, my first crepe, my first fondue.

My mother and father, who hadn't traveled much in their own youth, were determined to open the world to us. They took us to

Europe for the first time when I was seven. Every day, they would send me and my sisters into small shops to select bread, cheese, and chocolate for lunch. Although we sometimes ended up eating cheese that tasted like laundry soap, we learned how to use the local currency.

My parents carefully planned that trip and the many that followed to blend heavy hits of culture—museums, castles, and theaters—with wandering and outdoor fun. We went skiing in Switzerland, gaped at a snake charmer in a crowded Moroccan square, and visited hill tribes in Thailand. Dad insisted that his daughters learn to read maps, explaining that this would allow us to find our way anywhere on earth. We took turns being navigator, while my mother was relegated to the back seat. Each day, we were also required to write at least a few lines in our trip journals. My printed entries are a thread to my past, part of the tangle of memories—real, retold, and revamped—that comprise the legacy of self.

How do we become who we are? Until I was ten, I shared a room with Susan, older than me by three years. We lived in a state of uneasy détente, with an inviolate border down the middle of the room and negotiated neutral zones: the closet (on my side) and the door (on hers). She grew up to have five children, lives in a spacious, elegant house in a New York suburb, dresses well, and is a gourmet cook. Dale, three years her senior, is a lawyer with two children. Childless, I live more than three thousand miles away, in a house with barely functioning plumbing and windows that get sucked out by wind. I dress in jeans and pile pullovers, and if Doug, my designated cook, is away, subsist as I can or beg dinner invitations.

My sisters and I lead very different lives, but we can trace a common interest in far-flung cultures to our childhood. Dinners at our house were like board meetings-cum–social studies classes, with a steady flow of foreign guests associated with my father's work abroad. The three of us ate with the adults and were encouraged to engage in general conversation. Dale recalls a very reserved Pakistani woman unwrapping fold after fold of her red silk sari in response to our curiosity. We learned not to be intimidated by the titles attached to people's names but to search for the stories they had to tell.

I get my pragmatism from my father, who took an introductory psychology course as a college freshman and, concluding that it adequately explained the unhappiness of his childhood, eschewed further courses or years of therapy. I get my candor from him too, a habit that can create its own share of trouble. But I hope I also come by my parents' compassion and generosity. Because Alaska is so far from anywhere, friends often take on the importance of family. My mother and father have made my friends their own. When Nan and her husband were in New York to seek treatment for John's cancer, my parents insisted on putting them up; my childhood home became John's last home. When another friend was diagnosed with breast cancer, my mother jumped on a plane to come help take care of her and her four-month-old baby. I talk to my parents on the phone daily, often twice a day. Friends tell me this is not normal but I cannot imagine it any other way.

While I was chatting with dignitaries at the dinner table, Doug was plotting an escape from the chaos of the steak house. After six weeks, detesting city noise and hustle, he began hitching west. In the years before he could afford a car, he'd end up hitchhiking tens of thousands of miles, crisscrossing North America so many times that it became a personal geography. When he had fifteen cents, Doug would go into a diner and order tea, which he'd fill with cream. Then he'd garner all the crackers from the baskets on the counter and load them with free butter and sugar.

One morning, a stranger bought him a real breakfast, saying simply, "You can return the favor by buying a meal for another kid who needs it someday."

Doug came in off the road in North Dakota, where he had relatives on his mother's side of the family. They still ranched and farmed the land, known for "nine months of winter and three months of tough sledding," that their Norwegian ancestors had pioneered three generations before. But the relative who owned several farms offered no help, so Doug went to the three bars in town and asked every man on a stool for work. Most thought they might need somebody until they learned he was from Massachusetts. Eventually, Doug found a job gassing vehicles, turning weeds, picking rocks, baling hay, and hauling grain, seven days a week, from four-thirty in the morning to ten at night, for eight dollars and, even better, six farm meals a day.

After harvest, Doug journeyed only as far as Fargo before an aunt persuaded him to finish high school, which he did while working forty-six hours a week. He attended college mostly to prove to himself as well as to his naysayers that he could do it, subsisting on beans and cans of cat tuna.

Doug hitchhiked to Alaska for the first time in 1966, when I was eight. He arrived with $7.28 in his pocket, not enough for the YMCA, so he slept at the Rescue Mission. By then, he'd learned that if he didn't believe in himself no one else would, and he had made a habit of responding with dogged determination when people told him what he couldn't do. Alaska in pre-pipeline days didn't have many jobs, so he took what he could—longshoreman, firefighter, carny, housepainter, fisherman, carpenter, road striper, psychiatric aide. By the mid-1970s, he was chief ranger of a newly designated half-million-acre wilderness park behind Anchorage. Before the turn of the decade, he had created his niche as an avalanche expert, gaining international recognition.

But the man whose identity rests on his ability always to find a way failed to do so in his marriage, which faltered after seventeen years. In the mid-1980s, as I was tackling yet another project I knew nothing about—building a house for myself—Doug asked if he could camp on my land in the mountains above Anchorage. He needed, he said, just to wake up hearing birds sing. Before long, he and another newly homeless friend had set up their tents in the meadow out beyond the daunting piles of plywood. Soon, bachelor laundry lines stretched from tree to tree.

I fell in love with Doug because there was no danger of falling in love with him. To my practical mind, he simply was not a candidate for partner. I loved a lot of things about him. I loved the way his smile started at the corner of his eyes and spread down into his beard until the white of his teeth emerged like the moon. I loved his knowledge, his competence, his ability to cut to the chase, his gentle spirit. I loved the same things he loved—two hawks playing on air, the rawness of storms, dry grass blowing in the wind, the uncompromising beauty of the mountains. But love him in the definitive, lightning-strike kind of way, the mental billboard of a million white lights flashing: *This is the man I am going to marry and spend my life with*? No, I knew with certainty that wouldn't happen. He was older. He was divorced. He had three children, one of whom was still quite young. *Too much baggage,* my mental billboard said, in easy-to-read, oversized letters.

Doug perceives the world differently from me. The boy who failed geometry three times became a man who can find his way by shadows, who can glance at a heap of avalanche debris spread out over half a mile and announce how many DC-10 airplanes would make up the equivalent weight. If a logging truck passes him on the highway, he can almost instantly assess the number of board feet in its load. His sculptor's eye registers shapes and angles. When carving a piece of wood or bone, he removes everything that doesn't look like the image he sees inside. As a writer, I am accustomed to creating the image I want by adding words to a blank page. I think Doug discerned even before I did the dimension within me capable of being less absolute in my thinking, less judgmental of others, and wide open to whatever frontiers I could find.

I fell in love with Doug the same way I learned about avalanches: in increments, by observation, by discovery, by a series of small surprises. It may have been as we crouched to study snow crystals under a hand lens. Or during a long ridge climb that left us standing in the sun, looking down toward an arm of the ocean obscured by quilts of fog. Or maybe it was when Doug, a far better carpenter than I, arrived at my building site with power tools, offering free expertise. It could even have been when he helped me stuff insulation into the ceiling at one in the morning, but I doubt it. Still, it wasn't until we were on a search for a missing plane, and the Alaska State Trooper in charge of the mission asked if we would mind sharing a hotel room for the night, that I acknowledged an awkwardness that hadn't been there before.

As my house slowly gained shape, I found myself growing increasingly eager to see Doug at the end of each day. I kept more bananas around because he loved them. I liked the way his veins were raised across his hands and the way his soft, fine hair curled against the back of his head. I liked the confidence with which he tackled any job. We dug out the basement by hand, moving so much hard glacial till that Doug suffered prisoner-of-war tunneling dreams for a month. Together, we built super-insulated eleven-inch walls upstairs and down, to guard against deep winter cold and wind.

But the math kept tripping me up. When my mother was pregnant with me, skating on a frozen pond, Doug was thirteen, daydreaming about girls and anxious to leave home. When I was thirteen, thinking myself very grown-up for touring Paris alone during the day while my father worked, Doug was twenty-six, married and expecting his first daughter, Lahde. Now that I was twenty-seven, Doug was divorced and about to be forty. When he was seventy, I'd still be in my fifties. The age difference between Lahde and me is about the same as between me and her father. Only sixteen years separate Doug and my father. I was afraid of being pulled out of my bubble of youth ahead of time. I worried about disappointing my parents. I was afraid of Doug reaching old age before me, growing a potbelly, going bald, slowing me down, dying, leaving me alone. I couldn't help thinking of my father's father, who'd married a woman who was (an unfortunately coincidental) thirteen years younger. My grandfather died by degrees of Parkinson's disease for twenty-five years. I remember him only as a frail whisper of a man sitting in a darkened room, his thin, quivering hands folded into the empty space of his lap.

Though I pushed Doug away many times, he kept reaching for me, and it always felt right to be in his arms. He saw far more reasons to be together than even my most rational self could come up with to be apart. As a mentor, he'd encouraged me to learn through experience. Now it was my experience that gave me the confidence to trust my heart.

Regardless, I'm not sure I would have had the courage to fall in love with Doug anywhere but Alaska. Alaska diminished the risk, made everything seem possible. "You're going to build a house?" people would say. "Great! Where? When?" They never asked, "How are you going to build a house when you don't know a thing about vapor barriers, framing a wall, or putting on a roof?" When I announced a three-month rowing trip, I was met with enthusiastic advice and requests to come along, not "How are you going to take so much time off from work?" My friends would say, "So, Doug has three children. Tell us about them." It was as though Doug and Alaska were co-conspirators, each whispering in my ear, "There are no set boundaries here. Throw away your lesson plans, the limits are what you make them."

At the same time, Alaska has been uncompromising, showing me a lot of death. I need more than the fingers on both hands to count the number of good friends close to my age who have died in mountaineering, avalanche, fishing, and airplane accidents. I've dragged dozens of dead, unbending bodies out of the mountains. Such untimely deaths always seem ragged, with no chance to wrap up loose ends, say goodbye, or make sure important things are not left undone. A friend of mine from pastoral Vermont thinks Alaska a violent place, where people live too close to the edge. For me, though, it is a place that has helped teach me to love and live life less conditionally. Alaska is a big place that, rather than making me feel small, inspired me to grow into it.

Learning to accept Doug's love felt a lot like the trust falls I used to do as a teenage naturalist at an environmental school. I'd stand atop a five-foot stump, glance over my shoulder, and, keeping my body stiff, fall backward into the spindly, outstretched arms of diminutive sixth graders. The little gasp I'd try to hide usually came at the moment of commitment, when I knew that I couldn't return my feet to the stump.

When Doug and I teach people about avalanches, we train them to put all information to the "so what?" test. So what that different types of snow crystals fall out of the sky? Does this help backcountry skiers evaluate avalanche hazard? Not really. Is it important to be able to read snow surface patterns to determine which way the wind was blowing? Absolutely. This "so what?" perspective bled over into my personal life. So what that Doug had a hard time in school? So what that he had been divorced? So what that he sometimes wore clothes that clashed? Learning to love turned out to be like learning about avalanches. Each year, I look back and wonder how I possibly knew enough to survive the year before. But it is not so much that I have acquired knowledge over the years as that I have learned to strip away the clutter, to recognize what is most important.

We moved into "our" house on Valentine's Day 1986—not nearly as auspicious a date as it sounds, since Doug crashed my car the same afternoon. From the beginning, we were keenly aware of the need to cast separate shadows. But we also found new depth in tandem, complementing each other in spirit and knowledge. In some ways, our age difference has proved a benefit. Doug made me less competitive, more patient, less petty. Determined to spend his time well, he was not willing to fight over little things. He made me aware, by counterexample, that I was capable of manipulating not only by what I said but by how I said it. The fact that he doesn't fuss made me more self-conscious about fussing. I might have relinquished such habits of control on my own or with a partner my age, but it would have taken longer.

One of my offerings to Doug was the ocean. He'd grown up puttering on the water as I did, and likes to recall the sailing classes he took from Captain Bentley. This bearded holdover from clipper ship days once treated his pint-sized crew of eight-year-olds to a swig of rum after a vigorous squall. "Now down the hatch, laddies—and what'er you do, don't tell yer mams!" But in the intervening years of ninety-hour workweeks, cabin repair, and child raising, Doug had lost track of the sea—its sounds, its moods, its challenges, its peace, its constancy. At my urging, he bought a sea kayak and began to remember.

Only a few months after we'd replaced the table saw in the living room with furniture, the state of Alaska responded to plummeting oil revenues by terminating the public safety avalanche programs run by Doug and me. The legislators, however, were not powerful enough also to eliminate the state's burgeoning avalanche problem. Already conditioned by adversity to regard obstacles as opportunities, Doug tutored me to do the same. So we reacted to the loss of our jobs by creating a nonprofit corporation responsible for avalanche education and hazard management consulting, work we've done ever since. Our commuting time can be measured in seconds—we work from our house, in adjacent rooms.

There probably isn't a more stringent compatibility test than working together full-time. We are so often referred to as "DougandJill" that sometimes we suspect people think we are one person. Yet the circumstance of rarely being apart has allowed us to peel back successive layers of interference, ultimately giving each of us greater creative freedom. Our intimate collaboration feels a lot like sculling. To keep the boat moving in a reasonably straight line, we must stroke separate oars as one.

Our decision to marry was spurred by a tragedy. In December 1988, we were called to the scene of an avalanche accident. The victim turned out to be a friend who had spoken with Doug the evening before about the very instability that had proved so deadly. It took a struggle to ensure that Todd's fiancée, who as "girlfriend" had no legal standing, was treated with the same respect by law enforcement authorities as would automatically be accorded a spouse. In the piercing clarity that comes with such sadness, Doug and I were drawn to make our relationship as unambiguous as possible.

Via certified mail, we sent a mock subpoena on letterhead from the "Law Offices of Fredler and Fesston" to our friends Nan Elliot and John Hale. Then we fled town for the summer before they could refuse our request, which began:

Your presence is required in Larchmont, New York, on the occasion of the marriage of Ms. Jill A. Fredston, a single woman of backward vision and inner strength, to Mr. Douglas S. Fesler, a man of strong body, weak mind, and a founding member of Alaska Avalanche-Aholics Anonymous. The date will be sometime between the 1st and 22nd of October (1989), or sooner or later. Please reserve these dates on your calendar, further details will be forthcoming . . .

It seemed fitting to be married at my parents' house by the sea, for by then, several seasons of traveling along the margins of the ocean had done for us what centuries of exposure to waves and storms do to rocks. The ocean has a tendency to sort beaches by size, over time reducing boulders to grains of sand. Sharing weeks of days and nights without separation, sometimes driving our bodies beyond where they wanted to go, had helped strip us to our essential elements, smooth our sharp edges, and sculpt complementary perspectives.

Since Doug and I were beyond reach in Labrador, the wedding logistics fell to Nan and my mother. I'd told Mom that I harbored conviction about only two details: that Nan and John make the cake and that I not wear a traditional wedding dress. By the time we reached New York a few days before the wedding, four white dresses had somehow slithered into my closet. In the way of many wedding gowns, they featured tantalizing V necks. But fourteen hundred miles had melted twenty pounds from my frame, and I now had a chest that could double as an ironing board. As I reluctantly modeled the dresses, Mom, a fierce optimist, regarded the V necks plunging to my belly button and suggested that we take in the fabric here or there, but the situation was clearly hopeless. Doug fared only slightly better; the only item of clothing he wore at the wedding that wasn't borrowed from my father was his underwear.

When we discovered that we needed a copy of Doug's birth certificate for our marriage license, it seemed simpler to paddle the seven miles across the Sound to Doug's hometown on Long Island than to drive an hour and a half through the snarl of New York City. The city clerk on the other end of the phone evidently didn't agree, gasping, "You're coming by kayak?" Thanks to aggressive tugboat captains, the crossing proved some of the most dangerous paddling Doug and I have ever done together. As we pulled with relief into the Glen Cove harbor, one old man sitting on a park bench turned to another, saying with bravado and a slap on his friend's knee, "Here come a couple Eskimos from Alaska." When we confirmed half of his assertion, he began pounding on his friend's back, shouting, "I told you! I told you! I told you!" We asked for directions to city hall. "Oh, you can't walk there from here," they answered gravely. "It's two miles away." Deputizing them to watch the boats, we jogged to the town hall, where a group of fawning women nearly twice Doug's size commended him on his courage while I sat unnoticed on a wooden bench.

Nan, John, and other friends from Alaska laid siege to my mother's kitchen, taking four days to bake and construct a chocolate masterpiece with a hundred eggs and twenty pounds of butter. They decorated the layers with seals, whales, caribou, and moose, and topped the cake with a dashing duo in a rowboat negotiating whipped cream waves.

My mother was anxious about the ceremony. Nan and John had decided that because we lead lives of surprise, as officiators they would keep the ceremony itself a surprise, instructing us just to answer appropriately whenever there was a pause. Nan told

Mom that we wanted the ceremony to be funny. "Well," said my mother without a trace of humor in her voice, "funny can fall flat."

With guests gathered around a majestic oak tree on the lawn and John, a former U.S. Navy commander, in full uniform, Nan asked:

> If so many obstacles have beset these souls in their quest to be united, can *we*—is there any scurrilous sailor amongst us?—dare deny them a ration of rum, a clean new shirt, pressed pantaloons, a day in the sun and—yes, my friends—a bit of a kiss and a fond embrace to seal a deal that has been forged on the Mighty Main?

But we had secrets of our own.

When in the North, we had learned how to say "I love you" in Inuktitut, the language of the Labrador Inuit. On the morning of the wedding, however, after I had rattled Mom by disappearing for a long row, Doug and I found ourselves unable to remember the words or to locate our cheat sheet. "Look," Doug reasoned as we ran out of time, "no one in Larchmont is going to know Inuktitut. Let's wing it and make something up." So while friends and family thought we were romantically declaring our love for each other, we held hands and said, "Tufluk kabloona," for which the closest literal translation is: "Tough luck, white man."

I went to the woods because I wished to live deliberately,
to front only the essential facts of life, and see if I could not learn
what it had to teach and not, when I came to die,
discover that I had not lived.
—Henry David Thoreau, *Walden*

3

Rites of Passage:
Seattle to Skagway

WE SAT BOBBING in small waves at the edge of a bay three miles wide. I was rowing *The Mother Ship*; Doug was sealed into his sea kayak. For the past several miles, a forty-foot-long humpback had been traveling parallel to us, only about fifty yards away and roughly twice that distance from the boulder-covered shoreline. Whenever we stopped paddling, deep rhythmic breathing echoed our own, punctuated intermittently by the sharp smack of a flipper. Now the whale had disappeared. All we knew was that it was ahead of us somewhere in the open, sun-flecked expanse of water.

We talked quietly. I thought we should wait for the whale to surface so we knew where it was. "Come on, we could wait forever," Doug said. I bought a minute or two sipping water, fidgeting with small items, dabbing on sunblock. Unable to stall any longer, I pointed my shell toward the squat red cliffs on the far shore. As we began the crossing, with me in the lead, I kept sneaking glances over my shoulder, but the whale had seemingly vanished.

About midway across the bay, Doug broke the silence, observing that there was a line of small green bubbles emerging next to his boat. I glanced around. "Look, there are bubbles here too!" They extended from the port side of Doug's kayak toward me in a thirty-foot arc. Then Doug noticed that there were also bubbles advancing toward him from the starboard side. I felt the first flush of fear, accompanying a belated realization that the feeding whale was surfacing right underneath our unfortunately camouflaged blue-and-green-bottomed boats.

Humpback whales feed by swimming underwater, releasing a fine veil of bubbles that ring an area up to sixty feet wide. Fish and other small sea creatures evidently see these bubbles as a net and are herded toward the center, where the whale's cavernous mouth awaits them. We had blundered into this zone. Aghast, we saw a clear bubble, easily the size of a compact car, rising below the little bubbles and directly underneath Doug's boat. Just under this lens of whale breath, and no more than fifteen feet below the surface, the dark curve of the whale's body rocketed straight toward Doug like an elevator exploding from its shaft.

"Move!" Doug yelled—unnecessarily, as I was already throttling up to full power. With a *whoosh*, the whale burst from the water exactly where our boats had been a stroke or two before, right through the ripple marks left by our blades. In the time I took to blink, the whale's head reversed direction, arcing downward. It punctured the water less than two boat lengths behind me, and half that distance from Doug. Water streamed off the massive coal-black tail flukes in glistening ribbons. Doug, head down, his tan face red with effort, was planing toward me faster than I had ever seen him paddle. Still, he managed to find the

breath to instruct, "Take a picture, take a picture." "Screw you," I graciously replied. "I'm getting out of here." Then all that was left of the whale was a crease in the sea, a whirlpool of white foam, and a hint of dankness.

That evening, as we leaned against a driftwood log, we tried to reconstruct what had happened. When had we first realized that the whale was below us? How far away were we when it surfaced? Our conversation, which had started quietly, broken only by the sound of lapping waves, grew louder and more contentious until Doug exclaimed, "Jill, you're always exaggerating. That's not what happened at all." I listened in disbelief to his version of events. How could he be so sure when he wasn't facing the whale—when, in fact, he'd never even seen the whale?

Each of us was incredulous that the other could be so wrong. Doug suggested that we both sketch the scene, but the resulting scribbles only heightened our deadlock. Our pictures looked completely at odds, as if we'd met different whales in separate oceans. Frustrated with each other's intransigence, we lapsed into a silence with a hard edge, the unwelcome kind that bumps against bruised emotions like a poorly placed piece of furniture. I stared across the water, seeing little, acutely aware of Doug still hovering in my periphery while he diligently continued to study the drawings. I'd never noticed that he sucked in so much air so loudly. Where had he learned to breathe like that?

Suddenly, Doug began to laugh, a deep, resonating belly laugh that struck me as disrespectful. I resolutely ignored him as long as I could, then unleashed a glare that only intensified his hilarity. Before I could stomp off, Doug grabbed my arm. Struggling for words, he managed to convey that we had sketched identical scenes, only from what were essentially opposite sides of the same mirror. I had drawn mine facing backward, the direction I look when I row, and therefore toward both Doug and the whale. He had drawn his from the point of view of a kayaker, facing forward, with the whale behind him and me out ahead. Annoyingly, he insisted that I had drawn "upside down." Clearly, it was a question of perspective.

It was the summer of 1986, three years before our marriage, the same year we finished building the house I had begun alone, and only months after the state had dispensed with our jobs. Sixty-four days into the trip, we were well along the zigzag course we were paddling between Seattle and Skagway, at the end of Alaska's "Inside Passage."

Our intention was to row and kayak the narrow strip of nook-and-cranny seaboard that wiggles from the northwest corner of the contiguous United States through British Columbia, and back across the international boundary into southeast Alaska. It terminates at Skagway, a hurly-burly town of rough-hewn boardwalks and saloons that boomed in Klondike gold rush days and has experienced less rowdy rebirth as a summer tourist destination. For most of the way, with the notable exceptions of Queen Charlotte Sound and Dixon Entrance, it is sheltered from the open ocean by barrier islands and bulwarked on the inland side by the Coast Mountains. Regarding Inside Passage waters as protected or calm is a mistake, though, for they are regularly bullied by funneling winds and churned by opposing currents. When the ferry transits this route, also known as the Alaska Marine Highway, its motor thrums for five days and nights while it covers nine hundred miles, tirelessly negotiating point after rugged point, plowing through all brands of weather. Since we couldn't steam down the center of broad channels or travel around the clock, our trip would be much longer in both distance traveled and time.

My parents had visited in the spring, a reconnaissance trip to take stock of both the house that would have to stand up to 130-mile-per-hour mountain winds and the man who had moved into it with me. They seemed puzzled that our reaction to newfound joblessness and a fledgling mortgage was to go paddling for an entire summer. While they worried about potential hazards, we hoped that the trip would silence the static and recharge our souls. After dinner one night, my normally decorous mother took Doug aside and announced coolly, "If something happens to Jill, I'll kill you."

My parents were not alone in their doubt. On the ferry south to Seattle, the whispers began. Two kayakers had died trying to make it through Yuculta Rapids the summer before. Seymour Narrows had whirlpools that sucked down giant cedar logs and spat them out several hundred yards downstream. "Queen Charlotte Sound in small boats? Hell, I hate going through there on my sixty-foot fishing boat!" Even the language used to describe the inshore waters of the Pacific seemed harsh, laced with confidence-shredding terms like *rip*, *breaker*, and *bore*.

Our previous paddling trips had been more like vacations, two or three weeks long and a maximum of several hundred miles. Though the waters we'd be traveling were charted, our tolerances and abilities were not. Could our knees and bodies and minds withstand the strain of repetition? Did we know enough to make the hundreds of judgments required to keep us alive? We'd never spent virtually every minute of three solid months together. What would happen to our love in such close-quarter intimacy?

We were struck by the age of most of the tourists on the ferry. Many could no longer walk unsupported or easily see the white-headed bald eagles regally standing guard in the tops of tall trees, though they were coached to "look for the golf balls." I leaned against the ship's rail thinking about what would be left undone on my list when my own body started to fail. When I was seventeen, my father's mother emerged from days of incoherence and quite deliberately said to me, only hours before she died, "Don't waste your life the way I've wasted mine." I sensed these would be her last words, and they were. Her message fueled my determination to live otherwise, although surely our current enterprise wasn't quite what my grandmother had in mind.

Preparing for a long voyage is an expedition in its own right. Up to the moment of departure, we pay bills, look up the numbers of those capable of fixing the many things that could go wrong in the house, empty closets for renters, scrub floors, ready boats, sort gear, mend clothes, and pack food. When we're in preparation mode, the birch floor in the front room's bay window is food central. Breakfast collects on the left side of the window; zip-locked bags of granola, powdered milk, and high-calorie energy bars huddle together. While the pile might look haphazard to an untrained eye, every ounce of it has been stripped from its original packaging, cocooned in plastic, tallied and retallied, and duly recorded in the back of my journal. If I buy six overflowing carts of groceries, by the time I am done discarding the packaging and dehydrating what is not already dried, I will have no more than the equivalent volume of two neatly packed carts.

In March, I put our ten-tray dehydrator to work, drying spaghetti sauce, Doug's chili, salsa, barbecued chicken, tomatoes, peas, and anything else that has collected in the refrigerator. A bulky five-pound sack of carrots, when dried, occupies only half of a gallon-size bag. Dehydrated broccoli looks like miniature trees, and spinach is so light and crispy that it looks more like a substance customs inspectors should raise their eyebrows at than something edible. By drying food, we can carry twice the quantity, with less weight and more diversity.

I've had notable failures, like the time I sliced thick stalks of celery onto the trays and returned hours later to find only microscopic hairs. Or when I thought I'd try drying cheese and, as a grade-schooler could have predicted, ended up with dripping nacho material. Good homemade pesto never dries because it is so rich in olive oil, while reconstituted cauliflower could double for rubber balls. My most unanticipated success was yogurt; the sugary brands dry to the consistency of taffy and, without rehydrating, make a tasty snack. Healthier yogurts dehydrate to taste like cardboard. The dehydrator runs around the clock, scenting the house with an odd perfume and vexing Doug with its noise. He insists on shutting it into the tiny downstairs bathroom, a surprise to visitors assaulted by what appears to be a Sani-Fresh system in overdrive.

Our menu, long on rice and beans, would solve the problems of people with hemorrhoids and is perfect for those with dentures. No eating utensils are needed, other than a bowl and spoon for each of us. Knowing by mid-May exactly what we are going to eat for every meal until September is both demoralizing and liberating. When we do finally venture back into our cavernous local grocery store after months free of errands, we find ourselves the target of oblique stares as we stand gawking at vegetables. Often, overwhelmed by the bright abundance and variety, we make it down only an aisle or two before fleeing with a few coveted items.

Our boats may be the Chevrolet Suburbans of their genre but they are still taxed to fit all we need to keep ourselves warm, dry, sheltered, safe, and fed. The gear we need for a five-day trip—tent, sleeping bags, air mattresses, clothing, shotgun, water sacks, cooking paraphernalia, and repair kit—is roughly the same as for a five-month trip. What sinks the boat to the gunwales is food. Of the three-hundred-pound load in my boat at the beginning of a long trip (excluding body and boat weight), roughly two-thirds is food and cooking fuel. Two months of food for two people is the equivalent of twelve thirty-pound bags of cement. Shuttling all this food along with another fifteen sacks of gear up and down the beach every day and wrestling it into the boats is a form of mandatory weight lifting.

The most food I've ever packed at once was for three people on a hundred-day trip. It literally created a mountain that filled the back of my station wagon. When there are towns along the way, rather than shoehorning our provisions into the boats, we mail ourselves care packages courtesy of General Delivery. Most village stores carry only a limited selection of sugary and starchy food, at premium prices. We eat as much as we want each day (usually twice the amount at the end of a trip as at the beginning) and have yet to run out. Though we supplement our food supply with fish, wild greens, and berries, we don't forage as much as we could. After ten hours on the water, it is more tempting to boil noodles than to go catch dinner.

It is imperative to keep our food supply dry, not an easy task in an environment ruled by water. The keys to our success are plastic and duplication of systems. Every edible is swaddled in as many as four layers of plastic bags before being loaded into theoretically waterproof gear sacks called dry bags. All these sacks are labeled on the outside and color-coded so that we know exactly what is inside without exposing their contents to the elements. We've had the same system for so long that we don't have to think to find breakfast in the gray B-1 bag or supper in the orange S-1 sack.

On the seat in the bay window are the makings of our first-aid kit. Doctor friends have tried to anticipate everything we could do to ourselves. It doesn't take a lot of imagination to envision a need for the suture kit. Antibiotics are a necessary precaution, though microorganisms rarely cause trouble on our trips. Heavy-duty pain medication is intended for the truly hideous things that could happen. But most in demand for its anti-inflammatory properties is ibuprofen, which on the Inside Passage trip Doug fondly dubbed "Vitamin I" and the daughter of a friend calls "adult M&M's."

Freshly waterproofed maps are laid out to dry over the dining-room table and across the deck outside. Generally, 1:250,000-scale topographic maps are a good compromise between adequate detail and economy of space. Out in the shop, Doug packs a colossal repair kit, with enough supplies to completely rebuild a hull smashed in surf, coax a cranky stove back into service, or replace rowing wheels that are ratcheting along like flat tires. Doug can tape, lash, sew, glue, and patch with the best of them, a master of resurrection.

Sometimes, though, Doug fails. My tooth broke during the first week of a twenty-one-hundred-mile trip from Canada across the top of Alaska. It was a front crown, so all I had protruding from my upper gum was a vampire-like black spike. After we had exhausted the possibilities of the first-aid kit, I insisted that Doug make a foray into our repair supplies. He pulled out a variety of epoxies featuring prominent skull-and-crossbones hazard warnings in search of an adhesive with which to glue a chip of the crown back on. Nothing worked. Doug, who is about the least appearance-conscious person on the planet, told me it didn't look bad. And among the Inupiat, it was easy not to be self-conscious; their teeth looked much the same. When we returned to Anchorage in the fall, I went to my dentist, who was adamant that there would be no charge. "Anyone who would go around looking like this for three months deserves a free tooth," he said.

Upstairs, at least twenty books are stacked in a leaning pillar. We choose these carefully, as they are our only transport when storms pin us down. The first few hours of being stormbound are wonderful—we sleep, rest, and sleep some more. But after a day, paralysis and bedsores threaten. After 120 hours of lying side by side like mummies in our zipped-together sleeping bags, the tent roof flapping only a few feet above our heads, our grip on sanity weakens. We make occasional forays outside, but it is hard to motivate ourselves into already wet rain gear only to get drenched, frozen, or blown off our feet. During one inhumane storm along the Chukchi Sea, I refused to go outside, to eat or to pee, for three straight days. Our longest storm kept us penned for six days. In counting the cumulative number of weather days we've been tentbound over a span of fifteen summers, I discovered that we've spent over three months lying bedridden in a space smaller than the average hot tub. It's a wonder that we still love each other, and a tribute to some great books.

Also upstairs are our clothes, what there are of them. A summer's worth—even an Arctic summer's worth—would barely fill a laundry bag. On an average day of rowing, we change our clothes at least six times in response to fickle bursts of sun, wind, calm, fog, snow, or rain, but we're changing in and out of the same layers, day after day, month after month. When selecting our gear, we make two piles, one of things we absolutely need and the other of things we'd like to have. We leave most of the second pile behind.

Since I insist on renting out an immaculate house, usually we're still buzzed on toilet bowl cleaner when we leave. Departure, though, means freedom. Freedom from the tyranny of lists, the daily ritual of adding more "to do" items to the list of things still undone. Freedom from hearing the phone ring, let alone answering it. Freedom from choice and, temporarily, from a culture that equates success with having the greatest number of possessions, friends, and commitments to choose from. The longer I row, the better I understand Sue Bender's observation on the Amish way of life: "Making a choice—declaring what is essential—creates a framework for life that eliminates many choices but gives meaning to the things that remain."

The moment of launch, when at last we are standing by the water, our boats loaded with all that we will need in the coming months, is one of tremendous potential. Only time and geography stretch before us. It feels much like walking to the edge of a diving board, where, bombarded by a cacophony of splashes and shouts, you take one last preoccupied look around before you leap, arms outstretched, body arched. The instant you slit the water, you have entered a different world. The deeper you descend, the more completely the din fades away and the more aware you are of your own suspended breath. On long journeys, it can take us a couple of weeks to become completely submerged, to relinquish the clutter and adjust to living each day as an open slate. It is a time of decompression, of body break-in, of reorienting our ebb and flow to the wind, waves, and tides. It is a time to remember or to develop systems—the most efficient way to set up camp or load gear, the least awkward way to carry emptied boats over rocks that are slanted sideways, with ankle-sized cracks between them. We don't talk much when we paddle. Mostly, we listen and look, and occasionally, if we are happy, bored, or very far from others, we sing. As extra words between us fall away like autumn leaves, we find ourselves more and more free to hear.

Our paddling departure from Seattle, however, was less than promising. We were attempting to navigate by means of a city bus map, because the local stores had been sold out of anything more appropriate. As we hunched over its fanciful rendition of the shoreline, trying to decide whether we were closer to the red dot or the blue one, I was reminded of a conversation between Alice and the Cheshire Cat in Wonderland.

"Would you tell me, please, which way I ought to go from here?"

"That depends a good deal on where you want to get to," said the Cat.

"I don't much care where—" said Alice.

"Then it doesn't matter which way you go," said the Cat.

"—so long as I get *somewhere*," Alice added as an explanation.

"Oh, you're sure to do that," said the Cat, "if you only walk long enough."

By the second day, we had reached Whidbey Island. It was my twenty-eighth birthday, so we stopped in a small town to forage for chocolate cake. Still hampered by the bus map, we were unsure of the name of the town. Horrified that Doug actually wanted to ask someone, I insisted that we wander around and try to figure it out. Eventually, the name Clinton appeared on enough signs so that we felt safe in assuming it was our location. We grazed from a rotating case of desserts at a waterside café, then forced ourselves to leave while the doorway still accommodated our bloating bodies. Back on the beach, we untied our boats. "Look, Jill, a bird pooped on your seat," said Doug. Peeved, I snapped, "I hate when that happens," though it had never happened before. Wheeling around, I found an oversized chocolate éclair carefully balanced on my seat.

Later that afternoon, feeling as though I should mark my birthday by reflecting on the meaning of life, I'd instead find myself smiling about the éclair. When people comment wistfully that rowing must give time for intense introspection, I usually reply, "Yes, well . . . ," letting my voice trail off in a way that implies a subject too fathomless for brief conversation. How can I explain that I treasure these trips for the focus that comes with simplicity?

By the time we pulled away from the concrete ramp in Seattle, we had years of experience dealing with bears and hypothermia-producing weather. What we weren't prepared for was heat. Our cheese, normally refrigerated by lying along the cool bottoms of our boats, mutated into molten goo, and our skin sizzled almost audibly. As we neared the end of the last crossing to Vancouver Island, about ten sun-addled days out, we knew that we needed immediate shade. We beached our boats and, ignoring the ubiquitous summer houses, dragged ourselves under the branches of a large, eucalyptus-like madrona tree, where we lay panting, drinking tepid water from grungy bottles. Miraculously, the door of the nearest house opened and a ruddy-faced older man with pressed shorts and tall white socks emerged carrying two frosted bottles of beer. Our hearts thrilled as he walked toward us. I could feel my fingers closing around the cold glass, even though, much to Doug's continuing disappointment, I don't like beer. Without acknowledging our smelly, dripping presence on his land, the man came within a few feet of us before handing the beers to a young couple sitting waterside in an unscratched red canoe. They paddled away, then stopped before they had broken a sweat or reached water deeper than their belly buttons. "Oh, Daddy," shouted the man in the stern, in an aristocratic British accent, "we forgot the Elastoplasts." One hundred and eighty miles into our trip, hotter than any Alaskan should ever be, I didn't offer the requested Band-Aids.

Inside Passage waterways are flooded and drained every six hours by some of the biggest tides in the world. The difference between high and low tide averages twenty feet and can increase to over thirty feet depending on local topography and the phase of the moon. When all this water is squeezed from open straits into narrow channels, like water from an eight-inch main being funneled into a hose, the result is a turmoil of riotously strong currents, steep-sided standing waves, cliff-like overfalls, and giant whirl-pools capable of sucking large objects into oblivion or ejecting them as if from a slingshot. A small boater's best chance of survival in such a spot is to travel through at slack tide—that is, the variable sliver of time as the tide reverses direction—when the currents are the least strong. In some of the more notorious narrows, even whales have been observed waiting for the current to ease before swimming through.

It took twelve days to reach the first constricted spot. By the time we pulled in at the boat ramp two miles upstream of Dodd Narrows, we had been warned of our impending doom so often, it felt as if we were stopping in the anteroom before the gallows. Hearing the distant roar of water, we were happy to stall another hour and a half until slack tide, passing the time by fortifying ourselves with a poor excuse for a last meal.

Three old-timers were fishing nearby, but when we questioned them about the narrows, each answered in a casual drawl. It was no big deal, we could go through whenever we wanted. How could that be? What about all the stories? The third man, an arthritically humped figure in fish-smeared green coveralls, grew impatient when we pressed him. "I go through a few times a day, at any tide, in this," he said, indicating his leaky six-foot pram with its coughing two-horsepower engine. It had two bailing buckets in the bottom and no more than a few inches of freeboard when loaded. Even *Ikky Kid* would have challenged its status. "What the hell," exclaimed a sheepish-looking Doug as we walked away. "If a five-foot man can make it in a six-foot dinghy, let's go."

Ahead, the channel of smooth water bent into leaping folds; the sea had become a foaming rapids with irregular waves colliding at will. Our plan was to hug the left bank. If we could keep our boats at appropriate angles to the slightly weaker current there, a technique called "ferrying" in river lingo, we'd be able to stay pointed in the right direction. As Doug had demonstrated by moving little stick boats over diagrams etched into the sand, if I wanted to move closer to the left shore, I needed to turn my boat the opposite way so that the current would hit me broadside and give me the desired push.

My throat tightened as the rush of water began to crescendo. Unlike Doug, I had no whitewater experience. Without him, I would have fled back to shore and sold my boat for a Canadian dollar. I mimicked every angle change he made, so intent on his shoulders and his boat that the shoreline slid by unseen, a peripheral green blur.

The beginning of our passage was anticlimactic; it began to seem possible that this wasn't my last afternoon on earth. I relaxed—and in an instant was spinning in circles right through the biggest waves in the middle of the channel. Inadvertently, I had let my bow swing into a tongue of stronger current. "*Doouuuuug, hellllllppp!!!*" I yelled as spray soaked me. I couldn't hear him laughing as he scooted along the shore in total control, but I was certain he was already thinking about finding a more competent girlfriend. He had discerned that my actual hazard was not great. With no obstacles to run into, I faced not death but humiliation as the waves bucked me ignominiously around before dumping me back into water I knew how to handle.

We reunited at the bottom of the channel. Doug, without a drop of water on him, wanted to teach me how manageable, even fun, the narrows were, so he used the eddy current, a reverse flow of quieter water near shore, to paddle back up to the start and run it again. I was not in the mood for instruction, so I was secretly satisfied the next morning when his shoulder ached from horsing around.

Looking back, I can see the symmetry in being initiated into the art of ferrying at the same time that I was learning to navigate the twists and blind corners of the first no-holds-barred intimate relationship of my life. I had always accomplished what I wanted through action, control, and force of will. But negotiating competing currents of opinion and desire as a couple seemed to involve the same kind of angling toward a goal with finesse and slight course adjustments rather than powering straight toward it.

Intent on reaching Skagway, I'd lobby to row just a few more miles even if we had found the perfect beach, it was dinnertime, and our bodies felt as if they needed a crane to hoist them out of the boats. Doug was more process-oriented. We are here, right now, in this place, he'd say, in varying tones of patience, kindness, anger, and frustration. Tomorrow, we'll inch a little closer toward Skagway. And then he'd enlist my help in more important matters, like choosing the most appealing souvenir from a tantalizing array of speckled, egglike rocks on the beach.

We encountered the emotional equivalent of wind against current—a collision that often results in steep, pushy, drenching waves—when knifelike pains stabbed Doug's shoulders, or I was rabidly hungry, or we were both demoralized by headwinds. We said things we didn't mean or retreated behind thorny shields of silence. But even on this trip, before we had learned to read each other's moods without navigational aids, our spats were few, brief, and understood for what they were. In the end, we knew that we needed to paddle right next to each other, cook dinner in a single pot on a single-burner stove, and share the same tent at night.

Doug came to that trip with a disinclination to fight, describing himself as a "noncombatant combatant" who would fight if pushed far enough but who favored tolerance. I came with a code of conduct called "expedition behavior" that had been drilled into me as part of the National Outdoor Leadership School courses I'd participated in as a teenager. Expedition behavior was considered a teachable skill and a mandatory one, much like map and compass reading, vital for safety as well as enjoyment. It involves a conscious commitment to get along despite physical exigencies and personal idiosyncrasies. How much you dislike the way a person looks, smells, picks his nose, or flaunts her ego is irrelevant; it is your responsibility to be amicable and to work to diminish your own offensive habits, even if you are convinced you don't have any. The challenge usually makes me feel like Mother Teresa, virtuous and strong.

But it can be harder to be patient, forgiving, and reasoned with someone you love than with lesser friends. There is more at stake, and the time you have to get along is not as finite. In Greenland, Doug and I once spent five hours trying to cross a bay blockaded with broken ice. Having persuaded ourselves that we would succeed, we put too much effort into forcing a passage, so we had too little in reserve by the time we admitted defeat and turned around. Only when we were less than a hundred yards from the shore we'd left nearly nine hours earlier did Doug begin to vent. As is often the case, neither of us can remember what we fought about, only that Doug announced, "I'm leaving," and began rowing south. I watched him go, leaning against my back-rest and taking a quick, dispassionate mental inventory. He had the breakfast bag, the stove sack, and the fix-it kit. I had the tent, the lunch sack, our sleeping bags, and both of our wallets, including all our money, passports, and plane tickets. We were at least a hundred miles from the nearest village, in a foreign country. Without question, I had the better end of the deal. Doug evidently concurred, for within ten minutes we were kneeling next to each other on the beach, discussing what we wanted to make for dinner.

The Inside Passage, first populated by ethnographically distinct groups of Northwest Coast Indians, has long been a magnet for others attracted by its rich resources. Russians came in the mid-1700s, seeking the soft pelts of sea otters. After "the yellow metal that makes the white man go crazy" was found in Canada's Klondike in 1896, stampeders—and those who intended to make their fortune from them—crowded ships heading north. Huge schools of salmon lured Norwegian fishermen to settle along waterways reminiscent of their homeland, while loggers were drawn by towering stands of old-growth timber. These days, tourists come to see country shaped by ice and nurtured by abundant rain into a tangle of luxuriant vegetation. In between the scattered towns, most of which are accessible only by plane or boat, there are still relatively wild spaces. Green pools fed by hot springs waft sulfurous plumes of steam over forested slopes. Heavily fissured glaciers stream into the sea; majestic waterfalls plunge into deep fjords.

Each morning of the trip, we awoke to the sea, our ever-present inverse alarm clock. If the ocean was silent, we roused ourselves early, sometimes spooking a deer stepping lightly along the tideline or catching the first rays of sun spraying the treetops. If we could hear waves tumbling on the beach, we would snuggle hip to hip, soaking up extra hours of rest. When the sea was quiet but rain pattered against the tent, we faced a moral dilemma. Eventually, we shamed ourselves upright, knowing that the price of an ambitious trip was that, when able, we had to keep moving. Almost always, we first had to roll over on top of our pads, doing puppy-pose yoga stretches to limber our lower backs.

Each day, we'd paddle as far as we could or the sea would let us, whichever came first. Sometimes, that meant mere minutes of paddling, but usually we'd put in eight to ten hours, interspersed with floating rest stops and beach breaks, the day elongated at each end by the hour and a half of work required to break down or set up camp, shuffle all the gear above or below the tideline, and eat. We had numerous zero-mile days and a few where we slept as much as forty miles away from where we'd launched in the morning. Our daily mileage log in the back of my journal is a reflection of the weather's moodiness: 32, 1, 3, 29, 24, 9, 0, 12, 38 . . .

Our progress the first few weeks seemed infinitesimal, but that was only because I was using the wrong scale. I kept sneaking glances at our big-picture map to see how far we'd come in relation to how far we had to go. Gradually I began to focus on taking the measure of each day, not so much in miles as in moments— warm apple pie with a lighthouse keeper, naked baths in clear creeks, seal noses in the kelp beds, a Tlingit legend told in a lilting Native accent by a man who insisted upon taking us for a ride in his truck. There was Doug reading *David Copperfield* aloud while I cooked bulgur, and twenty miles of flat-water nirvana before ten in the morning. Most days were a rich collage. Sometimes, though, I'd reach a point where I thought I'd had enough—my left knee was barely bending, or Doug was cranky, or it was just too much like work to spend ten straight hours keeping my body going and my mind entertained. But then, inevitably, the sun would dance across the water or we'd beachcomb hand in hand, and I'd think, *ah*, this is why I'm here. And as the miles mounted together, the grandeur of the country grew, with fewer people and bigger, snowier peaks.

About twenty-eight days and 430 paddling miles from Seattle, we reached a group of low rocky islands in a narrow, quiet passage. On the high points of several of these, protected by shaggy tree boughs dripping with moss, were squat, square structures built by the region's Kwakiutl Indians. The newer ones were made of concrete blocks, but the older structures were built of planks split from logs. Inside the latter were bentwood cedar boxes, each made from a continuous piece of half-inch-thick wood shaped by a series of small kerf cuts, a technique now almost forgotten. The boxes, reinforced at the edges by sewn roots, were often decorated with the ceremonial crests of the maker's Indian clan and used as storage chests. As the owners died, they became burial boxes. In very old times, the box was then tied to a tree. Missionaries discouraged this practice, hence the small shelters. Femurs and skulls sat gently on the ground as the bentwood boxes decayed around them.

As we walked among the bones, Doug said, "When I die, rent an auger like they use for putting telephone poles in the ground and dig a hole about eight feet deep. Dump me in there, cover the hole with dirt, and plant a tree." I responded with my trademark "I don't want to talk about it right now," a phrase my mother sometimes claims was my first. I'm a card-carrying member of a youth-venerating society, where trying not to age is a competitive event not all that different from Little League or professional hockey. My strategy has been to keep my body hard and to use my time well, a relatively easy task on trips where most days are so vibrant and varied and full that each one feels like a week. But Doug kept pushing me to issue my own instructions. I thought for a while. "Put my ashes in an urn with a big window in it. Then put me on a shelf right above your bed and make sure the window faces out."

Near the islands of the dead is Mamalilaculla, an abandoned village that was once the winter home of the Kwakiutl. As soon as we pulled onto the beach, we felt scrutinized by dozens of pairs of silent eyes, although we saw no one. A bear had trampled fresh paths through the high grass and left behind steaming dung piles, but that didn't account for the palpable aura of suspended time. In the woods behind some old houses, we found a totem pole lying on the ground. A figure cloaked in green moss looked skyward with large oval eyes, hands folded around two stout knees. Toward the front of the beach, a leaning, weathered pole almost thirty feet high still stood. It bore a man with the head of a bear and a prominent hat, a sea serpent, a raven, and a killer whale far into the sky. The whale's fin pointed toward the sea, as if predicting the direction in which the pole would soon topple. We knew that the combination of figures told a story, but we were foreigners, trying to interpret a language that wasn't our own.

Sometimes, we stepped from the open glare of the beaches into thick forests where secrets seemed to hang in the canopy. Before our eyes could adjust to the dim light, we were aware of a musty fragrance, both dank and sweet. It was vaguely familiar, like the way dirty socks might smell after they had been stored in a cedar chest for centuries but more dimensional, more exotic, more pervasive. Underfoot, the forest floor felt springy, a spongy carpet of moss, needles, and decaying life. Slowly our eyes began to absorb detail—hanging moss resembling the beards of Hasidic men, gently waving ferns like those depicted on the backdrops of dinosaur dioramas. And then we saw the giants: shaggy-barked cedar trees and straight firs that made us feel like dwarves when we tried to stretch our arms around them. They reached to skyscraper height, with branches the size of trees blocking the sky. We spoke in whispers and light touches, conscious of our youth in the presence of ancients.

Using the magnifying lens on Doug's Swiss Army knife, we crouched to count the growth rings of downed trees. The spruce tree we leaned against while sharing lunch was six feet in diameter and roughly 680 years old. The ten-foot-thick cedar that fell across a wide ravine, forming a natural bridge, had lived a millennium. We estimated that, at these middle latitudes, it took roughly a century for a tree to add a foot of diameter to its girth.

British Columbia and southeast Alaska no longer host unbroken dark green slopes rising carpetlike from the sea. Industrial-scale logging has altered the look of the landscape and the rhythm of time. Stubby "poodle cuts" of slashed vegetation extend for miles over the tops of ridges and across broad, steep mountains. Dirt logging roads zigzag improbably from one scalped area to another. A recent clear-cut resembles a bombed zone. Almost nothing is left standing except brown, graying stumps about four feet high. Remnant trees lean at crazy angles into an otherworldly quiet.

Even the untouched forests became scrawnier and more weather-twisted as we approached Queen Charlotte Sound, the trip's true rite of passage. Although we had overcome all obstacles to date, including the six-mile Yuculta Rapids, where slack tide was only six minutes long, no one seemed to doubt that we would meet death in the thirty-eight miles of mainland coast that lie completely open to the North Pacific Ocean. On the seaward side, the nearest protection is offered by Hawaii; closer at hand, names like Cape Caution and Storm Islands hardly provide consolation.

Trying to beat the persistent headwinds that were chewing up Doug's shoulders, we had a number of obscenely early starts. Annoyingly, Doug feels it necessary at these times not only to cheer life but to do so raucously. A typical 4 a.m. start in a chilled tent went something like this: Doug, in far higher decibels than needed: "Good morning, honey, it's time to get up, it's a bee-*oooo*-tiful day." No response from me. Doug repeats his message. I reward him with a groan and a presentation of my rump as I wiggle to the far corner of our sleeping bag. After a few seconds, I feel my eyes being pried open manually, accompanied by instructions to open my eyes. Although my arms and legs are still ensconced in the sleeping bag, Doug cranks me to a sitting position. Usually, at about this point, Doug breaks into song or rhapsodizes about how terrific the birds sound or how great he feels. I don't talk, but I begin to move, albeit slowly and by rote. Doug says I have a coffee drinker's personality in the morning, complicated by the fact that I don't drink coffee. I counter that he should get a job with Hallmark.

Our last campsite before Queen Charlotte Sound was on a rock shaped like a turtle's back, the only place we could find that wasn't an impenetrable jungle of crooked, scrubby trees. I christened this tiny mound Edible Island because of the profusion of fruitless strawberry plants and wild onions. We could walk its perimeter in less than a minute; even the vertical relief was limited, with no margin for error between our tent and the high-tide line.

The morning dawned completely blue and calm. Although it seemed superfluous, we switched on our marine weather radio, which ominously warned of an approaching 995-millibar low-pressure system. Overly conservative marine forecasts are not unusual in British Columbia, where fishermen have lost their lives in unpredicted storms. But what really caught our attention about this forecast was its specificity: heavy rain, forty-knot winds, and seas building to three meters were expected in our area not by sometime midmorning, but by 10:30 a.m. precisely.

If we had stayed onshore every time there was a gale forecast, we would be landed immigrants somewhere in Canada. Since the water was table flat, we carried our boats down a natural rock ramp and began to load. By 9 a.m., we were ready to launch. Still wary, we took a few extra minutes to scope the horizon with binoculars. Everything looked perfect, though we both thought that just maybe we could hear the distant hiss of wind. We figured it was our suggestible imaginations, but we decided to be conservative and wait a few more minutes.

By 9:15, we thought we could make out a blue-black wind line on the horizon. It's often the small clues—a subtle change in the wind or in the other person's attitude—that keep us from being surprised by physical or personal storms. By 9:30, we could see the water beyond our protected group of islands begin to churn. By 9:45, the water around our rock was ruffled by a barely discernible breeze, and the water further out to sea was beginning to look frightening. We hustled our boats out of the water, carried all our gear back above the tideline, reloaded the boats so they would have ballast in them, and tied them down, bow and stern, using small cracks in the smooth rock dome as anchor points. Resurrecting the tent, we secured every guyline and added a few. By 10:15, we were battened down as if for a hurricane and more than self-conscious about overreacting. At 10:30 a.m. on the button, the first forty-knot gust of wind hit the tent, with rain following almost immediately. We dove into the tent with our sleeping bags, air mattresses, and books, and stayed there fighting boredom for most of the next two days and nights.

Cheered to be moving again after the gale, we reached the brink of Queen Charlotte Sound in three hours. It was day thirty-one of the trip, and, with five hundred miles on the back sides of our blades, we paused to decide whether to go or not. Leftover swells eight to nine feet high were sweeping by in powerful rolls, but we had a gentle tailwind from the southwest. Our timing was perfect for crossing Allison Harbor at slack tide, necessary because one of the swiftest tidal streams in the world, exceeding sixteen knots, rushes through Nakwakto Rapids six miles inland. Even at the mouth of the bay, the currents are considerable and, if they are running counter to wind or incoming swell, can create havoc in sea conditions. We couldn't see any breaking waves through the binoculars. The water didn't look terrific, but based on what we'd been told, we didn't think we could expect any better.

The first four miles were uneventful, although uncomfortably jouncy. I can see now that conditions built to a crescendo slowly enough not to immediately set off the alarms that would have alerted us to turn around. The deep ocean swells grew steeper in shallow water, the wind picked up and changed direction, the noise of the surf beating the coast a mile inland became increasingly intimidating. In time, we were rowing in fourteen-to-eighteen-foot swells from the northwest, topped by four-foot whitecaps angling in from the west. Adding to the Mixmaster effect were strong ebb-tide currents and waves reverberating off the shore. It was taking me several strokes to row up the side of just one swell. Unless Doug and I crested adjacent swells at the same instant, we went long seconds without seeing each other. If anything happened to either of us, it was unlikely the other could do anything. We were two people paddling alone.

I was seasick and more gut-wrenchingly, biliously afraid than I'd ever been in my life. And that was before we hit the suckholes, or "boomers," submerged reefs where the larger swells were feeling the ocean bottom and breaking in a ferocious display of boiling hydraulics that looked like inverted tornadoes and roared like jet engines. Because just the bigger swells were breaking, a given hole would explode only every ten minutes or so. We could see these holes open only when we were on top of a swell, and even then it was difficult to fix their location in a roiling environment without stationary reference points. Doug's forward-facing kayaker's perspective may well have saved us. He memorized the location of each abyss ahead and picked a route through the gauntlet that I followed, at times with swirling holes nearly two stories deep less than fifty feet off the end of each oar.

We rowed fifteen miles in this combat zone, unable to communicate easily because of the deafening, nausea-intensifying noise and our busy hands. I was sure Doug was weighing the only two options I could think of: paddling through the minefield in the dark, which was an hour away, or finding a place to crash in through the surf. Neither choice seemed remotely survivable. But then I caught a glimpse of Doug just as I was sideslipping the marine equivalent of an elevator shaft and saw that he was . . . singing. I stole a few more looks to be sure I wasn't hallucinating. Maybe I was perceiving conditions to be more desperate than they actually were. If Doug had hope, then so would I.

Burnett Bay had been marked by friends as a potential bailout spot on our map. We paddled its three-mile length of curving sand beach searching for a place to land, but it was being assaulted by five rows of eight-to-twelve-foot waves breaking in continuous parallel lines between the sand and deeper water. At the far end of the beach, there was a small island and a reef, which we studied closely, communicating by nods. It looked as if, with the right timing, we could barrel in through a narrow slot only inches wider than my oarlock riggers and land in much smaller surf behind this natural jetty. With the wrong timing, we could be impaled on the rocks.

The first part of the plan went fine. Multiple sets of waves were still breaking behind the reef, but they were half as big. Doug signaled that he would go in first; I watched him with my back to the sea, the stern of my boat pointing toward shore. Envy replaced empathy when he bent to kiss the sand after an unexpectedly easy landing. Once again, I relaxed my guard too early, letting myself drift too close to shore. Doug began to gesture emphatically toward the sea, his normally calm face hijacked by horror. I turned my body in time to see the green arch of a wave, much bigger than all the others, curl in over my head. In an instant, it deluged the cockpit with what Doug later calculated to be five hundred pounds of water (or, the way he thinks, a sixth the weight of a Toyota Land Cruiser) and splintered the half-inch-thick mahogany freeboard as if it were kindling. To avoid being rolled, I somehow cranked the boat around just as another outsized wave swept over me. My seat and legs underwater, I started rowing for land with the waterlogged strength of Clark Kent transforming into Superman. Doug met me in the last row of thigh-deep surf, wading in well over the top of his boots. Together, we bailed and dragged the drowning boat toward solid ground.

It was low tide on the gently angled beach, so before we could set up camp, we had to haul the boats and our twenty-seven bags of gear further than the length of two football fields to clear the tideline. We weren't complaining. I was content to spend years on this beach, which was covered with thousands of huge cedar driftwood logs, enough to build a good-sized town. With tears smudging my view, I watched the big blue Alaska state ferry glide effortlessly by, far out to sea. Then I told Doug how impressed and reassured I was that he had been comfortable enough to sing. He looked at me incredulously. "Jill," he said, "I sing when I'm scared."

That night, seeking relief from the incessant sounds of the sea, we carried our sleeping bags into the forest to sleep in a tiny, aromatic cedar cabin built by unknown hands. Two days later, there was barely surf on the beach. A remedial lesson: every notorious place has times when conditions are fine. And its corollary: success hinges on having a flexible plan and the patience to wait.

We finished the crossing of Queen Charlotte Sound in relative peace, though not without expending one last surge of adrenaline. I had taken the outside route around a small point while Doug, sleeker in his kayak, had elected for a shortcut through a jumble of rocks. As I swung toward where he was waiting, paddle resting across his deck, hands idle in his lap, I saw trouble. "Big whale behind you!" I yelled. Doug, assuming I was joking, didn't bother to turn around. There was no way a whale could be between him and the shore two stone throws away, or so he thought. I shouted more urgently and was rewarded with a silly hand-and-wrist wave, like a princess on parade. Only my last-ditch, fully frantic shout prompted action. Doug turned to see a thirty-five-foot gray whale heading straight for the small cove's only exit route, which was blocked by his puny green kayak. With the eggbeater stroke rate of a sprinter, Doug fled, allowing the whale to escape to deeper waters.

It isn't so much the whale I remember in reliving this moment as the upwelling of love, anger, and fear that seized me all at once. It only looked as though we were making the journey in two separate boats. The journey was ours, together, and the burden of having someone to watch out for, someone to care about more than myself, both deepened the risk and heightened the joy.

That afternoon, we lay without a shred of clothes on, sprawled on a snow-white beach littered with shiny mussel shells the size of our hands. We had just made the tender, timeless, supremely aware love of prisoners pardoned from death row. The sun-drenched beach sloped into quiet green Caribbean-like water so clear that we could see crabs scuttling along the bottom, ten feet down. We were happy, actually completely delighted, to be alive. Doug said, "The only thing that would make this beach more perfect is if someone brought us a fish." "Ha-ha," I giggled, "fat chance." No more than two minutes later, we heard the whine of an outboard engine. As a sixteen-foot fiberglass skiff pulled around the corner and drew close to our beach, we roused ourselves into shorts and T-shirts and went to meet it. Standing in the Boston Whaler, which was driven by her teenage son, was an attractive woman wearing nothing but a yellow bikini. She seemed oblivious of the huge expanse of ocean a few miles away, the lack of any local accommodations, or the need for survival gear. Explaining that the Whaler was the "runabout" for her larger yacht moored around the corner, she offered us a fish and a bag of Doritos. We are like Pavlov's dogs, conditioned by rewarding feeding experiences. Now when we see a yacht, we gleefully think food, maybe cookies.

In a quirk of political geography, Alaska is separated from the rest of the United States by a long sliver of Canada. Nine hundred and seventy-nine miles of paddling brought us home, back to Alaska and into Ketchikan, the state's fourth-largest city, population about fourteen thousand. Not surprisingly, since Ketchikan is deluged with roughly thirteen feet of rain a year, the day was wet and monochromatic. Even the skiffs that passed us had windshield wipers.

Near-constant rain escorted us north. To appreciate the conditions, try spending the day lying fully clothed in a bathtub, under a steady shower of cold water. For realism, add a fan to simulate twenty-mile-per-hour winds. After two unrelenting weeks on the receiving end of buckets of rain, we felt like creatures from the lagoon. Fungus and mold had transformed our rubber boots into biological wonderlands. Our peeling, corpse-colored hands appeared permanently shriveled, like albino prunes. Night after night, we squeezed water out of our balled-up tent, which smelled like a wet dog, before erecting it and crawling inside with our sponges. In desperate moments, we would carefully bring our blazing stove inside to create a sauna-like atmosphere. An aerial infrared view of the tent would have revealed naked, sweating bodies in the steaming interior, with cold, clammy heads extended out the windows to avoid carbon monoxide poisoning. Morning after morning, we willed ourselves back into already wet clothes so we could keep at least one set dry for emergencies. We staved off hypothermia only by having good gear that could still function when wet, by gobbling calories, and by moving constantly.

One morning, we glumly began yet another liquid day by bailing an inch and a half of rain out of our boats, but we cheered considerably when an orca with a tall, crooked fin glided directly across our paths, exhaling large plumes of mist. If the clouds had dropped any lower, they would have been draped over our laps, so the drone of a floatplane was an anomaly. Doug declared, "Anybody flying today has to be totally nuts." That afternoon, we reached a decidedly low-budget camp designated "Anytime Logging" on a cedar shingle. We were invited inside a stale, windowless trailer to dry our sodden selves. It was dark, but not quite dark enough to conceal all the pinups on the walls. The room was filled with tattooed, sinister characters who all looked like they were on their way to or from prison. One guy, with a beer in one hand and a joint in the other, commented, "Yeah, I was drinking beers in the back of the plane this morning when I looked down, saw two little boats, and thought, whoever is down there is fucking crazy."

By the time we reached Petersburg, Alaska's "Little Norway," condensation had crept inside our brains, short-circuiting any wiring for cheery morale or extraneous conversation. The docks, usually double-parked with fishing boats named for women, were almost abandoned, because the fleet was out fishing. This meant that we wouldn't be able to distract ourselves by visiting fishermen we'd been leapfrogging with since the border as they followed the salmon north. We sloshed up the boat ramp and exchanged a five-dollar bill for quarters at the café. Then the two of us crammed into a public shower intended for one, locked the door, cranked the faucet over to full hot, and spent the rest of the morning there. From time to time, delightfully warm, pink fingers would languidly drop another quarter in the meter.

The sun reappeared shortly after Petersburg. In celebration, we stopped uncharacteristically early on the end of Cape Fanshaw, a low-lying peninsula that protrudes into Frederick Sound. Though shiny, sculpted pebbles spoke of frequent waves, the sea was docile that day. As soon as we landed, we began to turn in circles, like chickens on a rotisserie, binoculars and cameras in hand. All around us were humpback whales, at least twenty-five of them, spouting geysers of spray, swimming with gentle undulations of their dorsal fins, leaping into clear sky, and slapping the water with their fifteen-foot side flukes and broad, notched tails. A mother and calf eased by, their sides touching. Only a hundred yards away, a forty-foot whale repeatedly torpedoed free of the water, twisted sideways in midair, and landed with a cannonlike explosion. Another whale, closer to shore, continuously and deliberately beat its tail against the water like a gong.

Around six in the afternoon, the whales disappeared and silence descended. There were no boats, no airplanes, no chain saws, not even the usual chirping of birds or lapping of waves. Doug poetically describes it as "so quiet, we could hear a flea fart five miles away." The only sounds we could hear emanated from us. But in the middle of the night, we awoke to a hum of very heavy breathing, interspersed with trumpet noises, resonant bass organ sounds, clicks, and whistles. It was as if we had hydrophone receivers inside the tent. The whale music went on for hours, lulling us in and out of sleep, permeating our dreams. At first light, we stood on the rocks at the water's edge trying to spot the pod of whales, but they were floating further offshore than we had imagined possible, given the clarity and purity of their symphony.

Another calm evening, we perched on a cliff of smooth yellow granite seventy feet above the water, watching sea lions feed below in a frenzy of growls and deep-throated barks. The next morning, a peaceful, blue-sky day, we paddled past Sumdum Glacier, which stopped far short of the sea, its white lobe framed by green. Doug's body was perfectly reflected in flat water along with puffy cumulus clouds, his tan arms rippling with definition. I thought, *Sumdum kayaker is passing Sumdum Glacier,* and smiled with pleasure. Now, when I pulled out the big-picture map, it felt bittersweet to see that all the strokes, miles, hours, candy bars, campsites, and weighed decisions had added up inexorably, until the Inside Passage was mostly behind us.

After seventy-two days of stops and starts, twanged muscles and begged backrubs, we were less than two hours from Skagway when we saw a gleaming cruise ship bearing down on us from the far end of Lynn Canal. All summer, these ungainly floating hotels for two thousand had passed us on their weekly transits of the Passage. But after 1,410 miles, we were fit and motivated, and we had a head start. Knowing that our eight-mile lead would quickly evaporate, we picked up the pace and pulled hard for town. We held a steady three-quarter power, with full-power sets of ten and twenty strokes that would have made my old coaches beam. We beat the *Island Princess* by a margin of yards, then jumped out of the boats to hug each other. To my disappointment, there was no marching band to greet us, only the car that we had parked three months earlier, which now had a cluster of bowling balls wedged beneath it. In a town lacking a bowling alley, the locals had improvised by placing pins in front of our car's sagging rear bumper.

We were not prepared for the letdown of reaching our long-anticipated goal. After a short tour of Skagway and its eating establishments, we were itching to set off again, but the ocean had ended in a wall of mountains. The limits of geography dictated an end to days defined by the sea and our own endurance or whims. With a jolt, we realized that we could no longer devour several pizzas at a time and unlimited ice creams with impunity. Settling aimlessly onto a bench, we watched the cruise ship passengers disembark and stream like penguins along the flat sidewalk toward town.

The car wouldn't start, even after we'd extricated the bowling balls. Without discussion, I began to push while Doug jumped in to turn the ignition. Not until we were halfway down Main Street did I view the scene from the perspective of the bystanders laughing on the boardwalks: a beanpole woman resembling Olive Oyl was pushing a rusting wreck while Popeye sat hunched in the front seat. Once the engine wheezed to a start, I climbed into the passenger seat and reached for Doug's callused hand. With his big beard, crinkled eyes, and brown skin, he was a reflection of the sea on a calm day.

We were not ready to go home, so we let the mountains pull us uphill on foot. From Dyea, a mostly abandoned town site behind Skagway, we followed the path of Klondike gold rushers who had used the Chilkoot Trail as a route into the interior at the turn of the century. Reaching the top of Chilkoot Pass on a rare sunny afternoon, we looked beyond white snowfields and blue lakes toward gray mounded ridges guarding the horizon. It was then that we resolved to return the next summer. We would put in at one of the lakes below us that fed the Yukon and follow the river all the way across Alaska and into the Bering Sea. From there, we'd strike out along the coast to Nome. "Seattle to Nome!" we declared, sealing the pact with a kiss.

During the twenty-hour drive back to Anchorage, we stopped to camp along the Yukon River. We arrived just at sunset. The far shore was black, too dark to let us distinguish individual trees, but the last of the sun lay reflected on the water, highlighting irregular polygons of current. With the night sky came green vibrations of northern lights, shimmering strongest to the north and west as if banners of fireflies were challenging us to a chase.

Merging back into our busier, hectic life at home felt like trying to accelerate onto a freeway in a Model T. The house seemed too big and too insulating. We felt adrift without sounds of the night or the rustle of changing weather, so we camped in our tent on the deck for a couple weeks to ease the transition. We found we had missed little while we were away except for family and friends. However, we did have renewed, intense appreciation for fresh fruit, running water, and a bed we didn't have to roll up every morning. An hour or two of exercise felt as inadequate as a stroll down the driveway. But even after we'd reentered the traffic of wider choices and greater commitments, we remained bound together by our time on the water. It was as though we had our ears to the same conch shell, finding strength and grace in a common rhythm.

4

Stream of Consciousness:
The Yukon River

DRIVING THROUGH SUNSHINE at three in the morning, we reached Tagish Lake in British Columbia on the longest day of 1987. One of several mountain-cradled lakes that form the source of the Yukon River, Tagish Lake lies less than twenty-five miles from Skagway. The Yukon River emerges modestly from the lakes as a narrow ribbon of blue-green water seeking the path of least resistance. But as it sweeps two thousand miles from Canada, arcing above the Arctic Circle and bisecting Alaska before finally merging its brown, silt-laden waters with the salt of the Pacific, it becomes the fifth-longest river in North America. In that distance, the river is blocked by only one dam, just below the lakes in the Yukon's provincial capital of Whitehorse, and crossed by road bridges only a few times. The Yukon isn't whitewater, a cocky tumult of froth and action. It is even more impressive in its timeless, understated way—a big river shaping an even bigger landscape.

The Yukon lies between the Brooks Range to the north and the snow-covered Alaska Range to the south. Seen from a satellite photograph, it appears to be a main artery fed by hundreds of veinlike tributaries. Home to beaver, muskrat, wolf, coyote, moose, fox, and bear, it pumps lifeblood through the heart of the land. Salmon fight swift currents to return from years at sea to their natal streams, where in quick succession they spawn and die. Huge numbers of birds congregate in the river's delta, a labyrinth of low, muddy islands, to feed, form flocks, and embark on their own round-the-world migrations. The river helps even the land migrate; it has been recorded as conveying a staggering load of 188 tons of silt per minute past one upriver stream gauge. Every second, it empties about 1.7 million gallons of water into the Bering Sea.

Though it is wild and relatively unaltered, Yukon River country is not wilderness. Humans crossed into the country from Siberia more than eleven thousand years ago, probably by a marshy land bridge that existed when much of the world's water was shuttered in ice. For generations, Athabascan Indians on the middle and upper river and Yup'ik Eskimos on the wider, slower lower river have lived and evolved their subsistence culture along Yukon River shores, reliant upon the life the river nurtures to feed themselves and their sled dogs. In 1898, 7,100 hand-hewn boats and rafts, offering transport for twenty-eight thousand hopeful Klondike stampeders loaded with equipment, checked in at the Canadian Mounties' post in Tagish. They were bound downstream for Dawson, where only a few would find what they sought. More than two hundred stern-wheelers plied the river between Klondike days and the 1950s. Today, though the region is not thickly populated, it is sprinkled with settlements. Many of the Natives, homesteaders, miners, trappers, dog mushers, and others who live along the river are intimate with its sloughs and eddies; they read the Yukon as if it is a book. Their hopes and needs and cultures are as integral a part of the landscape as the surrounding green hills and spindly black spruce trees swaying in the breeze.

My journal from that Yukon summer is relaxed, contemplative. For the first two thousand miles, from Tagish Lake to the Bering Sea, we didn't have to fight surf or even tides. Every few hours, we let the river carry us downstream while we ate, read, or lay against our backrests watching the scenery unfold at an easy six, sometimes ten, miles an hour. At the end of each day, we simply pulled out on a gravel bar in the middle of the river where the bugs were scarcest and tied the boats to a tent stake or bush. The Yukon's inexorable flow took us through village Alaska, a world light-years removed from urban Anchorage. If we'd chosen not to take a single stroke, we still would have had fighting odds of making it to the river's mouth once we'd committed ourselves to the current.

There were few moments of high drama, even counting the morning a black bear tried to run off with our stove sack as well as frequent encounters with German canoeists wearing enormous knives suspended from the waistbands of thick wool pants. What we remember most, after paddling the length of the river and tacking on another five hundred miles from the mouth around the edge of the shallow Bering Sea to Nome, are the people along the Yukon's shores and the lessons of the river itself. By the time I reached the sea, I knew that I could do far worse than to live life like the Yukon: Keep moving but find places to slow down. Don't go straight at the expense of meandering. Nurture others; accommodate both change and tradition. Savor the element of surprise. Be gracious, accepting, resilient.

The country is a study in contrasts. More than 150°F can separate gelid white winters from blazing green summers. While

the northernmost sections of the river are locked in almost perpetual winter dusk, they are flooded with light in spring and
summer. Hot, sunny summer days often darken into intense
thunderstorms, the kind that pelt rain and leave brilliant rainbows in their wake. Timbered slopes and sedimentary bluffs give
way to the flatness of the river itself. Though the river seemed to
rush us along, its waters sometimes rasping like sandpaper under
the hulls of our boats, it also slowed us down, helping us to notice
even the nuances of color in the pebbles on the beach. Many days
we felt as though we were at the bottom of a fishbowl—the sky
immense and azure, the clouds surrealistically fluffy, the quiet
all-encompassing. The Yukon is a perfect river to row backward,
for it tugs travelers back in time. Many of our experiences—sliding past abandoned sod-roofed cabins, startling a peregrine falcon
ruling the top of a clay cliff, or cooling our feet in a sun-warmed
pond in the middle of a sand bar—could just have easily occurred
in an earlier century.

Most of the guidebooks focus on the 460 miles between the
towns of Whitehorse, downstream of the often dangerously
windy headwater lakes, and Dawson, implying that the river
begins to lose its allure at the Alaska border. This is one of two
main reasons to discard the guidebooks, the other being that
rounding corners isn't as much fun when you've already read
what you will find. However, an advantage of this bias is that, re-
creating the stampede of old, most of the bowie knives and their
owners are concentrated in this upper stretch. Some paddlers
take out at Eagle, a huddle of log cabins lying just inside Alaska,
perched between the river and the end of a 160-mile-long
unpaved road open only half the year. We spent a Norman
Rockwell–vintage July 4 there, with root beer floats, sack races,
and kids on tricycles leading a delightfully corny parade. Just
downstream is Eagle Village, an Athabascan settlement where

weathered armchairs line the edge of the waterside bluff—clearly, most of the action takes place on the river. A few paddlers hang on until Circle, the last road take-out before the Yukon Flats, a braided sprawl of wetlands where the river elbows above the Arctic Circle. This is a stretch I can barely remember dreading because it proved to be a favorite. What I pictured as a wide, featureless, boring bug breeding ground actually reminded me of Cape Cod, with long sandy beaches and rounded points, a maze of tiny, intimate channels filled with bird life.

The absolute last road take-out is where the haul road to Prudhoe Bay and the Trans-Alaska Oil Pipeline cross the river. People floating downstream from there—and each year there are some, like through-hikers on the Appalachian Trail—are most likely heading almost another thousand miles to the sea, where they will either sell their canoes so cheaply that some delta villagers will use them as planters or arrange to haul their crafts home via barge or air cargo. We found that the longer we stayed on the river, the more its sounds and smells and horizons became the sum of our consciousness. And maybe as a result, the people of the river began to give us more of their time.

It was Uncle Al who revealed to me that I am, at heart, part Koyukon, one of eleven cultural groups of Athabascans in Alaska. When we first met him, though, three days downstream of the pipeline bridge, twenty-four days and twelve hundred miles from our start, he didn't seem all that wise. We'd pulled in at his fish camp at the invitation of a plump, cheerful woman in a faded blue kerchief and bright red riverboat with whom we had crossed paths in Tanana earlier that afternoon. The village had been the usual assemblage of dirt paths, aluminum skiffs tethered to the beach, and ragtag houses surrounded by chained dogs and moats of junk for which someone, someday, might find a purpose. The beer-breathed, hostile men bunched around the entrance to the store made sure we knew that as white people we didn't belong. Anxious to get to the ice cream we knew would be inside, we ignored their stares. But once we were back on the dusty riverbank, perhaps because we didn't have cameras hanging around our necks, most of the men straggled down one at a time to look at the boats and to talk about firefighting, boat racing, and the usual conversational pillar, fishing. We had only chatted with the woman while she was pulling the starter on her outboard, but amid the noise of the engine, we caught enough to know how to find her camp.

After stopping to cook dinner on a sandbar, we took the river's inside bend as directed. Just ahead, on a birch-covered hill, we could see the cluster of white canvas tents where Uncle Al and his family stay each summer to catch and prepare a winter's worth of salmon. On a log float tethered off the bank, the woman was standing awash in fish guts at a waist-high wooden table. Waving the bloody knife she was using to clean fish, she greeted us: "Boy, it sure took you guys a long time to get here." As she continued to fling blankly staring salmon heads into a bucket for the dogs, she introduced us to her much leaner, quieter husband. He took us on a tour past drying racks where slabs of red-fleshed salmon hung like laundry, through the corrugated-metal smokehouse pungent with cottonwood-smoked fish, around eight barking dogs and five little naked kids jumping in and out of the river, and up a hill, where he announced, "Uncle Al, I brought you some tourists."

Uncle Al was sitting cross-legged on the ground with the carcasses of two oil-stained chain saws in front of him. Though it was a hot evening, he wore a wool shirt that smelled of the forest, his skin the same tawny color as the river. With a somewhat baffled smile that couldn't have seen fewer than seventy summers, Al barely glanced at us before he asked Doug if he knew anything about chain saws. "A little," said Doug. "Well, maybe you can help. I've been working on these things for hours trying to get a working saw." The problem boiled down to this: One chain saw had a bad motor but a good bar for the chain. The other chain saw, a different brand but of similar size, had a useless, bent bar but its motor was functional. Uncle Al spoke with measured calm and patience, in the typically clipped Athabascan accent that emphasizes the front part of every syllable and makes the back part of each word sound as though it has been rear-ended. Doug regarded both saws seriously, then said, "Why don't you just put the good bar on the saw with the working motor?" Uncle Al removed his faded baseball cap and used it to slap his forehead with a flourish. "Why didn't I think of that?" he said, vastly amused that he had missed such an obvious solution.

Uncle Al was interested in everything—driftwood, rocks, people, things we'd seen along the way, how we loaded our boats, our impressions of the river. As we talked, it was apparent that his life had in itself been a remarkable journey. He'd been born into a people who needed to know how to make a fire to stay warm, who sewed clothes from animals they trapped, who roamed the land to hunt and fish in hand-built canoes. In his lifetime, he'd seen the influence of outside cultures, which had begun with the arrival of Russian traders on the lower river in 1838, spread through the country with traders, trappers, missionaries, gold miners, teachers, doctors, law enforcers, and back-to-the-woods settlers. He had cut wood for the double-decked paddle-wheelers that used to throb their way upstream but now lay rotting in various backwater sloughs, outstripped by motorized skiffs, barges, and bush planes. Uncle Al had grown accustomed to living in a house in the village, with electricity, running water, satellite television, and telephone communication, but he was adamant that he didn't need such things.

"I don't know about this TV," Al said, and I remembered eating with a Native family upriver in the hardscrabble village of Fort Yukon, a place that made Tanana look effusively friendly. They ate salmon strips in silence while flipping channels between a game show and the Iran-Contra hearings. "Our ways are drowning in alcohol and disappearing in front of the television," Al lamented. "Young people don't know the old songs; most are too weak to understand what they have lost. They need to be like the salmon who know how to find their way back from the ocean to the clear streams where they were born."

Many of the old songs honor wildlife. In Koyukon tradition, living and nonliving things were endowed with spirits, and animals had distinct personalities. If an animal was not treated with respect—if it was unappreciated, pointed at, or disparaged—it might refuse to be caught, and the people would starve. To Koyukons, the natural world was a source not only of life but of spiritual power; the natural and the supernatural were entwined. A person in nature was never alone; he moved through a world that was aware, endowed with signs, and easily offended. Birds and spruce trees and hills were all part of his community. Uncle Al had been taught by example not to say that he was going hunting. He would put on the appropriate clothes, pick up his rifle, and head out overland or by boat. Those around him knew his intentions by his actions, but if he did not speak them aloud, the caribou or moose did not. His success depended in part upon whether the hunted animal deemed him worthy enough to die for.

I looked at Uncle Al. There wasn't much resemblance between us. His eyes were dwarfed by owl-like glasses, his gnarled hands looked as though they could fell trees without a saw, his hearing was poor. But somewhere in my evolution, I had learned, at least a little bit, to act like a Koyukon. When Doug and I are in the middle of a long, exposed crossing, I might think to myself, *Wow, I hope this calm lasts, conditions are perfect, I think we are going to make it all right.* I will never, ever announce this out loud. Doug mocks me for being superstitious; I am simply trying not to antagonize the spirits of the ocean, the powers behind the wind. Doug, true to his Norwegian heritage, is more of a Viking. In the middle of the same crossing, he will say, "Sure is lucky that the seas are flat and the wind isn't blowing, because we could get nailed out here." Inevitably, within minutes, the wind will start to howl and we'll be fighting for our lives. When I point out that the Koyukons have managed to outlive the much more flamboyant Vikings, Doug throws back his head and laughs.

I am too much of a scientist to believe that Doug causes conditions to change. I am also aware that explanations for everything do not exist, that any individual's perception of nature or, for that matter, any reality is influenced not just by what he sees but by what he has been taught to see. When I was an eighteen-year-old naturalist at the Grand Canyon, I once had a near-riot in a group of adults I had assembled on a point to watch the sunset. As the maze of ancient rock below began to glow pink in the day's last light, one man muttered, almost to himself, "Jeez, this would be a great place for sanitary landfill." When the others attacked him, I intervened, speaking of linked ecosystems, describing cause and effect. Somewhat to my surprise, I was sympathetic to his perspective. He was a garbageman from Chicago who had spent his whole life finding places to put the city's trash. In front of him lay one of the biggest holes in the world. In what I can remember of my answer I also see the seeds of Koyukon philosophy: There is great merit in trying to move through familiar and unfamiliar worlds with understanding and reciprocity, without causing unnecessary offense. Before the man from Chicago filled the Grand Canyon with trash, he needed to learn the intricacies of a new place. Instead of writing him off as stupid, I needed to make an effort to comprehend the experience that had shaped his perception.

More than half the humans on earth now live in cities, in habitats created and ordered by man. So it is hardly a surprise that we tend to manipulate nature, and to treat it as an entity outside of or separate from ourselves. It may be, as the conservationist Aldo Leopold observed, that "we abuse land because we regard it as a commodity belonging to us. When we see land as a community to which we belong, we may begin to use it with love and respect." One of my favorite books, *Powers of Ten,* has no words, only pictures. It begins with black views of the galaxies and then, an order of magnitude at a time, draws closer and closer to Earth until we see Lake Michigan, Chicago, a marina, green grass, a family picnicking, a hand, skin, capillary vessels, a cell, and so forth, spiraling ever inward. By tightening the focus, we are able to see both more and less.

But these were thoughts that would surface once I was back on the river. For now, we were talking fishing. Uncle Al's family had caught sixty-five salmon that day, with a fish wheel that they'd built and mounted on a raft moored to the bank. Like the many other wheels we'd seen, it had two mesh scoops that were bolted to opposite sides of a center axle and rotated perpetually by the river's current. As each scoop in turn was raised into the air, it dumped its catch into a holding box. Most of the families we had met on the trip had complained of a poor run, even with multiple fish wheels and nets in the water. Uncle Al explained that there had been some disagreement about who had the right to put their fish wheels where. Not wanting to fight, he had moved his wheel to a spot where there had never been one before. Everyone thought he was crazy, but he'd been watching the spot for years, and thought the fishing might be good there. This story has stayed with me as I have tried to leave less and less room for conflict in my life. Often, I've discovered, it is most productive to move my own proverbial fish wheel.

The generous light of summer allowed plenty of time for our conversation with Uncle Al to drift through the seasons. In Koyukon country, the lengthening days and increasing warmth of spring are a time to hunt snowshoe hare, the dovelike ptarmigan, and returning waterfowl, along with bear and caribou. May heralds dramatic change as, in a cacophony of creaks, booms, and rifle cracks, the river bursts free of the cast of ice that has encased it since October. During breakup, great blocks of ice hurtle downstream, shearing trees along the bank, sometimes massing into solid ice jams that cause flooding. Fish are the focus of summer, when many families heap their belongings into skiffs and leave their villages for camps scattered along the river. Whitefish and trout can be found in tributary streams; the first salmon usually reach Koyukon country after mid-June. Later summer is a time for gathering blueberries, crowberries, and cranberries by the bucketful. By late August, fall has arrived. The birch trees yellow and the tundra reddens. It is a time of renewed hunting for the larger mammals like moose, which have also benefited from a summer of plentiful food. Snow is on the ground by September or October; trapping for mink, marten, fox, and other furbearers begins in November. Winter brings days of dusk and periods of deep cold, the kind that freezes a tossed cup of coffee before it even hits the ground.

We talked as we strolled back down the hill to the river's edge, where Uncle Al stood admiring Doug's kayak. Hefting the double-bladed paddle in his upturned palms, he commented, "I've always wanted to try one of these." At Doug's invitation, he slipped nimbly into the cockpit, pausing only briefly to listen as Doug explained that the main difference from the canoe stroke

Al was used to was that, with a kayak paddle, he needed to push on one side while pulling on the other. My reservations about shoving this small old man who had never kayaked before into the current dissipated instantly. In one breathtakingly fluid motion, Uncle Al took off upriver, paddling with exquisite speed and grace.

Uncle Al was gone for quite a while, and when he returned, he only reluctantly traded places with Doug. In parting, he took a long moment to hold our hands between both of his. Then he slipped a fat silver salmon into the kayak's cockpit, between Doug's feet. "God bless you," he said. "Journey far, but remember your home." In an instant, the current carried us out of sight.

On that visit, Uncle Al told us several Koyukon legends from *Kk'adonts'idnee,* which has been translated as "Distant Time." Raven, the glossy, raucous acrobat of the sky, figures largely in these stories, as creator and trickster. It was Raven who created the earth. At first, the rivers he made flowed upstream along one bank and downstream on the other, but deciding that it was too easy for humans to drift in either direction without having to paddle, Raven altered his design.

Like any river, the Yukon has more subtleties than first appear. Its waters do not all flow at the same speed or even in the same direction. The river accelerates on the outside corners of bends, flows faster in mid-channel and on the surface than on the edges or at depth. Along the shore, it has slack zones and eddies, places of reverse current where migrating fish gather to rest and locals like to place their nets or fish wheels. The river constantly presented me with choices. By reading its swirls, I could use the current to best advantage—going up, down, or across stream as I wanted rather than committing myself blindly to the predominant flow. Or I could relinquish control, submitting to the river's whim. The parallel to navigating the irregular flux of life is obvious. What is less apparent is how hard it can be to feel the force of the current pushing until you try to row against it. In life or on rivers, awareness of what is giving momentum at any one time is essential if you want to avoid getting pinned against an undesired shore.

When we paddle, we take our sometimes humbling lessons where we find them. One day, a bag of garbage taught us about persistence. We saw it at nine in the morning, at first mistaking it for our third swimming black bear of the summer until we noticed it was too shiny and didn't have ears. Hurrying past it with regret that we didn't have room for the litter on board, we scanned for mastodon tusks as we moved between ancient cliffs. We stopped to wash clothes in a village of leaning cabins, setting off again in the afternoon under building thunderheads and paddling past fish camps, straight paper birch trees, and meadows of tall purple fireweed. About fifteen minutes before landing for the night, after more than forty-five miles of shoreline, we again passed the bobbing bag of garbage, cheering ourselves for winning the race. And then, as we were brushing our teeth, we saw a speck out on the river that binoculars confirmed to be the same black bag. We never saw it again and can only assume that it arrived somewhere before we did.

A week and roughly 270 miles after our visit with Uncle Al, beyond the bend where the river makes a major turn to the south, we pulled through low, rounded mountains into the village of Kaltag. Though it was so early in the morning that steam was still rising from the water into cooler air, the village was awake. A number of people were in skiffs just offshore, while others walked back and forth along the beach with bowed heads or stood quietly in watchful clusters. Our arrival was barely acknowledged. On landing, we learned that the men in the boats were dragging the bottom of the river with treble hooks, hoping to snag the body of a man in his twenties who had drowned a few hours earlier. He had tried to leave the village in his skiff but was so drunk that he had forgotten to reinsert the drain plug. While he tried to start the motor, the boat filled with water. Like many rural Alaskans, he was unable to swim and probably died a hundred feet or less from shore. The prevailing opinion—a consensus based upon too much experience—was that if the body wasn't recovered that day, it would float to the surface within a week.

Feeling very much outsiders, we stood in a corner of the beach talking with the man's fourteen-year-old brother, whose black hair hung low over his eyes like a veil. In a soft voice filled with resignation, he explained that it was village custom to set the boat adrift and burn it with gasoline so that it wouldn't kill anyone again. "Why burn a several-thousand-dollar boat?" Doug asked, stopping himself from adding that it wasn't the boat's fault. "It is our way," answered the boy, elaborating that the village would then gather for a feast at which the family would present gifts to everyone in honor of their lost son. The boy invited us to the pot-latch, but it was clear that we should leave.

The summer we floated the Yukon, there were ten such alcohol-related deaths in this region. By the time we reached Kaltag, we'd already passed several raw bluffside graves topped by heaps of plastic flowers. Some of these deaths were suicides; others, like the one in Kaltag, were labeled accidents. Studies from this same period, the mid-1980s, showed that ten times as many young Alaska Natives as Caucasians would take their own lives. There was a one-in-ten chance that a fifteen-year-old Native male would commit suicide, or at least try to do so, before he reached twenty-five. Statistics, however, cannot capture the grief and anger and numbness we saw etched into those faces in the dawn at Kaltag. They cannot convey the weariness of a culture being eroded by forces as undeniable as the river itself. Nor do they show the currents of hope that nevertheless persist.

The Native culture that binds individuals to the land and to one another has been beset by Western institutions, diseases, and values. Subsistence, the term commonly used to describe Native dependence upon what can be gathered, hunted, and caught for food, shelter, and clothing, was traditionally far more than just a lifestyle. It has long provided an economic and spiritual base for the culture, a life that centered on sharing, humility, and respecting nature. For some villagers, unemployment checks and boredom replaced the subsistence framework. With limited local work opportunities, others sought full-time or seasonal jobs outside the village, on forest-fire crews or in construction.

Drinking is one way of numbing the turmoil of change. With it has come a huge increase in accidental and self-inflicted deaths, along with domestic abuse and other violence. Under the influence of alcohol, many Natives have frozen to death within sight of their villages, drowned by falling overboard, or died in high-speed snowmachine collisions. In the wake of this widespread destruction, there has been a growing sobriety movement in which some communities have attempted to assume more control over their lives through sovereignty. Many have voted themselves "dry." Native elders like Uncle Al have been a moral compass in trying to rekindle their people's sense of independence, self-esteem, and purpose, in part through the teaching of traditional skills.

As I stood in Kaltag's disturbing silence, I remembered another Distant Time story related by Uncle Al. Raven first made humans out of rock, but determined that to be too easy. So he created us again, this time out of dust, and we became mortal. The finiteness of a lifetime adds intensity to our search for truth, for beauty, for happiness, for love, for ourselves. I've begun to understand that death lends meaning to life, that it adds weight to the choices I make about how I want to live and who I want to be. The oceans seem even bigger and more compelling because I know I can never fully explore them. The same is true of the mountains, the forests, and the rivers. There are so many kinds of time. Distant Time. Geologic time. River time. Lifetime. So many ways to measure time: in eons, change, minutes, miles, seasons, growth, tragedies, disappointments, accomplishments. Working on the Greenland Ice Sheet, I routinely held in my hands inches of cold ice core representing ten thousand years. Seventy or eighty years, however, is an awkward span, its boundaries almost too comprehensible.

On the lower Yukon, only a few hundred miles from where the river has emptied into the sea for 40 million years, we slipped from Athabascan into windier, more open Yup'ik Eskimo country. Under often stormy skies, the hills recede and the brown river slows. Forty-four days from Tagish Lake we reached the Yukon's delta, a place of cool rain, salt air, high swamp grass, and boot-sucking mud.

Anxious not to intrude and eager for sleep, we try not to camp in villages, where adults and packs of unsupervised kids alike tend to keep noisy late-night hours. But in Kotlik, a Yup'ik village only ten miles from the ocean, we had to make an exception in quest of a place where we could stand without sinking. Three curious rubber-booted children watched us wrestle our gear through the muck. After much foot-shuffling, the bravest of them mustered the nerve to creep close to Doug, whose big, full beard is a rarity among Alaska Natives. "Are you Santa Claus?" the five-year-old asked. Doug bent to a crouch, looked directly into the boy's glistening eyes, and answered kindly, "No, but he's my brother."

In villages, we are almost always greeted first by the children. They tell us where the store is or take us to the post office. Often too shy to speak, they lead us by running ahead, their giggles trailing after them. After they've climbed inside our cockpits or been chased away from making a seesaw of my oars, they start asking questions. The most common is "Where are your kids?" In village Alaska, where fifteen-year-olds are often mothers, my small questioners usually can't fathom that I don't have any children. Tired of giving the same answer, after a while I'll joke, "Well, Susie is in the blue bag, Billy is in the gray bag, and Johnny is over there in the orange bag." Wide-eyed, they'll ask if my kids can come out and play. "No," I say, "they're napping. But if you want, you can carry them up to the top of the beach."

In Kotlik, the kids gingerly held out their arms like miniature forklifts and carefully toted their loads through the mud. When they went home, they surely told their parents about the gussuk paddlers who kept their children in colored bags. Gussuks—a Native expression dating back to the days of Russian "Cossacks"—are white people. Maybe an elder commented, as did one old man when we asked him about the impact of anthropologists in his village, "I've been studying the ways of white people my whole life. They are strange."

We asked our onlookers in Kotlik if they knew Andrew, a local man who had worked with Doug many years before. Word spread, and before long Andrew came to our boats to invite us to supper at his family's house. Like most Yukon Delta settlements, Kotlik copes with a lack of solid ground by means of a network of slanting wooden boardwalks on stilts. The boardwalks connect the houses, a washateria where we spent the afternoon doing laundry and taking showers, and a few community buildings before yielding to the flat expanse of waving grass.

Andrew met us at the door of his house and asked us to wait outside, as his "old man" was going to the bathroom. In a one-room house in a village where indoor plumbing exists only on TV, this means that the "honey bucket" is in use. A few minutes later, his father appeared, shuffling carefully down the steps of the house to empty his galvanized pail into a larger container surrounded by a sludge of spilled waste. While standing outside, Doug noticed a fifty-five-gallon drum positioned to catch rainwater from the roof. Flecks of industrial paint floated on the water's surface.

Andrew's father, Philip, was close to eighty and frail. Cataracts had almost completely robbed him of his vision. He kept pushing a can of baby formula toward me, urging me to make myself a drink; he had mistaken it for powdered Kool-Aid. Philip spoke only Yup'ik, but he could speak volumes with his hands. Although he had a gentle, understated demeanor, it was apparent that his failing body housed a treasure of knowledge. He was one of the few living elders who knew how to build a skin kayak, a process he described in detail at Doug's urging, with Andrew translating as necessary. A hunter would make his kayak three and a half times the span of his outstretched arms; the width of the cockpit was one and a half times the distance from his elbow to his fingertips. Philip emphasized that the boat must fit the hunter, for it would become an extension of him. He paused for a moment, smiling with almost childlike glee, for he had realized that he didn't need to explain that to us. The rocker, the curve of the keel, was three fingers higher at each end of the kayak than in the midsection. The ribs were steamed, bent, and tied with caribou sinew, and could be made of any type of straight-grained driftwood found in this muskeg country.

When we asked how the seal skins were sewed together to cover the frame, Philip deferred to his wife; that was a woman's job. She spoke in singsong Yup'ik, her work-thickened hands moving so dexterously as she demonstrated the stitch needed to make a waterproof seam that they looked like dolphins swimming through the air. The old man radiated pride describing the special concoction, with urine as its main ingredient, that the Yup'ik from this region used to treat the skins so that they would be both durable and waterproof. Years later, in Juneau, we attended an exhibit of Native kayaks collected from around the Arctic. There were kayaks from Siberia, Alaska, Canada, and Greenland. The kayak from the Yukon Delta was the oldest in the exhibit, dating back to the 1700s—and it was the only one with its original skin still intact. Philip would not have been surprised.

Andrew's mother served goose stew, saying, "I make it this way, but I don't know how gussuks do it." She put her hand on my shoulder, speaking so softly that Andrew leaned to catch her words. "I think you will like it, though, because you are of the river." We ate mostly in silence, with the crowd of people living inside the small house. Having spent time with other Native families, we knew that they don't feel compelled to fill quiet with continuous conversation. New teachers in the bush sometimes don't realize that children are answering the questions asked of them by simply raising their eyebrows in affirmation, or wrinkling their noses to indicate dissent. Once, when a Native storyteller was asked by the humorist Garrison Keillor what could be learned from his culture, his answer—which came, of course, only after a pause—was "quietness." Quietness is less about not talking than about learning to listen and being attuned to nonverbal clues. It is a state of watchfulness, a heightened awareness of the sough of wind on the river and the honking of geese overhead.

We were cursing that heightened awareness, however, and praying for quietness later that night. The only nonliquefied ground we'd been able to find for our camp was on the edge of the gravel airstrip. A group of roaming kids, all under the age of ten, found us at two in the morning. It was still light outside, and we were the closest thing to a video arcade within hundreds of miles. They made an increasingly aggravating game of unzipping our tent door to laugh at the exhausted gussuks trying to sleep. First we tried ignoring them; then we tried politely asking them to leave; then we resorted to yelling. Eventually, we thought to tie the door shut from the inside with a piece of parachute cord. Later in the morning, one of their mothers, wearing a flowered calico parka with a wolf ruff, brought a gallon of freshly picked salmonberries in wordless apology.

The next day, we paddled into the ocean. After an uninterrupted diet of current for two thousand miles, it felt like molasses. Andrew's mother was right, though. I did feel of the river, with some of its strength and a bit of its resilience. The river speaks a language rich in verbs—it is constantly rippling, sliding, eddying, burbling, and bending. Perhaps for that reason it made me feel very much alive, conscious of myself within an ever-changing mosaic of time and space.

Four years after the Yukon journey, on the Mackenzie, another northern river that we'd hoped would be as wonderful as the Yukon but was not, I dreamed of a friend's death. I'd known that John Hale and his wife, Nan, the masterminds behind our wedding, had flown from Alaska to seek treatment for John at the same cancer hospital in New York City where my mother would later be a patient. By the time we left, they were already staying at my parents' house on Long Island Sound. The prognosis for John had been relatively optimistic; at least, no one had said he would die soon. But while we were camped on an isolated black silt beach, I had a dream, so vivid it woke me, in which John said goodbye with one of his trademark snuffling doggie kisses in my ear. I had my hands on Nan's shoulders, which were moving like the ocean.

In the morning, I almost didn't tell Doug about my dream. When we are far away from the people we love, it is easy to become paranoid about all the things that might be happening to them. That worry can cripple a moment, a day, a trip. It is not the way we have chosen to live our lives. I couldn't shake the dream, though. And despite Doug's reassurances, from Tuesday night to Sunday, over a stretch of almost 250 miles, I thought about little except reaching a telephone. When we finally pulled into Fort Norman, a small Canadian Arctic village, there were no public phones, but a curiously transplanted Ibo tribesman from Nigeria let me call from his house. My mother picked up after only one ring. "John died last Tuesday morning, didn't he?" I blurted. "I thought you would know," she answered softly.

I ran back to the sweltering hot mud bank where the Mackenzie River flowed past my feet, unseen through a blur of tears. My thoughts were a jumble of wishes. I wished I were with Nan. I wished I had followed my hunches and gone back East to be with her and John. I wished I weren't stuck on this wide, boring, slow-moving, buggy river. I wished that I didn't have to climb back into my hot boat and grind out more hot miles. I wished that Doug, who was off trying to help an Austrian buy a new paddle, would hurry back down to the boats, where I waited, sobbing and frying.

When Doug returned to the river, we pushed off into a light current. Something broke inside me, and, shirtless and sweat-drenched, I rowed as if possessed. There was no way that Doug in his kayak could match the pace. Soon, he was a dot in the distance upon which I fixed my eyes. I pounded down the river, covering forty miles in four hours, oblivious to my surroundings and seized by racking heaves. Finally, utterly drained, I pulled onto a beach and waited for Doug to come gather what was left of me into his arms.

We lay awake for most of the night, reminiscing, reminding ourselves that John's life, the sum of his energy, wisdom, and humor, was a tributary to ours and the lives of so many others. I spooned close to Doug, keenly aware of our hearts beating in unison. With fleeting clarity, I wished for nothing but to be exactly where I was.

When I ask friends to draw time as they perceive it, some sketch a straight line with an X at each end, others scribe a circle. In my most satisfying moments, I see time as a river, the way the Yukon and the elders along it taught me. The water keeps moving whether I stand on the shore and watch it flow by, let myself get carried by the current, or actively steer a course down or across the river's shifting channels. And when I reach the end of my journey, others will just be beginning.

"I'm very brave generally," he went on in a low voice:

"only to-day I happen to have a headache."

—Tweedledum in *Through the Looking Glass,* by Lewis Carroll

There is a strength one rises to in rare moments, a stretch of cunning or physical ability.

And there is a strength one pares down to, a tundralike patience, self-denial,

or determination. Both can occur as often in the inner city

or on a college campus as in the Amazon.

—Diane Ackerman, *The Rarest of the Rare*

5

Big Surf and Bad Bears:
The Chukchi Sea

WHAT'S A NICE GIRL FROM NEW YORK DOING *standing knee-deep in surf, blood-splattered to the elbows, watching for grizzly bears while dewhiskering a dead walrus?* That was the only thought tracking through my freezing brain. Any notion of who I thought I was or wanted to be had been chased away by a much grosser reality.

I had gotten to this place innocently enough. The previous September, arriving in Nome just ahead of the first gusts of storm season, we'd been greeted by two crusty old miners sifting the black sand beach for gold nuggets. Declaring themselves the official welcoming committee for couples who had paddled the four thousand miles from Seattle to Nome, they presented us with a marble hastily procured from their waterfront tent, a dilapidated A-frame pitched just above the tideline and festooned with a "For Sale" sign. Our benefactors also insisted upon treating us to lunch.

Looking seaward as the four of us walked into town, I saw a point in the distance and was sneak-attacked by a pang that I wouldn't be rowing around it. After sixty-nine straight days of river and ocean, we had just pulled our boats out of the water for the last time that season. We weren't even halfway through our cheeseburgers before Doug and I began to explore the idea of returning the next summer to extend our wanderings from Nome to Point Barrow, the northernmost finger of the United States.

A friend once commented that she wished she could do the kind of trips we do but was inhibited by fear. "How do you deal with it?" she asked, as if *it* were a two-headed, fire-breathing monster with wickedly sharp incisors. She brought to mind Mark Twain's words: "I have had a great many troubles, but most of them never happened." Most of the time it isn't real fear that seems to cripple people; it is the worry about all the bad things that *could* happen. Will we get cancer or Alzheimer's or not have enough money to live on when we are old? What if the boat swamps or the ice breaks or the plane crashes? Uncertainty is nearly always at the root of such anxieties. Allowed to run free, our imaginations can be depended upon to conclude the worst. This is the kind of worry that Gavin De Becker, in *The Gift of Fear*, calls a form of self-harassment, "a way to avoid admitting powerlessness over something, since worry feels like we are doing something."

The summer of 1988 along northwestern Alaska's Chukchi Sea affirmed the importance of controlling our minds as a way to manage our lack of control over clearly present danger. It wasn't the moments of pure fear, when the grizzly's paw was pushing against the tent door or Doug was getting pummeled in the surf, that were the hardest to deal with, for then all we had to do was react. It was the insidious stress that comes with being in a state of continual alert against adverse potential. Most bears, when skinned, are said to look startlingly similar to humans. As individuals, our most vulnerable inner core is usually carefully sheathed by bravado, pretensions, and assumptions. Coping with agitated cold water by day and bad-tempered bears by night is a sure, though not necessarily recommended, way to accomplish a kind of metaphorical skinning. Hardship strips us to little more than pink flesh. For better or worse, the raw fibers of which we are made then lie more clearly exposed.

The first challenge that year was just getting out of town. A springtime of large avalanches with a penchant for annihilating power lines kept us working well past the solstice. It was July 20 before we found ourselves standing in the din of a cavernous Anchorage air cargo terminal, facing a choice of freighting our boats that night to Kotzebue, north of both Nome and the Arctic Circle, or waiting another day until they could fly to Nome. Either way, we, along with forty-five days of food, would follow on a passenger plane a few hours later. We shuffled our feet on the grimy floor, asking each other, "I don't know, where do *you* want to go?" Eager to get going and not sure that we had enough summer left to accomplish our original goal, we chose to head north along the Chukchi Sea from Kotzebue.

Kotzebue, a town of several thousand, sits on a spit of dust and gravel that has been inhabited by Inupiat Eskimo for centuries. At this edge of the Arctic, the country consists of enormous expanses of sky, sweeping tundra and grasslands, distant rounded mountains, and, of course, the sea, which is frozen in winter and moody in summer. It is treeless land that looks old, weathered, wise. Almost perpetual wind stirs the grasses into motion, an undulating, animated tapestry in green, brown, and onion-purple.

The plane we arrived on also brought a small crowd of tourists, all wearing colorful "Native-style" parkas provided by the airline and clutching certificates proclaiming that they had crossed the Arctic Circle. We happened upon this group a few hours later in Kotzebue's Museum of the Arctic. The visitors stood in a knot at one end of an oversized room, snapping photographs of three silent Inupiat elders who were up on a stage demonstrating traditional activities—sewing fur clothes, cleaning hides, and playing with a fur-covered "Eskimo yo-yo." The stage was backed by a fanciful mural depicting heavily glaciated country not even remotely resembling any terrain within hundreds of miles. A stuffed white wolf snarled from a corner, a dead polar bear had a vacant look in its eyes, and an Arctic hare was missing one ear. We thought we saw the faintest glimpse of a smirk on the face of a stuffed snowy owl.

The first sunny days slipped by in a rejuvenating rhythm. We breathed deeply of space and silence and, as gently as possible, broke the news to our paddling muscles that their winter hibernation was over. One calm day we swam, albeit briefly, in a dazzling blue freshwater lake, which we shared with a sandhill crane while an owl called from an unseen perch not far away. On Cape Krusenstern, we explored a fan of former beaches curving parallel to the present shoreline. They are now gentle benches sprinkled with lagoons, ponds, and soggy tundra. The cape is an archaeologist's paradise where artifacts from successive periods of habitation have been unearthed. The oldest artifacts, furthest inland, were last touched by human hands around 6000 B.C. Everywhere we looked, we saw rocky, grass-covered mounds, the remains of old sod houses. Also, big piles of discarded beluga whalebones—vertebrae, jawbones, and surprisingly tiny teeth stained reddish brown by the soil. We found modern relics as well—snowmachine cowlings, fishing floats, and even the remnants of a basketball court near a tar-papered cabin.

On the fourth day alone, our animal tally totaled eighteen dead walrus, one dead and four live grizzly bears, two live seals, one dead polar bear, three dead whales, and one live porcupine as bristly as Doug. Dead walrus had already become a commonplace sight on this journey. Traditionally, when walrus were hunted, the entire carcass was used—the hides for boats, the oil for light and heat, the meat for food. Now walrus are illegally shot by a few younger Native men for the hundreds of dollars their tusks yield, while the rest of their bodies, sometimes weighing more than a ton, are discarded. Such waste causes Inupiat elders to shake their heads in disgust. Within days of washing up on the beach, the mottled gray hides are raked with claw marks of grizzly bears and pecked by seabirds and ravens. All summer, I tried to restore some measure of dignity to the animals by placing long, smooth pieces of bleached driftwood in the empty sockets where their tusks should have been. Doug did the same, driven less by sympathy than by vengeance. He hoped the decoys would waste the time of the killers who cruise the area in small planes or ATVs (all-terrain vehicles, which resemble dirt bikes with three or four knobby rubber tires and which proliferate in predominantly roadless bush Alaska), scouting for slain victims that have sunk before they are separated from their tusks.

We found the polar bear, with its head and claws cut off, in front of a backdrop that looked like the painted white rocks in polar bear cages at zoos. He was big, at least nine feet long even without his head. The weather soon began to turn joint-stiffening raw. After lunch the wind accelerated to a low-pitched wail, inciting the water into a riot of seven-foot waves and leaving no question that the time had come to bail out. Precisely when we needed it, we found a narrow channel through a sandbar in the barrier beach that allowed us access to the more protected waters of Kotlik Lagoon without our having to execute a surf landing. That flush feeling of luck didn't last long.

Kotlik Lagoon. Either of us can say the name more than a decade later and the same desolate images come to mind. A dull sky and a pervasive spookiness. A craving for hot drinks and dry, pliable fingers. The sensation that if the earth were flat, this would be the elusive, much-dreaded edge.

Cruising the inside beach, we found the dead grizzly bear with four enormous fang teeth. We'd only just taken refuge in the tent and our books when the incessant throbbing of surf was broken by the sound of revving motors. Two modern-day cowboys roared up astride four-wheelers, rifles slung over their backs. Words burst out of them like pressurized steam. They were off-duty construction workers from the terminal facility of a nearby lead and zinc mine. Bundled up against the weather, they had been nearly on top of a grizzly bear feeding on a dead walrus on the outer beach before they saw it. The bear, as startled as they were, had taken off inland, brushing right past our tent.

Exhausted from being pitched around by waves and staving off hypothermia all day, Doug and I quickly fell into a coma-like sleep. In the middle of the night, the sound of very heavy breathing and occasional snorting began to filter through to my consciousness. Doug says he was vaguely aware of a gentle nudging against his feet but didn't register alarm until he heard me asking hopefully, "Doug, is that you?" He sat bolt upright and found himself looking out the partially unzipped tent door into the biggest, brownest set of eyeballs he'd ever seen, less than his arm's length away. By this time, I was also sitting up. Noticing that a paw the size of a frying pan was pushing against the tent door, I yelled, "Hey, bear!"

One advantage of having what my friends kindly label an "unusual voice" is that I am always in possession of a strikingly effective bear deterrent. Without panic, the bear withdrew his paw, backed up a few feet, turned to give us a rear view, and lumbered off. In case the bear circled back, Doug grabbed for our 12-gauge shotgun. In sorry fact, on this trip he seemed to be almost as attached to this tool of last resort as he was to me; it had become his constant companion and sleeping partner. Five more times during the night we woke up slinging "Hey, bear!" beyond our nylon walls, toward the gravel crunching menacingly around our elbows, toes, and heads.

The weather allowed us to move only in fits and starts. Long before we had paddled the ninety miles to Kivalina, however, this village of about 250 mostly Inupiat residents announced itself by increasing concentrations of floating or marooned Pampers, cans, and plastic. We had scarcely pulled up on the beach in front of the cluster of boxy, generic-looking houses when a teenager bicycled up to us with a miniature skin umiak, or boat, nestled inside his coat. The word was out: tourists had hit town. What Doug really wanted was a miniature kayak, so we attained directions to the house of the local master. These days, it is much easier to find Inupiat who know how to make the models rather than the kayaks themselves.

Nearing our destination, we asked a man who stepped outside his house if we were on track to find Oscar Sage, Sr. He nodded and waved us inside, where he showed us a twelve-inch kayak cleverly constructed with scrap-wood supports, a covering of caribou intestine, and sinew threads. A paddler clad in white canvas, with an orange Styrofoam face and a caribou-antler pipe, sat stoically in the cockpit, his hands covered in mouse-fur mitts. A miniature harpoon was strapped to the deck. After we had purchased the kayak and were talking around the kitchen table, another man entered and introduced himself as Oscar Sage, Sr., brother of our host. He invited us to his house next door. We didn't want two kayak replicas, but it is awkward not to buy something when you are sitting on cardboard boxes inside the artist's cramped home, being stared at by its numerous tenants. So we ended up with another kayak from the real Oscar Sage, Sr.

Only eight miles out of Kivalina, we became seriously storm-bound. The tide, which is usually less than two feet in the Chukchi Sea, rose eight feet, and the waters reached about 175 feet up the beach. Fifteen-foot waves crashed relentlessly, and our boats, tethered in the tundra behind the beach, were floating. This portion of the Arctic is technically a desert, with an average of only six inches of precipitation a year. Over the next forty-eight hours, we received enough rain to get the area at least temporarily reclassified as semitropical. Winds of forty-five miles per hour, punctuated by higher gusts, contorted our tent into shapes not commonly pictured in equipment catalogues, plastering it with sand and making the poles whine. The collective roar of surf and wind sounded like the runways at Chicago's O'Hare Airport on a holiday weekend. Yellow sea foam covered the beach and scudded over our tent in clumps. On our little gravel knoll, we were about the only thing in sight that wasn't partially submerged.

During the peak of the storm, in the middle of the second night, we were both awakened by a loud pop that could have been a gust of wind snapping the tent fabric—or something tripping over one of the tent strings. Conditioned by that point, we let loose with a "Hey, bear!" and, hearing nothing more, went back to sleep. About an hour later, Doug crept outside to relieve himself and started to laugh, prompting me to ask in a growl what was so funny at four in the morning. Looking down, he had seen two large hindpaw prints immediately next to the tent. Scanning upward in search of the front prints, he'd found them on *top*

Sunset near Nanaimo, British Columbia

On the Yukon River *(Doug Fesler)*

Night visitors on the Yukon River

Alaska Peninsula *(Doug Fesler)*

Home for the night, southeast Alaska

A Greenland
iceberg in Labrador

In northern
Labrador
(Sunna Fesler)

Rowing the east
coast of
Spitsbergen
(John Bauman)

The hanging whale
(Doug Fesler)

Greenland
(photo on right
by Doug Fesler)

Inupiaq man
near Barrow,
Alaska

Hauling *Princess* across the Beaufort Sea

Ooze of garbage and guts near a
Greenland cabin

(Doug Fesler)

Grizzly bear track

Lunch break along Søndre Strømfjord, Greenland

of the nylon tent, about twenty-five inches above my head. Evidently, the bear had been testing the thin fabric with its paws when we scared him off. I shuddered briefly, then relapsed into sleep. My mother asks incredulously, "That's it, you went back to sleep?" But we couldn't come up with any better options. We were grateful when the storm released us the next day and we could continue north.

It's hard to credit now, when safety and warmth allow our minds the luxury of freely ranging thought, but in risky circumstances we have learned to cope by not thinking too much, and relying on our instincts. On this trip, we were too exhausted, too scared, and too cold to worry about what *might* happen; we needed to harbor our energy for dealing with actual crises as they arose. It became routine for us to wake up, react to an intrusive bear, and roll over in our sleeping bags, although sometimes we snuggled closer together in what has been given the unfortunate name of a bear hug, thankful not to be traveling solo.

We'd always smugly asserted that most people with harrowing bear stories just don't know how to camp and react around bears, and we still aver this is the case more often than not. We are religious about never eating in the tent. Instead, we cook downwind of camp and below the tideline to minimize the possibility of lingering food smells. But given even worse weather than usual, the Chukchi Sea grizzly bears were finding little to eat other than roots, parka squirrels, and long-dead walruses. When we could get off the beaches they used as thoroughfares and onto the tundra behind, we could usually make it through the night uninterrupted. In many places, though, there were unscalable cliffs or steep, crumbly mud banks with permanently frozen lenses of ice, or draining, quarter-mile-long beach hauls. Sometimes we carefully balanced objects in strategic spots so that they would make loud noises when they were knocked over, but these elaborate early-warning systems proved to be little more than a psychological safeguard. The bears never showed any interest in our boat or our food, just our tan-colored dome tent. Doug was convinced it was my socks that drew them in; certainly they were potent enough to have applications in chemical warfare. I maintained it was his fermenting rubber boots. Quite likely, to an inquisitive bear, our tent bore a striking resemblance in both smell and shape to a bloated walrus. It reached the point that, emerging from the tent one morning, we were startled to find two sets of fresh grizzly bear prints intersecting with our footprints from the night before only because one of the bears actually seemed to be afraid of us. We could tell from the heavily indented toeprints and the greater distance between them that it had galloped away.

We are accustomed to dealing with wilderness hazards by gathering data that helps us to reduce uncertainty and by building an arsenal of strong skills, but with these bears, we had to admit a degree of powerlessness. Just because their visits were nearly certain, we had to continually remind ourselves, didn't mean that the outcomes of our encounters were predetermined. Sometimes it was impossible to keep images of disfigurement and impending death at bay, especially in Alaska, where horrific bear stories are passed around like popcorn and any residents of duration, including us, are bound to know several people who have been mauled. If we were vigilant enough to make ourselves stay in the present, though, we bought ourselves breathing room, even a sense of freedom. This kind of mind control, more critical than physical conditioning, isn't as difficult to achieve as it sounds when the need for it is so apparent. It is sort of like chemotherapy: the notion of choosing to inject poison seems completely untenable until it is presented to you, or your mother, or your closest friend, as the best and maybe only chance of surviving cancer.

Of course, all this mind control would have been superfluous if we had just left and gone home. But we weren't exactly traveling in Europe, with rucksacks and a rail pass that enabled us to hop around as we pleased. The few villages along the coast were widely spaced, and most were serviced by bush planes too small to accommodate our boats. Also, despite the reality, we felt committed to the *idea* of the trip, to linking together as much of the coast of Alaska as possible.

The morning we found the paw prints of the fearful bear, our ritual good-luck kiss before launch failed us. The surf wasn't outrageously big, but each wave crashed onto the beach in a frenzy of white foam. Assisted by a timely push from Doug, I made it out, wet but intact. Sitting beyond the surf zone, I watched him prepare for battle, positioning his bow in the suds of the breakers.

On flattish beaches, the trick is to thrust yourself into the water at the crucial time without getting stuck, so as Doug climbed into his kayak, he had his paddle in one hand and a driftwood push stick in the other. He had just secured his spray skirt around the cockpit rim when an unexpectedly large wave crashed directly onto the bow, machine-gunning him with gravel. As the water surged around his boat, he made a valiant effort to break free of the beach, thrusting forward with his hips and pushing for all he was worth with stick and paddle. But a second wave pounced on the bow and swung his boat around, leaving it vulnerably broadside to the waves. A third wave landed directly on top of Doug, caving in the neoprene spray skirt and instantly filling the boat with water, eliminating all hope of escape. I could no longer see Doug, just the rolling, capsized kayak getting smacked by every incoming wave. In kayaking shorthand, he was getting "Maytagged"—thrown around as if inside a washing machine on spin cycle—but he managed to fight his way out from under the boat and skyward. We both took much-needed gulps of air. Unconsciously I, too, had been holding my breath.

Staggering to his feet, Doug grabbed the stern line before the strong undertow could pull his submerged kayak beyond reach. Trying to pull it up onto the beach felt like attempting to beach a whale, but he waved me back out when I rowed in to help—the waves in deeper water were reasonable for traveling and there wasn't much point in both of us getting stuck on the wrong side of the surf. Stopping occasionally to lunge for pieces of gear that had been washed out of his kayak—a blue stuff sack here, a water bottle there—he dragged the boat beyond the bite of the waves. Only then did he begin to vent. I couldn't hear him, but I had a pretty good idea of what he was saying from the gestures he made as he stomped on the beach, picking gravel out of his ears. He tugged his spray skirt off over his head in one angry motion, then pulled dripping gear bags out of his boat and flung them to the ground. While I shivered in my drifting boat, he bailed, bailed, and bailed some more, a sponge in one hand and a bucket in the other. At last he repacked his kayak and squared off again in the surf. Emerging on my side of the breakers, still roaring frustration, he looked like a lion shaking foam from its mane.

As a result of this debacle, we devised a new surf exit method I dubbed "the eternal tug of salvation." Doug would push me out with a slack line attached from my boat's stern to his kayak's bow. Once I was beyond the surf and he gave me the ready sign, I'd start rowing seaward with power, providing the needed momentum to yank his heavy boat out of its sitting-duck position.

By midafternoon the next day, we found ourselves traveling alongside green hills, buoyantly alone in the middle of what seemed to be untouched nowhere—an illusory perception that shattered abruptly at the mouth of Ogotoruk Creek. There was rusted junk scattered all over the tundra, along with some drooping Quonset huts and a tracked vehicle parked next to a dirt airstrip. What was this place? Who had lived here, and when? Why had they trashed it?

We were to learn later—though not until we'd heard it from a few independent sources did we believe what at first seemed surely a tall tale—that this was the site of Project Chariot. In 1958, the Atomic Energy Commission and Edward Teller (prose-lytizing father of the H-bomb) were looking to demonstrate the peaceful use of nuclear energy. They reasoned that a good way to do that was to detonate multiple thermonuclear bombs underground simultaneously in the Arctic. The explosion, 160 times greater than the one that shook Hiroshima, would create an unneeded deepwater harbor that Teller graciously offered to configure in the shape of a polar bear if desired. Of course, the result might initially be hard to see under a radioactive cloud that could rise as high as thirty thousand feet.

The Inupiat living nearby, dependent upon the land and sea for subsistence, were informed of this plan almost as an afterthought. A few biologists, Native leaders, and environmentalists banded together to mount a fight. Defying stacked odds, they won. Project Chariot was never completed, though it will be a long time before the remnants of the site studies—including shallowly buried nuclear waste—disappear.

When we pulled even with Ogotoruk Creek, we did not see a nuclear wasteland but a small, unremarkable stream bisecting a pebble beach covered with sea booty from the recent storm—driftwood, Styrofoam floats, dismembered starfish, and a dead walrus. Something about the walrus looked different. It took a moment to register that this one still had its head and tusks. We couldn't tell if it had died naturally or had sunk before it could be recovered by its killer. Doug and I looked at each other. He had long wanted to carve walrus ivory, but a law intended to help curb the lucrative practice of "head-hunting" for tusk money makes it illegal for non-Natives to buy raw ivory. This was clearly our chance.

We landed, hurried ourselves into extra clothes, and rolled up our sleeves. Our implements were woefully inadequate to the task at hand. Doug sharpened his Swiss Army knife to a razor-thin edge, but it practically bounced off the walrus hide. We were beginning to understand the persistence required of a grizzly bear to claw repeatedly at a hide in order to break through to meat. Our bone saw was only about an inch wider than the broad skull of the walrus, so Doug was reduced to tiny, almost futile back-and-forth motions. Meanwhile, I retrieved the vise grips from the repair kit and began to extract Plexiglas-like walrus whiskers from the pug snout, trying to ignore a nagging sense of reproach.

After about fifty minutes and several knife-honing sessions, we had our head mount, complete with two beautifully smooth, curved twenty-inch tusks. Neither of us was anxious to go diving into the opposite end of the walrus to retrieve the oosik, the impressively large penis bone that fascinates many humans. We cleaned off the gore, ran a few fast laps, breath steaming, to get blood back to our extremities, and pushed off to put distance between us and the fresh bear bait.

Having reassured each other that what we had just done was legal, we had paddled less than a mile when we saw our first small boat of the summer approaching. (We'd been asking Natives why we hadn't run into other boats and they had always given us the same unsettling answer: "Too rough.") When the two hooded men in the bouncing, inflatable Zodiac identified themselves as U.S. Fish and Wildlife Service biologists, we were disconcerted. Doug, with the still oozing walrus skull in garbage bags on the deck of his kayak, posed a hypothetical question: If white people were to find a dead walrus, would it be legal to harvest the tusks? Yes, said the biologists, as long as the tusks were registered within thirty days of returning home and were not sold. When we revealed that the question was not purely theoretical, the men berated themselves for not heading out to scavenge firewood earlier, as they would have beaten us to the treasure. Still, they repaid our tip about the still-available oosik with an invitation to dinner at their camp.

The next morning, recharged by pizza and warm baths in a galvanized tub filled by the bucketful, we reluctantly declined an offer of pancakes, knowing that we should try to get around Cape Thompson before the winds cranked up for the day. We continued along rumpled cliffs that started just beyond Ogotoruk Creek, our eyes following dark coal seams and gray swirls of layered rock up into a shroud of clouds. Low arches eroded into the base of the cliffs formed a bowling alley for waves. We were intrigued enough by the landscape to be willing to paddle in the nauseating confusion of the combat zone, where waves reverberating off the rock walls met fresh recruits. Screeching, milling seabirds—cormorants, murres, gulls, puffins, and guillemots among them—circled overhead, first a few, then hundreds, and finally thousands. This was their summer home, and we were invaders. Black-legged kittiwakes with yellow beaks plunged toward us, bombarding the water with streaming strings of droppings. It was only a matter of time before we suffered a direct hit, so we sought refuge under our parka hoods and kept moving.

When the cliffs ended abruptly, we followed the arc of a wide gravel beach until, seeking calmer seas, we portaged over the top of it into a lagoon. Rare tailwinds sent us flying, powering us as if by magic. The water was little more than ruffled, and the sun made fleeting, tantalizing appearances from behind a mass of clouds. From a polygon pattern of tundra drooping over the eroded edge of a bluff, three sets of little ears emerged. Curious and unsupervised, the wolf pups attached to the ears rolled, pounced, and played tag outside their den, less than twenty feet from us. A few hours later, we encountered three armed off-road warriors popping wheelies on their ATVs and accelerating at gravel-spewing speeds. When they asked us if we'd seen any wolves, neither of us had any trouble lying.

We camped within sight of Point Hope, a place where Inupiat people have lived since prehistoric times, calling it Tikiraq, which means "forefinger." A fifteen-mile bulge in the coastline, the spit is really a low-lying triangular framework of gravel that holds back the sea with its outer edges and contains several large lagoons within. It is an exceptionally strategic spot from which to intercept a host of sea mammals, including whales, walruses, and seals. Seabird eggs can be collected from the cliffs to the south and the inland rivers provide good fishing.

The sun escorted us into Point Hope the next morning, as did three large, splotchy gray whales. Some people stopped to stare as we approached. They were dwarfed by towering snow fences erected on the lagoon side of town, reminders of harsh winter winds that can transport enough snow to envelop the houses in dense drifts. We were close enough to shore to hear two elderly women speaking to each other in Inupiaq when a skiff zoomed by us at twenty-five miles per hour. Though they were seconds away from a head-on collision with the beach, the family inside sat ramrod straight. Peering stoically ahead, the middle-aged man standing in the stern looked like George Washington as portrayed crossing the Delaware. A moment before impact, he casually tilted the motor and the boat careened, screeching, onto the gravel beach, like a flat stone skipping across water, and stopped about twenty feet above the water's edge. The family disembarked as nonchalantly as if they were stepping off a streetcar. Our arrival was markedly less dramatic.

The eight hundred residents of Point Hope are renowned for being proud defenders of their culture, adapting to new technologies but unwilling to forget the old ways. Until the 1940s and 1950s, most of the region's people lived in semi-subterranean sod houses with driftwood or whale bones as structural supports. Now the houses are aboveground, built of wood and connected to power lines, but it is not uncommon to find modern-day Inupiat skinning seals in their living rooms while *Days of Our Lives* blasts from the television. If we had flown into town, they probably would have ignored our presence, having been analyzed, interviewed, and second-guessed ad infinitum by white people. As it was, some of the younger men were hostile, hurling barbs at us with their eyes and body language. However, our mode of transportation seemed to afford us some degree of credibility, and we soon had a small crowd around us asking where we'd come from and where we were going.

Doug found himself in the paradoxical position of teaching the Inupiat how to kayak. One man in his late fifties, with a dark, weathered face that radiated stoicism, was especially eager to learn. He knew that his father and grandfather had used kayaks to hunt, but he'd never sat inside a boat smaller than his skiff. Doug coached him on basic paddle strokes and helped him into the kayak. The man was only a few strokes away from the security of the beach when he asked in a guttural staccato, "You sure this boat isn't too tippy?" In time, nervousness gave way to a grin of contentment. Meanwhile, I tutored an athletic fellow willing to endure the pitfalls and humiliation of learning to row. He fell off the sliding seat, bashed his hands together, and wove a circular course. But both men wanted to keep practicing, so we gave them a few last pieces of advice and went off to do errands.

Laundromat gossip revealed that it had been a rare 75°F in Point Hope on the Fourth of July, but the pack ice had still been fast against the outer spit. At the post office, we mailed our walrus tusks off to a bighearted friend who had agreed to pick them up. (Though we thought we had done a good job of cleaning the skull and wrapping it in excessive layers of plastic, the box arrived in Anchorage reeking of death and dripping blood. When our friend showed up at the post office to claim it, only some fast talking on his part prevented him from being arrested and our box from being confiscated.) We blithely continued to the store, where we cruised aisles stocked with Twinkies, Cheerios, and Coca-Cola, looking for something we wanted to eat. We settled on Eskimo Pie ice cream, adding to the irony of the day. I made the ritual phone call to my parents, committing a few sins of omission for their sake. While I wrapped myself around the receiver, trying to hear them over the clamor of ATVs and tethered sled dogs, they described the elegant dinner party for ten they were hosting during a record-breaking heat wave.

We camped a short distance out of town and were awakened in the morning by a boatload of rowdies in their twenties who had not yet been to bed. One of them, underdressed in a thin windbreaker, had been shivering violently and appeared to be in a drug- or alcohol-induced haze. When Doug asked him if he was okay, he answered acerbically, "What does it matter? I'm going to die soon anyway."

We took advantage of tailwinds to whip the remaining nine miles down Point Hope's lagoon in less than two hours. The locals had told us that we could stay in sheltered water as far as "Ate-a-boat." Puzzled, we'd asked for clarification, but they laughed and said we would know the spot. In time, we came to a wrecked wooden boat, cocked on one side. It looked like a packer, once used for hauling people and freight. Closer inspection revealed the name *Ada* printed in faded letters on slowly disintegrating timbers.

Outside the lagoon's confines, the water was still too rough, so we pulled out on the far side of the channel to open water, beyond easy range of three-wheelers cruising the few miles from town. Meandering fox tracks told us we were not the first beachcombers of the day. Doug found a perfect walking stick and, squinting through his magnifying glass, counted ninety-five closely spaced rings within the circumference of a cigar. Once the trunk of a spruce tree that had survived nearly a century of harshness, it had almost certainly drifted from Siberia. That night we dozed off listening to wind and waves. We were jolted from sleep by two, possibly three, gunshots, followed by the distinct whizzing of bullets over our tent. Staying low and out of easy view, we peered through an opening in the tent door trying to spot our assailant. We saw only the exhaust end of a three-wheeler peeling back toward Point Hope on the opposite side of the lagoon entrance. Though we were certain that the shots had purposefully been aimed high, the message was all too clear.

When we finally ventured back into the open sea, leftover storm waves and swells joined forces, surging to eight feet or more and creating the kind of jumbled water that reduces rhythm to a concept. I just tried to keep the boat pointed in the right direction and think about something other than being seasick and far from home. Before long, however, the landscape was more than enough to distract me. We were approaching the Lisburne Hills, the western edge of the Brooks Range, which rises from the ocean, traverses the width of Alaska, and, taking no notice of the border, saunters into Canada. On the seaward side, cliffs of banded rock drop abruptly into the water while more gradual ridges stretch inland. Crooked spires along the shore, reminiscent of the canyon country in the American Southwest, alternate with long, white sandy beaches that elsewhere in the world would attract scores of vacationers with pale bellies.

Changing winds were causing the water to darken and waves to pitch up at random angles. The contours of the land and greenness of the tundra drew us to shore, and we soon had an idyllic camp set up near small, clear Angolik Creek. We purposely erected the tent in a spot surrounded by plate-sized flat rocks, comforted by the idea that any approaching bears would make as much noise walking on them as we did. Then we hiked up nearby 922-foot Iviagak Mountain, leaning into brisk winds, chirping back at parka squirrels, and carefully stepping around little patches of moss. Iviagak is an Inupiaq name, meaning "breast." The U.S. Geological Survey, attempting to use local nomenclature on topographic maps, assigned the name to the wrong mountain, but in an area with a remarkable number of breast-shaped mountains, it is easy to understand their mistake.

On Iviagak's spine, we hunkered from the wind inside a circular rock wall that, judging from the pattern of well-entrenched orange and black lichens, was built long ago. It may have been intended as a blind for hunting caribou or a lookout for whales, or it may simply have been a windbreak, but the vantage point it offered was seemingly infinite. Our eyes were drawn along the inward curve of the beach, then rose over folded tundra to the slanted tops of the headlands. In the distance, cliffs gathered into a barren plateau that was softened by a plume of cottony cumulus clouds. The expanse of sea looked storybook blue, fringed by a neat white comb along the shoreline. Our boats and tent provided scale, betraying the illusion that the surf was small and innocuous.

Landbound again the next day, we set off for 571-foot Cape Dyer, opting to take the high route across squat bluffs that lined the beach. In this harsh climate, the vegetation kept such a low profile that a tall blade of grass barely reached our ankles. Sunken into the tundra here and there were piled circles of flat rock. Some were the remains of old Inupiat shelters, others were graves. The sun finally broke through the clouds unequivocally, taking the sting out of the wind while we sat knee to knee on top of the cape, previewing the next stretch of coast with shared binoculars.

The next morning at five, we were jolted uncompromisingly out of oblivion by two potent whacks. So much for our theory that we would hear an approaching bear. Under siege, our tent crumpled instantly. The front door ruptured open and nylon drooped around our shoulders like a shawl as our tent poles shattered. We shouted our most uninviting "Hey, bear!" in unison, and there was no third blow.

Uncertainty hung in the silence. Was our assailant circling for another hit? Thinking it likely, Doug grabbed the shotgun and did a Rambo roll out of the ruins, landing on his feet and looking every bit a stuntman—except that he was stark naked from the waist down. I couldn't help but laugh, aware it might be the last sound I made. The bear, however, had decided that we were definitely not something dead and was loping down the beach, leaving us happily alone.

Oddly, our moments of real danger are usually accompanied by little more than a surge of energy and quickened heartbeats. It is only after we no longer need our instincts that the more terrifying "what-ifs" penetrate our psyches. By this point, though, we were experts at distracting ourselves, and we quickly became absorbed in the problem of resurrecting our tent. Each of the poles had broken in three places. Every place there was a break, the pole had also snapped through the tent and the rain fly. In all, we had twelve fractures in the poles, twenty-four nylon tears, and a twisted front zipper. We always carry a spare tent pole and a few splints, but we didn't have nearly enough to deal with destruction on this scale. Later in the day, we would spend hours searching for straight pieces of driftwood and bone with which to improvise splints. Dental floss and duct tape took care of the rips, pliers repaired the zipper. Though it looked like the home of voracious carnivores, with weather-bleached crane legs and seal ribs protruding from the pole sleeves, the tent would soon prove that it could still withstand freight-train winds.

Neither of us was inclined to go back to sleep, and as the sea was looking uncharacteristically reasonable, we decided to end our stay at Angolik Creek. An hour after the siege, I was packed and wandering a couple hundred feet from Doug when he whistled an alert. I looked up and saw a grizzly bear about three football fields down the beach galloping toward the boats and Doug. It was easy to discern by his lighter color and larger size that this was a different bear from the one that had just demolished our tent. It was probably four or five years old and about six hundred pounds.

We regrouped at our boats. Doug suggested that I get the gun out of my completely loaded boat. When I am afraid or in the midst of crisis, I grow surrealistically calm. In mountain rescue situations, it is as if I have a third eyeball mounted toward the back of my head, slowly rotating and absorbing detail. I see things very clearly, and a sequential plan of action unfolds in my mind like a slow-motion film. It plainly occurred to me that I could just launch, leaving Doug, who was not nearly ready, stranded on the beach. Then the bear stopped about 175 feet away and stood up on its hind legs, craning for a better look. I scrambled to unearth the gun and pumped a round into the chamber, while Doug stockpiled an arsenal of fist-sized rocks.

We knew we were in trouble when the bear's honey-colored fur prickled and his shoulders rotated forward and down. He dropped back onto all fours and charged us, at terrific speed. Standing our ground, we tried to make ourselves look huge, but for the first time all summer, my "Hey, bear!" went unheeded. I resorted to our marine flare pistol and fired a round in front of the bear's nose, taking care not to overshoot—a mistake that could have the nightmare result of scaring him toward us faster than he was already moving. The orange smoke had about as much effect on him as blowing soap bubbles.

A creek about seventy-five feet away was the dividing line for action. It probably took less time for the bear to reach it than it took you to read the previous paragraph. The bear crossed this scrimmage point without slowing, ripping up the sand. Doug grabbed the shotgun out of my hands, put it over his head, and ran at full tilt toward the bear, yelling and gesturing like a wild man. The bear's eyes seemed to widen, and his enormous paws splayed—the ursine equivalent of a double take. Then, in one fluid motion, he spun around and sprinted inland across the tundra. We watched him until he shrank into a dot. I suggested to Doug that at least he could have warned me. "I wasn't sure what I was going to do until I did it," he responded. "I felt like I was back in high school, where I learned that fighting is as much about bluff and posturing as action. It seemed like the only way to make him reconsider before he came so close that we'd have to shoot." I wouldn't be surprised if, to this day, the bear suffers nightmares of attacks by a rampaging two-legged creature with matted hair and a ragged beard.

For a change, we were happy to push off through surf. Sunshine and flat water worked a transformation in our mood as we edged along almost continuous pinnacled cliffs, accompanied by thick-billed murres flapping along determinedly, their black feet projecting straight out behind them. From the magnificent safety of our boats, we spied on a coffee-brown grizzly leisurely sniffing his way up a hillside. Near Cape Lisburne, the clamor of thousands of birds set the sky in motion and made the cliffs ring. Inhaling as infrequently as possible to avoid being overpowered by the stench of guano, we rounded the prominent bulk of the cape and ran into our old friends, headwinds and choppy waves. Dripping clouds moved in to join the party. As we powered into higher gear and donned appropriate clothes, we were astonished to see a golf ball nestled in the finger-shaped pinnacles at the top of the cliffs. In country of such expansive scale, the golf ball turned out to be the white dome of an Air Force radar station positioned watchfully westward toward what was then the Soviet Union.

We were able to travel four out of the next six days. A few porpoises and seals surfaced to monitor our passage, and a fearless fox pup, grizzly bear, and wolf did the same from their waterside vantage points in the tundra. Overhead, two jaegers mounted a screeching raid on a lone gull's lunch—the gull chased them off using aerial maneuvers a fighter pilot could only hope to emulate. We celebrated the sighting of our first live walrus, but it was a young one that had gotten blown onshore during the last storm and looked as if it did not have long to live. During a lunchtime hike, we intersected a grizzly bear thoroughfare, activating our own early-warning radar, the hairs on the backs of our necks. Individual paw-sized depressions had been worn into ground so hard that when we scuffed our feet back and forth like fitful horses, we barely made any impact on the vegetation. Such trails, which occasionally have been observed elsewhere, appear to have been created by bears following exactly in one another's footsteps for years on end.

Our arrival at Point Lay after 345 miles of paddling was marked by a number of deflating changes. For one thing, the country flattened into a low, almost featureless coastal plain. We had trouble finding the village, which was not at the location marked on our map. Unlike Point Hope, with its rich tradition and reason for being, Point Lay seemed to be populated by 150 people who came from and wanted to be somewhere else, despite new metal-roofed buildings and signs of ongoing construction everywhere—a school, a health clinic, a garage, and a fire station. Doug waited an hour and a half at the cubbyhole of a post office at the back of the store, only to be charged what seemed like an outrageous sum of sixty-seven dollars to mail three boxes home the slowest way possible. The confused young clerk did not inspire confidence but she assured Doug that this was the right amount. After Doug left, he realized he had forgotten to send something, and reluctantly returned. He struck up a conversation with another man in line, mentioning his doubt about the postal charges. Blowing his cover, the man revealed himself to be a postal inspector in town investigating the contractor for incompetence and looking for thousands of dollars of unaccounted-for funds. He marched into the office and reweighed the boxes himself, ascertaining that Doug had been overcharged by fifty-three dollars, which he insisted on repaying out of his own pocket, before evicting the clerk and closing down the place with a padlock.

That evening, the village's public safety officer, Mike McCarthy, took us on the grand tour. We drove by the old town sites, the dump, the sewage disposal area, the freshwater lake that is the town's water supply, the radar station, and the jail in less than twenty minutes. Then we went to Mike's house to spend the night. His wife, Betty, who was afflicted with multiple sclerosis, had been in Point Lay for only a month. She was trying to adjust to the inhospitable climate and a way of life in which plastic buckets substituted for flush toilets. Harsh is a pitifully inadequate word to describe a place where, a few winters later, a resident would be eaten by a malnourished polar bear cruising the dark gravel streets. Betty expressed amazement at our travels; I was dumbfounded by her courage. When she offered to make a pie if I could help her cut the apples, I almost knocked my chair over lunging for the nearest knife.

In the morning, the McCarthys fed us a big breakfast and waved encouragement from the beach as we launched. I was not heartbroken to leave Point Lay, but looking at photographs Mike took that morning, it is hard to know what motivated us to continue our trip. Everything is gray—the sky, the water, the smudge of land on the far side of the lagoon, the gravel we were standing on, even my boat. The only contrast is provided by Doug's yellow kayak and the brightly colored layers of clothing protecting us against a windchill well below freezing. Rising northwest headwinds let us grind just far enough to make it impractical to row back to the lasagna dinner we'd been invited to, though not far enough to keep from being tortured by the prospect.

Over the next few days, we alternated between sitting out the weather and inching, little faster than we could have propelled ourselves on hands and knees, against round-the-clock north winds. There were certainly occasional highlights: another live baby walrus—this time a healthy one—sleeping on a mud bed; another day, a multitude of ringed seals inquisitively surfacing around us. The seals belonged to a somewhat unusual population of about a thousand that summered in a lagoon rather than drifting further out to sea with the pack ice. But our daily mileage totals stayed in the single digits, our frustration mounted, the tundra yellowed, the water in our bottles froze, and snow dusted our boats. One morning, as we were plodding almost futilely along, I asked Doug what he was thinking about. He replied, "Getting to Point Barrow." When I asked again a few days later, he gave me the same answer.

We were engaged in a race against winter, and we were losing. My prospects in the accompanying battle against boredom didn't look encouraging when, lying stiffly on my back, tentbound again, I sped two-thirds of the way through my last book. Appropriately enough, the book was Roland Huntford's *The Last Place on Earth*, about Scott and Amundsen's struggles to reach the South Pole. Two passages struck close enough to my core to merit recording in my journal. The first was the reaction of Bjaaland, a member of Amundsen's team, when he first sighted the midnight sun:

One could wish one's home here in the icy regions where the sun shines day and night. One would think that it was everlasting summer here if it were not for the chill [in the air] that speaks of ice and desolation.

The second, also from Bjaaland, seemed prophetic:

Now we are ready again. I hope that it won't be a fiasco like the last time ... If I emerge unscathed from this journey, I must see that I get out of polar exploration. It's hardly worth the trouble ...

The winds that were holding us back were also pushing the pack ice toward shore, reducing the area of floatable water. On August 22, Doug suggested that we head back to Point Lay and fly home. I resisted, fixated on our goal of making it the last 120 miles or so to Point Barrow. But the truth of the matter was that we weren't having fun anymore—in fact, we hadn't had much fun yet.

We had always prided ourselves on savoring the *process* of traveling and exploring rather than focusing on reaching a particular place. Yet I had a surprisingly hard time giving up the goal. Doug kept asking, "Why do you want to keep going?" My only answer, "To get there," echoed like an empty cliché even to me. I couldn't quite shake the notion that quitting equaled failure and weakness. Doug, ever rational and remarkably skilled at separating reality from his ego, kept chipping away at my pride. How was this different from teaching people to evaluate avalanche hazard by making decisions based upon data rather than upon their desires? he asked. Finally, with surges of misgiving but mostly of liberating relief, we turned around near Icy Cape, appropriately named by British explorer Captain Cook when he was forced to make his own retreat southward in 1778. Rocketed by tailwinds and glorying in their novelty, we covered in hours the distance that had taken days of demoralizing struggle.

Our decision to quit proved to be a wise one. Thick pack ice quickly moved in, trapping three large gray whales in a small lead of open water near Barrow and preventing them from migrating south. Amid vaudevillian fanfare fed by worldwide press coverage, millions of dollars were lavished in an enormous rescue effort that freed the whales.

In a dizzyingly short time, we found ourselves back in Anchorage, where we marveled that we could wear shorts and sleep through a night without being sniffed by a grizzly bear. Of course, no one cared that we hadn't reached our goal; most were surprised we had persevered as long as we had. We weren't really aware that we were still under strain until six months later, when I awoke one night to find Doug's hands around my neck in a chokehold. On trial for murder, he would have had difficulty convincing a jury that he had simply been fending off a grizzly bear in his sleep.

Two summers later, our renters had their own unrehearsed drama with bears. We'd left the house in the care of friends who were fearful of bears, their fear heightened by the fact that we live in a place called Bear Valley. We'd assured them that bear sightings weren't common, moved out, and headed for southeast Alaska with two of Doug's daughters. End of Act I.

Act II, Scene 1: It is two o'clock in the morning. Caryn and Bret (our friends) are sound asleep in their room when Bret awakes to heavy rasping and wheezing noises. He awakens Caryn and tells her that he thinks her mother, visiting from New York, is having some sort of respiratory problem. Caryn, thinking that her mother is choking to death, rushes naked out of bed. At the top of the stairs, her worst nightmare is unfolding: a grizzly bear cub is running up the stairs toward her. She does exactly what one is supposed to in these situations—holds her ground, waves her arms, and talks loudly to the bear. But the bear is only five months old, only slightly larger than a bushel basket, and doesn't know that it is supposed to be afraid. So it keeps coming. Caryn retreats to her bedroom and locks the door. She yells to her mother, who also locks herself in. From their safe havens, they hear a pandemonium of thumps and crashes. The cub is knocking our collections of bones, rocks, and plants off the downstairs windowsills in an effort to find an egress anywhere it sees light because the door through which it entered has swung shut. It also keeps trotting up and down the stairs, whining, crying, and leaving frequent, indelible trail markers.

Act II, Scene 2: Mother bear and two more cubs are outside the house vigorously seeking a way in. The big sow has gouged deep claw marks into the deck and managed to push in not only the basement door and window but their wooden frames as well. Mama is very unhappy; foam is dribbling out of her mouth. Now it's time for action, but Caryn and Bret are not excited by the idea of chasing the cub out of the house. Every time they try to venture from their safe haven, the cub comes upstairs to investigate the noise. So they do the only thing they can think of. They call 911.

Act III, Scene 1: The first Alaska State Trooper arrives on-site. Since we live about seventy-five feet below tree line in the Chugach Mountains on an old homestead road about a half hour from town, this does not happen as quickly as in the movies. The Trooper rolls down his squad car window and hears Mama grunting and snarling just downslope of the main door, swatting the alder bushes and making loud popping noises with her jaw—all clear signs of an angry bear. He elects to remain securely inside his vehicle at the bottom of the driveway and radios for backup.

Act III, Scene 2: Backup arrives, possibly after stopping for doughnuts and coffee en route. Under cover of a high-powered rifle, the Trooper who drew the short straw hurries onto the deck leading to the door, climbs onto an old wooden whiskey keg, and pushes the door open with a long pole used for dip-net fishing. Sensing freedom, the cub hurtles past him.

Act IV: Caryn's mother insists on cleaning the house before going back to bed, a foul project that takes hours. Caryn and Bret call our contact number in Juneau and leave a message for us to call immediately because an emergency has occurred at our house. A friend relays the message to everyone we know in town.

Before we arrive in Juneau a week later, we've heard the message six times from passing boaters, some of whom are friends of friends of friends who have been alerted to watch for us. I've had hours to sort through the awful possibilities, coming to grips with the notion that the house burned down. The mental list of what I will miss is detailed, but much shorter than I would have thought. When we reach the docks, Doug heads for a pay phone at the top of the ramp while I secure the boats, watching intently for his reaction. He listens for a long while, then breaks into spasms of laughter, his stomach convulsing, tears racing down his cheeks. He is doubled over, almost to the pavement. I cannot fathom what kind of emergency could be so funny.

Epilogue: The carpet cleaner has little luck with the brown spots on the carpet. Caryn's mother goes to Denali National Park, famous for its wildlife, and doesn't see any bears. And now the sad part. Mama and her cubs continue to frequent the valley for several weeks, mauling an occasional dog and pilfering dog food. Mama is shot by the Troopers. One cub is sent to a research facility in Washington, and two, including our intrepid guest, are shipped to the St. Louis Zoo. We return home, not realizing we have underestimated how traumatic this episode was for Caryn and Bret. Trying to get into the house is like penetrating Fort Knox. But after we have made our way past several new bolts and barricades, we are home again.

It is precisely what is invisible *in the land* . . .

that makes what is merely empty space to one person, a *place to another.*

—Barry Lopez, *Arctic Dreams*

6

At the Dark Time, Pull the Cord:
The Mackenzie River to the Arctic Ocean

MOST OF OUR JOURNEYS begin as thin lines we trace with pointed fingers across the surface of a map. What we see on paper is only a bare representation of the physical attributes of the landscape, the sprinkling of place names providing hints of human history. In our minds, the map raises as many questions as it answers. Who lives in the small villages with the hard-to-pronounce names? Which way does the wind usually blow? What colors shade the land, what sounds and fragrances give it life? In murmurs, we fill in the shadows with expectations of what we will find.

A map is a portrayal of place at one point in time. Change is inevitable, the one constant of nature, though the changes may occur at imperceptible rates and civilizations place a premium on permanence. Political boundaries and cultures change in a process we label history. Landforms evolve and disappear, climatic alterations occur. The changes are linked, in a web as complex and round as the earth itself. Adaptation is the name given to the adjustments made by living things to ensure survival. The philosopher Herbert Spencer said, "A living thing is distinguished from a dead thing by the multiplicity of changes at any moment taking place in it."

Travel is the next step, a way to make a link between features on a map and what is actually there. For us, the value of travel is not so much in leaving one place or reaching another as in the knowledge that when at last we go home, we will not return to exactly the same point. Travel takes us outside of ourselves and deeper within. It reminds us that despite geographic vastness, all places are connected to all others, with simple elements like air and water in common.

Traveling is often perceived as glamorous, but our experience is more evocative of the word's French root, *travail*, meaning hard work or arduous effort. That is part of the romance, though undoubtedly not what my sister Susan was visualizing when she remarked, "It must be so romantic for you and Doug to be able to spend the whole summer together paddling."

Our trip down the Yukon River had inspired us to follow the course of another long river. The Mackenzie seemed a compelling choice, a stout blue line cutting boldly through northwestern Canada. Draining more than a million square miles north of the Great Plains, roughly 20 percent of Canada, the river draws waters from as far south as the Alberta Rockies near Jasper and conveys them to the Arctic Ocean. Deh Cho, the Indian name for the Mackenzie, means "great river."

Led by Native guides, Alexander Mackenzie, a Scottish fur trader with the North West Company, canoed the river's length in 1789. He did not find the Northwest Passage he sought to put on the map and was not at all enamored of the country, reporting that his group was "nearly suffocated by Swarms of Musquit-toes." Continuing in the same unflattering vein, Mackenzie deemed it "unpardonable in any man to remain in this country who can afford to leave it." Though he is credited with opening up the western Canadian Arctic, he was actually being shown a route the Indians had used for years as a transportation corridor, much as it still is today. The river figures prominently in subsequent accounts of fur trading and northern exploration, stories that have held both Doug and me captive since childhood. Even Sir John Franklin had traveled the Mackenzie's length on his second Arctic trip in 1826, before his continuing quest for the Northwest Passage killed him and all his men.

To reach the headwaters of the river in 1991, we drove east for three days out the Alaska Highway from Anchorage before turning north on a narrow road so dusty and tedious that we began to think Mackenzie had overstated the region's appeal. Dust and bugs gave every surface of the car and the boats on the roof rack a texture that resembled no-slip surfaces in the bottom of bathtubs. Rarely did we have a view longer than the edge of the road, which was lined by straight yellow-barked trees and scrawny spruce, although the occasional bison perked us up. The attraction that excited us enough to actually stop and take a photograph was one of the "dust-free zones." In the picture, Doug stands next to a road sign marking the start of such a zone, his hair so matted and filthy that it looks like an abandoned bird's nest, the red Volkswagen Rabbit behind him caked so brown that it could be mistaken for a boulder on wheels. Our rattled brains required all surviving cells to deduce that these slicked sections of road were intended to give vehicles enough visibility to pass. We never saw another car, but for us these zones were brief respites from being vibrated and suffocated, chances to remember that we had a life before this road and to contemplate turning around.

We were creatures of our plan, however, which was to put in at the town of Hay River in the Northwest Territories, float its namesake river a short distance to Great Slave Lake, work our way along the lake's shores until we felt the tug of the Mackenzie, and follow the river 1,120 miles to the sea, roughly the distance between New York City and Omaha, Nebraska. From there, we would turn west and paddle into Alaska, traversing its north coast to the village of Barrow. Time permitting, we were hoping to make the short hop down the northwest coast to Wainwright, close to the termination point of our bear-ridden 1988 trip. There were certainly less demanding ways to hook these two trips together than to start 2,100 miles away in Canada, but none of them held the same appeal.

Great Slave Lake, the deepest lake in North America, seemed all sky. It also appeared to host every mosquito in the universe. We quickly relearned an important rule of the North—not to spit inside the head nets we sometimes wore on land as a last resort to keep the hordes of mosquitoes whining an incessant, high-pitched chant for blood from drilling into our eyes, noses, and ears. Every other inch of personal real estate was covered with heavy clothing. One swat of my glove-covered hand against my forearm would produce fifty flattened corpses. On the drive north, we'd been so intimidated by the multitude of kamikaze insects on our windshield that we had stopped in a village and commissioned an elderly Dene woman via sign language to sew a disconcertingly coffin-shaped enclosure out of window screen material. It was our best prospect for being able to cook and bare parts of our body for the execution of basic human functions without sacrificing flesh and blood.

We traveled only a short section of the lake's southern shore before the river gently began to draw our heavy boats downhill. The second morning of the trip, we happened upon a brand-new, standing-room-sized tent that at first we mistook for a heat-induced mirage. Easily six times more spacious than ours, it was erected on an island so swampy that we wouldn't have chosen to camp there unless someone was holding a gun to our heads. Pulled up next to the tent was a spanking new aluminum canoe loaded with bulky ice chests. A man and a woman were jumping around on the end of a small gravel point like fish out of water, waving frantically. We thought they might be having some sort of medical problem. "Thank God you've come," the man said as we closed to within earshot. "I've been calling on the radio all day to find out where we are."

Doug and I could barely look at each other for fear of laughing. We were afraid to ask the man how he thought the receiver of his call could help them. From Los Angeles, he and his partner had come seeking a wilderness paradise and instead, mostly for lack of skills and knowledge, they had paddled straight into purgatory. They had planned this trip for two years, taken sabbaticals from their jobs, driven north, unloaded the canoe, and had their truck irrevocably shipped by barge from Great Slave Lake all the way to Inuvik at the river's mouth. It had taken them eight days of paddling to cover a distance that had taken us less than eight hours. They were truly stranded, at the start of a more-than-thousand-mile river intersected by road in less than a handful of places. We had the feeling that they would do almost anything to be anywhere else.

Doug and I helped them as much as we could, resisted their pleas to spend the night (only partly because it was ten in the morning), encouraged them to head back to Hay River, then continued downstream. We never heard anything more about them, which we could only hope was good news. I imagine they survived, though I wouldn't make the same assumption about their relationship.

For the first third of the river, we also cursed ourselves for not arranging to be somewhere else. The bugs were relentless, the heat was overwhelming, and the channel so wide that we couldn't see from one bank to the other. Between high-water levels and low-lying terrain, there wasn't much land to be seen from the river. The contour lines were so far apart that it looked as though even the map was yawning. My mantra was: "I'll never have to paddle here again." We sang, played Twenty Questions, and counted eagles overhead. I became so desperate to amuse my parboiled brain that I bungie-corded Wallace Stegner's *Angle of Repose* to my feet and read while I rowed, not an easy task. Sometimes it took three or four strokes to snatch a complete sentence, but that was of little consequence. We treated this first part of the trip like a workout, figuring that, if nothing else, we would beat our bodies into shape. Each morning, we sprinted down the beach trying to shake the airborne paparazzi before catapulting into our boats. In eight days, we rowed 339 miles, with only minor help from current. At night, our sunburned bodies threw off so much heat that we might as well have had radiators in the tent. The only romance I was interested in was with my tepid water bottle, which I rolled back and forth across my steaming forehead.

Thankfully, swamp symbols on the map gave way to shading indicating vertical relief and terrain features with names like Old Lady's Ghost Creek Mountain. A limestone island allowed us a naked, bug-free lunch. I stowed my book and laid aside my mantra, beginning to anticipate the curves ahead. Doug, with his usual nose for treasures, doggedly hunted around old trading post sites, foraging for celerylike stalks of fresh rhubarb so that he could cook huge pots of tangy sauce. We sniffed our way to hot springs pitted with orange-white calcite domes that towered over my head, spouting fountains of water. Not knowing that many

Dene avoid this spot, believing it to be haunted, we marveled at the lack of footprints.

Thick fossil beds of coral and shells were layered in bands of sedimentary rock along the riverbanks. Some were brachiopods—clamlike bivalves that lived roughly 300 million years ago, when what is now the Mackenzie Basin was covered by shallow sea. The area may be submerged again in a wink of geological time; along with Lake Baikal in Siberia and northwest Alaska, it is considered a global "hot spot." In the last hundred years, temperatures in these areas have risen by three times the global average. In the Mackenzie region, drier summers and warmer temperatures have contributed to larger forest fires and thawing permafrost.

The river narrowed and funneled us between steep limestone ramparts. Bison watched our passage, and the water vibrated as dozens of tundra swans with wings regally outstretched took simultaneous flight, leaving grapefruit-sized footprints on the beach. Maps of the lower Mackenzie depict a ten-mile-wide, fan-shaped web of thin channels haphazardly winding toward the ocean. Though the lines on the map remain blue, by this point the Mackenzie carries so much silt that it is the color of rich chocolate ice cream. We read the maps with artistic license, knowing that the river's load of sediments continued to shift and settle even as the ink on the maps was drying. We also knew that the roughly 4,700 square miles of delta provided opportunities to get lost for the rest of our lives. At every intersection, we chose the westernmost passage, anxious not to get marooned amid miles of boat-grounding shallows.

It would be difficult to design a more ideal breeding ground for bugs. Around 40 percent of the delta's area is covered by shallow lakes and ponds because underlying lenses of permanently frozen soil inhibit drainage. The same attributes make it a paradise for migrating waterfowl. Moving clouds of cranes, swans, and geese cast animated shadows across our path. Tiny gray cygnets bobbed in the water, while their concerned parents circled overhead. A female moose stood belly-deep in the water, no doubt driven there by voracious insects.

When I climbed into my boat at 9:30 a.m. on day twenty-five, I vowed not to leave it until we had reached the ocean. In time, the country began to open up and settle down, rolls of foothills and mountains behind us and nothing but flat ahead. A few scraggly but tenacious spruce trees grew in sheltered depressions, until they too yielded to the latitude and the realities of exposure only six miles from the sea. An occasional aluminum motorboat, driven by Natives en route from the delta village of Aklavik to fishing camps or to the ocean to hunt white whales, passed with a *vroom*. After fourteen straight bone-bruising hours in the boats, we reached a wide shoal bay bordered by low tundra and turned toward the sun, which was still high in the sky.

It is easy to be misled by the Beaufort Sea into assuming that few people have ever before stood on its shores. Harsh weather and incessant wind have shaped country that brooks no compromises and provides no reassurances. It seems almost a miracle that such apparent emptiness can persist in today's world. The beauty of the region presents itself not spectacularly but subtly, over time, in ethereal lighting, isolated flowers, wolf tracks on a long gravel beach, and breezes that keep the mosquitoes at bay.

From the sea, the coast is nearly invisible, distinguished only by a thin rim of tundra and intermittent mud bluffs grinning white smiles—underground ice exposed by erosion. Battering storms have taken bites out of parts of the shoreline, leaving the tundra hanging like a carpet that has lost its floor. Further inland looms the wall of mountains known as the British Mountains in Canada and the Brooks Range in Alaska, which spawn fast rivers that flow north from the Continental Divide and spread as they cross the coastal plain. Offshore, skinny barrier islands, barely higher than the sea that surrounds them, parallel the coast like string beans laid end to end.

The flavor of the Arctic coast might best be captured by stripping away verbiage so that what remains is as spare and unadorned as the landscape itself. Given only ten words, I'd choose *exacting, dynamic, flat, windswept, icy, vast, otherworldly, penetrating, moody*, and *stark*. The problem with transposing familiar language to an unfamiliar landscape is the judgments the words imply. *Bleak* is a word commonly chosen to portray unsheltered, barren, treeless land by those of us who come from treed, hilly places in more temperate climates. It shouldn't be assumed to mean boring, ugly, or expendable. It is impossible to know the places we visit as well as we know the places where we live; there is less time to develop personal relationships or to comprehend the nuances of what we see. We would do well, though, not to assume that others see the world exactly as we do and to bear in mind how alien and inhospitable our own landscape might seem to visitors from the North. Witness the words of Mabel Ruben, a woman from Paulatuk, a village on the coast east of the Mackenzie Delta, as quoted in Ulli Steltzer's *Inuit: The North in Transition*:

> When I saw all those straight lines in the pictures in books and in the movies, I thought they were making it up. Then I flew to Edmonton. Who would ever think of making those streets all

straight and putting them trees all in one row, and even the flowers? And when I was flying over the land and was looking down, up here it is just one big land, down there it is all in pieces like one big puzzle.

Despite appearances, the region has a rich human history stretching back more than a millennium. Near the delta, it is home to the Mackenzie Delta Inuvialuit. Traditionally, their seasonal transition between fixed winter villages and more migratory spring and summer camps coincided with the movement of the wildlife on which they depended for sustenance. In winter, they lived primarily in excavated houses built of driftwood and stacked turf blocks. When traveling or hunting on the sea ice, they sometimes built the domed snow houses or igloos that most people associate with the word *Eskimo*, despite the fact that these were only built in certain regions by certain Native groups. By mid-June, much of the population dispersed to fishing camps and, later in the summer, to whaling camps along the coast, traveling from site to site in umiaks, the large wood-framed boats covered with bearded seal hides, which were propelled primarily by women using single-bladed paddles. Summer dwellings were skin tents stretched over willow frames and secured at the base by a circle of rocks. Meat was dried on wood racks or stored in permafrost cellars dug into the tundra. The population of the Mackenzie Delta Inuvialuit is estimated to have numbered around twenty-five hundred in 1850. Though available estimates are incomplete and conflicting, it is known that this group was one of the largest in the Canadian Arctic in aboriginal times. But more widespread contact with the outside world exacted a deadly toll.

In 1888, a white man named "Little Joe" Tuckfield was outfitted in Barrow with a whaleboat, a year of supplies, and an

Inupiat crew to investigate a report of whales near the Mackenzie Delta. Tuckfield returned in August 1889 with news that he had spotted whales "as thick as bees." The rush to exploit a new whaling ground was on. By late 1889, Yankee whaling ships, which had been harvesting bowhead whales in the Bering Sea since the late 1840s and near Point Barrow since the 1870s, took advantage of newly developed steam power to push east. The first of these boats to succeed was the *Mary D. Hume*. She returned her long-haired, tattered crew to San Francisco in 1892 after two winters in the Arctic, an absence of twenty-nine months, carrying $400,000 worth of whalebone—a cargo worth more than $6 million today and one of the most profitable in North American whaling history. Too small to carry tryworks used for boiling blubber, she had harvested only the baleen, or head bone, of thirty-seven whales, a wasteful, timesaving practice unfortunately adopted by a majority of the fleet because whalebone outvalued whale oil more than fivefold. With their baleen used for corset stays, bowheads were early fashion victims.

By 1894–95, fifteen whaling ships were wintering at Herschel Island, a nondescript, windy crescent about a mile offshore and just west of the delta. It offered a reasonably protected anchorage, and Pauline Cove became a motley community with a wildly diverse population of nearly fifteen hundred at its height, and a trade jargon made up of mix-and-match words from Native dialects, Danish, French, English, Polynesian, and other languages. The Royal Northwest Mounted Police moved in, minus their mounts, to ensure Canadian sovereignty and establish order, a formidable task given the widespread drinking, debauchery, and corruption. One whaling captain gained notoriety as the "kindergarten captain" because of his practice of "renting out" Native girls only eleven to fifteen years old. Herschel Island's heyday lasted from 1890 to about 1908, its decline precipitated by the invention of spring steel and the resultant collapse in the price of whalebone from five dollars to fifty cents a pound.

Attracted to the island by access to trade goods such as gunpowder, flour, clothing, and, tragically, alcohol, Natives hunted animals not just for their own food, shelter, and clothing but as commodities for trade. The settlement required a prodigious amount of game—sometimes more than two thousand caribou were taken in a year. But Mackenzie Delta Inuvialuit, like most Native groups, had little to no immunity to infectious diseases and became particularly vulnerable as they began to settle around trading posts and whaling stations rather than living in less concentrated nomadic camps. They fell victim to scarlet fever and measles in 1865 and suffered a major epidemic of measles and influenza in 1900–2. After about 1880, tuberculosis and syphilis were common. Cultural assimilation also took place as a result of Natives immigrating from Alaska during the whaling era. Alcohol and firearms contributed to the demise of the original Mackenzie Delta population, which was estimated at 250 in 1905 and had dwindled to a mere 10 by 1930.

Our second day on the coast, we pulled into Shingle Point, a gravel spit where in 1889 Natives boarded seven whaling steamers that had just dropped anchor, the first ships in these waters in thirty-five years. Like their ancestors who had established summer fishing and hunting camps here, a number of families were congregated in clusters of plywood shacks. Further down the beach, several women, their heads wrapped in once brightly colored scarves, and an old man were setting out fishnets. One man invited us in to tea, decrying the destructive impact of television on his culture while delighting in his discovery of the persistent threads of shared heritage at a recent circumpolar conference, when Greenland and Canadian Inuit began singing the same song. Everyone who dropped by gave us an introduction to his or her cousin living further west along the coast. Not coincidentally, many of the last names were the same, and a good number were old New England and Long Island names. I wonder if the Gordons, Browers, Bodfishes, Hopsons, and Leavitts back East know that they have relatives in the High Arctic, a legacy of whaling days.

Continuing west, we came to a scoop of land cut by a river drainage. Though we couldn't see the back of the bay, the *pop-pop-pop* of repeated high-powered rifle shots and the racing of outboard engines indicated that a pod of beluga whales had been trapped in the shallow water near shore. Here's how an observer described such a hunt in 1880:

> The beluga are hunted in kyacks [sic]; a dozen or more natives take up the position near the entrance of some bay, where they can see them as they come in with the tide. As soon as they have passed, the natives paddle out behind them, and, by shouting and beating the water, drive them into shoal water, where they are easily dispatched with flint spears.

Motors have replaced paddles, guns have added killing power. Outsiders tend to disparage modern methods, as though technology should have stood still for authentic Natives. Or they question the need for continued subsistence hunting at all, particularly whaling. Yet subsistence is a line back through time, before cash-based economies and outside influences began to erode tradition. The cultural need for a connection to land and sea may be even greater now than in centuries past.

We knew all this. We also knew the gaze of a beluga whale surveying us from a few feet away and the deep cork-popping noises, clunks, and high-pitched whistles of unseen belugas offshore. Some of the men who had whizzed by in skiffs had invited us to the hunt, but not wanting to see the waters turn red, we paddled on without stopping.

As we passed low tundra hills, more mud bluffs, and minia-ture mountain valleys, Doug proved himself to be a great provider. I heard a startled yelp and looked over to see a fish leap onto his spray skirt. He calmly grabbed it and bashed its head into the side of his kayak, as though fish routinely sacrificed them-selves on his lap. Dinner was secure, even if it was only an eight-inch herring.

The bowhead population, though still listed as endangered and carefully monitored, survived both the era of commercial whaling and the advent of oil drilling, with numbers healthy enough to allow a sustainable harvest by Natives. The spring and fall subsistence bowhead hunts remain a pivotal focus for com-munities along the north coast; for many Alaska Inupiat families, the meat and blubber account for more than a quarter of their annual protein. In late May 1992, crews from Barrow landed a battle-scarred, fifty-one-foot bowhead whose fluke stretched to seventeen feet. Estimates are that it weighed over 100,000 pounds. Buried in the whale's blubber, under a scar about six inches deep and ten inches across, was a stone harpoon tip, a weapon supplanted by the iron tools, ammunition, and darting guns introduced by commercial whalers in the 1800s. What little scientific data existed previously estimated the longevity of bow-head whales at sixty to seventy years. Given that most hunters don't pursue bowheads younger than about twenty years because of their small size, the whale killed that day, with meat so tough that even hours of boiling didn't soften it, may have been well over a century old.

But the whale didn't die without inflicting grief. A block-and-tackle system set up to haul the whale onto the ice near shore failed, whiplashing a thirty-five-pound pulley into the crowd that had gathered to help pull. Two Barrow women were killed. Some villagers perceived the whale as having a powerful spirit. Others saw no connection between the whale, the accident, and a poor spring whaling season. Most were reluctant to verbalize their feelings to outsiders. In the end, what may have helped to sustain them was the tradition that respect and generosity will bring bounty. The hunt the following fall was a success, a cause for grateful celebration.

As we moved through country where Stone Age weapons are found in whales killed by people living in houses with satellite television, we felt like travelers in a time warp. Only a little more than eighty-five years before us, after completing the first marine transit of the Northwest Passage, a goal that had killed so many others, the legendary explorer Roald Amundsen had been forced to spend his third consecutive winter in the Arctic. With his Norwegian herring boat *Gjoa* frozen in the ice off King Point, near Herschel Island on the Canadian coast, Amundsen and his seven men took a week to build a house that became home until the ice released them the following July. Now, we wandered among the purple lupine and hip-high bushes of King Point that Amundsen had thought luxuriant compared to even sparser vegetation to the east. Though we looked, we couldn't find the mounded turf grave of one of his men who hadn't survived the winter.

If Amundsen could have returned to King Point with us, he probably would have thought the area largely unchanged except for the absence of masted whaling ships and the oil rig waiting for action not far offshore. But if he had sat and talked with our companions, a father and son who had motored over in a boat from Shingle Point in search of caribou, he might have been surprised that the middle-aged man could no longer speak his native language, having been punished as a child for doing so in school, and that the son hoped fervently for oil drilling on the Canadian coastal plain, as it might provide local employment. Amundsen might have smiled to see Inuit cook whale blubber in a microwave or use the high towers of now-abandoned Cold War radar stations to scout game, but I doubt he would have been surprised at their continuing pattern of adapting resources at hand to their needs.

Amundsen drove a dog team over the frozen sea from King Point to Herschel Island in late September 1905, hoping to get news of home from the whaling captains. We paddled over for much the same reason, passing a large ringed seal lying on a slanted piece of ice and blinking passively, letting me draw closer than it should have. Perhaps it was too old, or had seen too much to care. Our first layover day in a month was spent exploring the old settlement at Pauline Cove, now occupied by the Canadian park service and complete with what has to be the best sauna on the north coast. Wardens zipped into bright orange survival suits scooted about in skiffs where the schooners used to lie at anchor, while carpenters worked to restore the leaning community hall.

On Avadlek Spit, a long beach projecting away from the bulk of the island like the handle of a frying pan, we discovered archaeologists on hands and knees excavating two dwelling sites that predated the whaling community by as much as four hundred years. Minutes before our arrival, they had unearthed an intricate fishhook made from a beluga whale tooth. Roughly an inch long and about half the diameter of a standard pencil, the hook had two tiny, slanting eyes made of copper. It was the copper, also used to fashion the barb, that had the archaeologists so excited that their words tailgated together. Copper was evidence of early trade between Inuit in the western Arctic and those living in the Coppermine region further east.

Four Aklavik men in their twenties and thirties, hired as part of the dig team, had lashed together a wooden tripod like the ones local hunters climb to scout for whales, except this one was used to provide an aerial vantage point for photographing the site. Proudly, they gave us a tour around the perimeter of the house lived in by an ancestor they'd dubbed Forgetful Joe. In contrast to the discarded, broken implements that were the norm, they kept discovering tools in perfect condition. It was as though Joe had tucked his favorite stone scraper under the raised bed or wedged a newly shaped harpoon point between two timbers and absentmindedly forgotten about them.

We woke the next morning to the sound of sifting dirt and launched from the archaeologists' camp in mist so thick that we might as well have been blindfolded inside a refrigerator. The pervasive, vertigo-inducing fog heightened the sense of the exotic we already felt along this isolated, almost featureless coast, where relief the height of a person appeared mountainous and time seemed a vacillation between fast-forward and reverse. At one stretch, we paddled nine straight days without being able to see further than a hundred feet; most of that time I felt lucky if I could see Doug a boat length away. Traveling without visual reference points in those days before handheld global positioning systems was an exercise in trusting fate, each other, and the magic of our compasses, which were reliable as long as we kept the cooking pots and shotgun away from them.

Once, when Doug was a park ranger, he and a patrol partner were caught by a ground blizzard far back in the Chugach Mountains. Hunkering behind the windshields of their snowmobiles, rime ice coating their goggles, they tried to work their way out against fifty-mile-an-hour winds and driving snow while being mercilessly buffeted by unseen roughness in the trail. Doug was all concentration, focused on following the faint blur of his partner's taillights, keeping his machine under control and himself on the machine. Jiggling and shaking, he figured he was driving about twenty miles per hour when the strangest thing happened. His partner stood up, dismounted, and wallowed over to him, looming larger in the storm until he was standing right next to Doug's moving machine. Incredulous, Doug realized that though he'd been accelerating, he wasn't actually going anywhere. Like his partner, he was stuck, with his machine nosed into a hollow, its suspended track spinning in circles.

Paddling in Arctic coast fog was sometimes like that. Were my oars pulling through water or walls of air? Were my eyes open or closed? Were those lumps shaggy musk oxen or driftwood logs? Were they moving, or were we moving? At dinner, would we find ourselves back where we ate lunch? And if we did backtrack, would we know it? One evening, walking along a fog-shrouded beach, we came upon a polar bear track so huge that Doug could put both of his size 12 extra-wide rubber boots inside it with room to spare. The sand in the center of the print was still dry, indicating that the bear had sauntered by only minutes before. Spooked, we peered into the fog, but everything looked whiter than ever.

The fog not only altered our sense of space, it reset our biological clocks. We slept until noon, when the sun, though still unseen, had enough presence to dry a little of the condensed air soaking our tent fly as well as the outsides of our sleeping bags. Lunch was usually around 5 p.m., dinner at midnight. This put us on "Inuit time." (When we find a laundromat in a northern village, we're no longer surprised if its summer hours are noon to midnight, and we have grown accustomed to seeing packs of little kids roaming freely at 1 a.m.) We learned to fight fog with fire. Often, we built two a day, one at lunch and the other at dinner, grateful for the quantities of silver driftwood imported north by the Mackenzie and west by the coastal current. We'd dig a

shallow pit in the gravel, torch small wood that would burn completely, and huddle around the flames while wolfing food, thrilled
to be both motionless and warm. Before leaving, we'd cover the
glowing ashes with a thin layer of gravel, snatching a few
moments of luxury by sitting until we had radiant rear ends.

Leaving Avadlek Spit, we began to get a hint of why the Inuit
invented kayaks instead of rowing boats. The appearance of a
fogbow, a delicately colored arch with a faint spray of rainbow
colors, portended the emergence of the sun, which sheared
through the fog at lunch, reenabling our sense of sight and
revealing an entirely new world of vibrant, sparkling lagoons.
Further inland, rounded mountains rose in folding tiers behind
the flat coastal plain. And ahead of us, floating on blue water, was
white ice.

Rumors that the pack ice was still thick near land had reached us
when we were still far up the Mackenzie. Normally, the Beaufort
Sea remains permanently frozen about fifty miles offshore, but in
summer the sea ice closer in breaks up, shifting at the will of
wind and current. This would prove to be one of the worst ice
summers in decades; impassable ice would prevent supply boats
from reaching some villages, and winter fuel would have to be
air-freighted in at great expense. But we didn't know this yet.

At first, we had no trouble crafting our way through the floes.
Then the patches of open water became smaller, as if herding us
from a six-lane highway to a four-lane road to a single country
track. Trying to scout a route from our seats only a few inches
above the waterline was like navigating a tricycle through a fleet
of tractor-trailers. After a few days, when we found ourselves on
the equivalent of a bike path, with open water becoming more of

a concept than a reality, we stopped to climb a rare hill for perspective. The view was sobering. An unbroken sheet of ice stretched all the way to oblivion. It was not flat and smooth like a skating rink, but rather a jumble of blocks, most more than six feet thick, some the size of two-story houses, that leaned against one another at odd angles.

We could see a tiny ribbon of open water between the beach and a heap of grounded pressure ridges just offshore, where winter storms had shoved the ice into conical piles thirty feet high. Even to reach this lead, we would have to walk on water, jumping from one frozen block to another. We were not going to be able to paddle the Arctic Ocean; we would have to manhandle our way across it.

We couldn't tell how far the lead extended, maybe half a football field, maybe more. I felt like Alice staring down the rabbit hole toward Wonderland. Like her, I knew without much considering that we'd follow this channel to wherever it led. As we entered it, gliding quietly in our boats, I even felt that somehow, without finding the magic bottle that said "Drink me," I'd been shrunk to exactly the right size. The distance between the gravel and the ice was merely inches greater than the span of my oars.

The lead was a world of its own, a thin section of emerald-green water two feet thick over a shelf of pitted ice that was still frozen to the gravel bottom. It was a quiet, calm place given dimension by subtly rich hues of purple, blue, green, white, gray, and black, and insulated by the breakwater of pressure ridges from the grinding, grating ice outside. Within this world, there seemed to be only beach, ice, sky—and us. Then we noticed the point of a V in the water bubbling steadily toward us until it revealed itself as a smooth-skinned baby seal attracted to the lead for the same mobility it offered us. It pulled even with my oar and docilely climbed onto the painted blade for a rest. Schools of char bumped against our hulls while seabirds bobbed along the fluted edge of the ice shelf, their bodies mostly hidden in shadow. To our vigilantly scanning eyes, every yellow-white hump began to resemble a roaming polar bear.

I refused to make proclamations about how long the lead would last. To my distress, Doug felt no such inhibitions. Occasionally, we had to wrestle the boats around a jam of wedged blocks, but a few hundred feet grew into a mile, then more, while I held my breath along with my tongue. The magic carpet ended at Clarence Lagoon, only four miles from the Alaska border.

Characteristically, we didn't acknowledge defeat immediately. When the lead became too constricted to paddle, we pulled yellow rubber dishwashing gloves on over our wool gloves and "lined" our boats along shore, tying a loop of rope from bow to stern and walking them like unwieldy dogs. We were not unhappy when it was clear that we could go no further. It was July 20. There were at least a few weeks left before winter, and we had plenty of food. We could wait for the tides and winds to move the ice. Resident loons on the lagoon behind us filled the air with haunting song, and caribou danced in the tundra, their antlers prominent against the sky, their hooves obscured by waving yellow grasses. If we grew restless, the strip of coastal plain had narrowed so the mountains were only fifteen hiking miles away, though we knew they would be guarded by legions of mosquitoes.

Braced for a long wait, we slept most of our first morning at Clarence Lagoon, reading into the afternoon before bothering to get up for breakfast. When Doug finally unzipped the tent door, I heard him say, with a touch of wonder, "Toto, we're not in Kansas anymore." I sat up quickly. The sheet of ice that had looked so solid and uncompromising the night before was completely gone, having been tugged out to sea by winds we hadn't even heard.

Another day, having gone to sleep beside a mostly ice-free bay, I awoke to Doug commenting, "Uh-oh, we've got a little problem." One look told me that unless I wanted to go ice-skating, I could stay in bed.

We snuck into Alaska in the dead of the night, except that on July 22 in the Arctic, 2 a.m. looks like day. The border was marked by a rickety tower, a lone caribou backed by distant pink mountains, and a staring wolf whose curiosity was prolonged by Doug's faint clucks and wounded-rabbit squeals. There was no customs station, no change in topography, no fence to impede the movement of winged, hoofed, or swimming creatures unfamiliar with the concept of artificial boundaries. Yet there are lines on the map beginning at this 141°W longitude mark that could affect the future of this same wildlife, for it is the edge of the Arctic National Wildlife Refuge, more than 19 million acres of wild habitat—braided rivers, mountains, lakes, bog, and tundra—set aside for protection by Congress. ANWR, as it is commonly abbreviated, includes the calving grounds of the Porcupine Caribou herd, roughly 150,000 animals strong, and a rare 125 miles of coastline not open to oil development.

The opening of ANWR's 1.5-million-acre coastal plain has been the subject of righteous debate in recent years. Pro-development forces argue that drilling can and has been accomplished without destroying habitat, that energy resources are vital, that domestic production decreases dependence on foreign oil. They point west, to the vast oil fields centered on Prudhoe Bay, which are estimated to be the richest in North America. Income from royalties provides as much as 85 percent of Alaska's budget, and annual dividends of almost two thousand dollars to every Alaskan man, woman, and child. Environmentalists shout, *Stop!* Don't compromise the last vestige of shoreline and premier wildlife habitat to extract oil reserves estimated to last only two hundred days. They assert that as much energy leaks through windows in the United States as flows through the eight-hundred-mile Trans-Alaska Oil Pipeline from Prudhoe Bay to Valdez annually, and that pushing for increased energy efficiency could create more jobs than drilling. Unlike the Gwich'in Athabascan, who live inland and fear for the caribou, many coastal Inupiat, including the whaling captains, aren't opposed to onshore activities, given the existing track record and spectacular profit. Most are, however, vehemently against offshore drilling and seismic testing because of the potentially catastrophic impacts of a spill and the disturbance to bowhead whales, whose migratory route, they claim, has already been pushed further north.

ANWR is often represented to be pristine wilderness. The undeveloped lagoons, spits, and water-pocked flats its coast comprises are wilder than most places and rich in life, but like almost everywhere we have traveled, they have not been immune to the influence of man. Whenever we thought we saw the bulk of a musk ox, it usually proved to be just another fifty-five-gallon drum. Many of the beaches are heaped with thousands of these, some still at least partially full of toxic substances. They are a by-product of the Cold War, when radar stations reliant upon their contents were built approximately fifty to a hundred miles apart in a defensive line across the Arctic from Alaska to Greenland. In the intervening years, tides and storms have licked away at the stockpiles. Leaning against our boats, we counted 307 drums in one location; it was no mystery how nearby Drum Island derived its name. A cleanup is underway using federal Superfund dollars. Though thousands of drums have been removed, a staggering number remain.

Kaktovik, on Barter Island, is the first settlement west of the Alaska border. Scurrying between laundromat, post office, showers, and telephone, we met Daniel Akootchook, an Inupiaq Santa

Claus with a rounded belly and a life-embracing smile who insisted that we come home with him for dinner. He cooked us whale blubber, white-man style (in a microwave) and Native style (steamed in a saucepan), amused at the way our unaccustomed jaws flounced away as if tackling rubber. Daniel plied us with more food every time we emptied our plates, and topped off the feast with cinnamon rolls. Showing us his well-worn bird book, he said, "I don't study them, I eat them."

We didn't leave Daniel's house until well after eleven at night, intending to paddle just far enough to find a place to camp. As we pulled out of the harbor, a man on a three-wheeler approached. It was Daniel, with Native-style parka, leathery broad-cheeked Inupiat face, and video camera in hand. In a reversal of stereotype, he had driven out to film the white people—tuniks, in local vernacular—paddling through icebergs under the midnight sun.

The kayaks designed by Native groups vary depending upon the intended purpose and prevailing sea conditions. Along the north coast, kayaks were designed not so much for rough water as for hunting from the ice edge, so they are narrow and very maneuverable. Such maneuverability is key, particularly when the gaps in the ice look like a slalom course set by a demented drunk. Even rowing backward, with protruding oars and riggers, I could make it through most of the same slots as Doug in his kayak but with considerably more neck action, effort, and time. Once, he slipped nimbly through a slender opening that was rapidly being slammed shut by wind-pushed ice. Not wanting to get stranded, I followed him. But the ice on one side was too high to allow my rigger to clear. With the ice threatening to crush me against this wall and snap the aluminum rowing frame, I pulled a maneuver I would think I'd imagined if Doug hadn't been a witness. Using every one of my 125 pounds, I somehow canted my 120-pound, twenty-foot-long boat at nearly a 90° angle and, head almost against the ice, shim-mied it through the hole. Fear is a powerful drug.

We had good ice days and bad ice days. On good days, we made forward progress, though typically not in a straight line. On bad ice days, we slipped, scrambled, and heaved our boats like con-crete sleds. What looked like solid ice from afar proved to be a congregation of floes with water between them, so moving the boats required hour after hour of leaps of faith. I could handle up to four-foot jumps without much of a problem, especially if I was starting from a high block and landing on a lower one. The big-ger jumps were more problematic. One afternoon, Doug coaxed in his most encouraging voice from the far side of such a jump, "Come on, Jill, you can do it. Don't think, just fly." His extended fingers were at least six feet away, and the uphill, sloping landing was precarious at best.

It is not easy to stop thinking after a lifetime of being condi-tioned to do so. I jumped, but, losing confidence when I needed it most, tried for one last step before I pushed off, breaking through a thin skim of ice near the edge. Falling into 30°F water is proba-bly the closest I'll ever come to being vacuum-packed. Most of the air was sucked out of my lungs in one long, excruciating, involuntary gasp. The only thought I can remember is: *It's lucky I'm not a man*, a flashback to Doug's offhand comment at dinner the night before that a man's testicles would shrink into his body with the shock of such cold. I'll never know whether I would have had more profound thoughts, because as my arms and legs turned into sandbags, Doug slid his kayak toward me. I draped myself across the deck, and he reeled me in like a fish.

Off came my wet rubber boots, socks, long johns, wind pants, polypropylene shirts, pile jacket, parka, ski hat, and gloves while Doug ransacked my clothes bag for dry replacements. We had been trying, as a precaution, not to have both boats and both of us on the same piece of ice at the same time. Now, as I stood stark naked on a thimble of the Arctic Ocean, there was no choice but to throw such caution to the same winds that were flash-freezing my body through convection.

Dry again but unnerved, I lobbied for dragging our boats over the wet sand and gravel beaches. So that's how we found ourselves harnessed like mules, leaning side by side into freezing head-winds—sleet, snow, and blowing sand in our eyes, banging against each other with every step. It's an understatement to say the boats didn't slide well. Fifty steps, then a break, then fifty more steps. We counted to ourselves, no breath to spare, thigh muscles quivering. We'd haul one boat, then the other, each half full so that they were light enough to pull and so that we didn't ruin their hulls. Then we'd return for the rest of the gear, loading what we could into our empty backpacks and hanging the remaining gear sacks on yokes we made from driftwood sticks. During rests, I'd lie flat on my back and find myself obsessively picking out leads in the clouds. We traveled like this, on and off, for several weeks. One really grueling day we worked for eight hours, traveling nine miles in three round trips to gain a discouragingly pitiful linear distance of only one and a half miles.

On trips we read mostly nonfiction, often about the region where we are traveling. This can be a liability. When we were stopped by an endless expanse of ice floes piled against one another like upended moving vans, it was not a morale booster to pass the time reading an account, written merely a hundred years before, of explorers stranded under similar conditions on a beach only five miles away. Nor was it inspiring to read that ultimately they became so frail with hunger that they were forced to eat their boots.

Along the Beaufort Sea, I sped through our book supply at an alarming speed, until the only one left unread was Deborah

Tannen's *You Just Don't Understand: Women and Men in Conversation*, sent to me by my mother. It describes in great detail the different perceptions and styles of expression of men and women—how, for example, when a woman says X at a cocktail party, the man she is speaking to might interpret Y. The nearest cocktail party was probably hundreds of miles away, and I had a good handle on what the only man in the vicinity was thinking even before he said it. Moreover, I had been wearing the same long underwear for two weeks and didn't have to exert my sense of smell to know that Doug was doing the same. Near-freezing temperatures had discouraged us from bathing, so my hair was plastered to my skull in helmet mode. Outside, the wind was gusting over sixty miles per hour and blowing snow was collecting in the lee of our tent. The ocean was frozen solid. I had few other options for entertainment than to read the book, but every attempt made me feel like a lone dog at a cat convention. I resorted to reading the first-aid book cover to cover.

Near Prudhoe Bay, the ice eased, although the fog returned, fed by expanses of cold, open water topped by only slightly warmer air. Like phantoms, we slid past the causeways, raised buildings, drill rigs, seismic trails, oil flares, roads, and well-stocked cafeterias. The few workers we met shook their hard-hatted heads in wonder that anyone would choose to be a tourist along this coast. Near Oliktok Point, where there was a saltwater treatment plant, the two men who found us mainlining chocolate in a snow squall met with no resistance when they insisted we come inside. The place felt like an alien space station, with dry surfaces and gloriously unlimited hot water. Only in the shower did I discover that I had frost-nipped my toes chalky white during the day. They had the flexibility of frozen fish sticks.

I wanted to go home, to call my mother, to feel the sun, to sit under a tree—to do just about anything but stumble around in the fog like a conscript. Yet in the kitchen, having a snack, wiggling my now pink and tingly toes, I found myself defending the virtues of this coast to our hosts, who saw it as nothing but a grim place they viewed from the safety of the station. This feeling of protection from the unforgiving elements would prove illusory several years later, however, when a polar bear came crashing in through a window and badly mauled a worker.

It was actually a relief to leave the plant's tropical climate in the evening and head across wide-mouthed Harrison Bay. We planned a wide arc to skirt the murky shallows at the mouth of the Colville River, which were rumored to extend more than five miles from shore, hoping to reach land again in about thirty-four miles. We took a northwesterly bearing for the first three hours, then veered west, and finally south. Trying to factor the influence of wind into our course and estimate our location from elapsed time, we figured one hour, including quick breaks, equaled five miles. During the sixth hour, we were looking hard for land and wondering if our course had taken us anywhere near where we wanted to be when we came upon three toothless old Inupiat men gaping at us from a battered skiff filled with fishnets. It was 1:30 a.m. "Are there radio towers anywhere near here?" we asked hopefully, for this was the landmark we'd used to map our bearings. They pointed in the direction of the invisible antennas, only a hundred yards away. Just because something can't be seen doesn't mean it isn't there.

The Barrow map, our twenty-fourth in fifty-four days, looked like many of the others. The flat land, shown white and contourless, was splattered with blue, representing thousands of irregular ponds, so that the coastline resembled a swatch of decaying lace held to the sky. Or picture hundreds of irregularly shaped teacups arranged on a shallow tray, all filled to the brim. The area described by the cup edges is land, the rest is water. You are on the North Slope. Chances are the wind is driving snow into your face and your fingers are freezing. Put on every last layer you have and turn up your collar.

What you can't see on paper are the phalaropes swimming in circles near shore, the black-and-white snow bunting fluttering in the doorway of the tent, the fresh polar bear tracks in the sand, or the bounty of weather-bleached whalebones scattered like driftwood. It is August 13. Try to feel the exhilaration of a rare blue-sky day that seems a scorcher, though the thermometer reads only 50°F. Helped by a tail breeze and well-scattered ice, we paddled a whopping fifty-six miles on this day, all the way to Point Barrow, the northernmost protrusion of the United States. At midnight, we rounded the corner into the Chukchi Sea, rays of sun emanating through a pink glow, Arctic terns careening in the orange space between the water and the clouds. Close your eyes and hear bowhead whales bugling not far away. If you have a good nose, take a deep breath. You might detect a change of weather in the air.

The next morning we awoke to thirty-mile-per-hour winds from the direction of the ice and powerful, steel-gray waves. The sun had slipped back into hiding. It was only thirteen miles to Barrow, but the miles were reluctant to slide by. Though we ground away diligently, we noticed that the town bus kept passing us on its rounds. Swallowing our pride, we pulled the boats onshore and, with dirty laundry in tow, took the free bus into town.

For Barrow to seem a metropolis, you may have to have sweated, shivered, and grunted your way out of the heart of Canada and across the top of Alaska. A motley collection of houses is surrounded by dogsleds, slabs of whale meat, bloody plastic buckets, polar bear hides, truck carcasses, bicycles, umiaks, skiffs, and more. Perched about three hundred miles above the Arctic Circle, with a population of over four thousand, the town sees eighty-four days elapse between the last sunrise in May and the first sunset in August. Satellite dishes aimed south appear to be pointed toward the ground.

As the regional headquarters for North Slope communities, Barrow has prospered by charging property taxes to oil companies. Among other amenities, the town has an insulated water and sewer system called a utilidor that cost more than $700 million, which is rumored to factor out to at least $400,000 per toilet. In 1991, though, it still didn't have a laundromat, which meant that after much searching and pleading, we ended up in the back room of the taxi office washing our clothes. Barrow did have a hotel and several places to eat, so we treated ourselves to a Mexican dinner. We felt hardened and content. Another couple had arrived in town just ahead of us after completing a shorter trip and were publicizing their effort on local radio and in the newspaper. When people asked us if we were "the kayakers," we said no, and pointed off down the street.

We made it halfway through dinner believing that this was the end of the trip. The day's rough weather had pushed the pack ice back onshore in the usual chaotic heaps, and locals were saying that conditions might not change now that the fall storms were rolling in. We were disappointed but also a little relieved. I was still plowing through my pile of beans when two men from the local barge company came to our table and introduced themselves. Within moments, they had offered to transport our boats back to Anchorage if we made it to Wainwright, roughly eighty-five miles down the coast. In straightforward water, this would take only about three days, but we'd forgotten what unfrozen ocean looked like. We told them we'd think about it, but we knew we wouldn't be able to resist trying.

We did more talking in Barrow than we had for two months. An exchange student from Brazil described his impressions of the United States, based wholly upon life in Barrow. A scientist told us how four city blocks in Washington, D.C., had reeked for weeks after the liquid from a drum containing a walrus specimen for the Smithsonian Institution was dumped down a drain. We learned that a helicopter used to ferry crews out to an oil rig 175 miles offshore in the Chukchi Sea had been bought from Manuel Noriega's regime for $9 million and rented for $6,000 an hour. At a late-night Native dance, we surprised ourselves by crying. In the elemental beat of the drums, the heat of crowded bodies, the articulated motions of performers young and old that evoked familiar images, we could feel the power of the landscape.

It was well after midnight by the time we walked back to our tent, which we'd set up north of town toward the point. Just as we were crawling in, a shiny pickup truck pulled over on the edge of the road and idled there. When we walked over to say hello to the elderly Inupiat couple inside, they asked, "Aren't you cold sleeping out here?" and took us home for caribou stew, muktuk, walrus, Wonder bread, and tea. It must have been at least 80°F inside while Warren played a drum made of whale-liver membrane and chanted a song about hunters in a snowstorm who couldn't find their snow house. He was an ardent advocate of the oil companies, for they had enabled him to enjoy a much higher standard of living than his parents.

The next day, the tuniks were the source of great local entertainment as we hauled our boats across the ice in front of town. Someone asked for my autograph on a matchbook. Every few hours, the same trucks came by to check our progress or give us tea. They also offered rides, but by now we were committed to our own power. By the end of the first day, we reached the town limits, which had been in sight since morning.

It took five days to lurch fifteen miles, of which we paddled less than two miles and hauled the rest. My arms felt like pulverized meat and Doug was stooped as a crone. An Inupiaq man in his fifties or sixties, his face a map of hard living, walked over to visit from his fish camp. He said he wasn't worried about getting his aluminum skiff back across the ice to Barrow; one of the borough's rescue helicopters would sling-load it for him if need be. "Got any marijuana?" he asked, and when we said no, "How about whiskey?" We offered him a foam pad to sit on, but he said, "I don't need that. I'm Eskimo."

Along one of the most fatiguing, muscle-cramping, desperately hopeless stretches of ice-tangled coast, we found a faded orange life preserver. Underneath Russian writing, in barely readable English it said, "At the dark time, pull the cord." We looked at the vest again, then at each other, then at the ice stretching as far as we could see, and collapsed into laughter. There was no cord or even a place for one. After more than eleven hundred miles of river and roughly nine hundred miles of ice, we had found the perfect rallying cry.

For the next week, we heard the telltale sound of Rice Krispies on the tent almost every night, which meant that we would begin the next day by scooping fresh snow out of our boats. At least the ice had thinned enough to paddle. On August 25, as we approached Wainwright, we noticed a crowd of about sixty collecting on the beach, and a swarm of three-wheelers. A truck drove alongside, tooting its horn. Doug, facing forward, reported more details. He saw people standing on rooftops, running and gesturing, some even jumping out a window. We figured something special must be going on, but it wasn't until we punched through small surf onto the beach and people reached to help that we realized the crowd was waiting for us. Word had gone out by CB radio that the kayakers were coming. For the first time in days, I felt warm all over.

God made Labrador in six days. And on the seventh, he threw rocks at it.

—Old Newfoundland saying

7

If I Were a Place:
The Coast of Labrador

IF I WERE A PLACE, I'd be Labrador: improbable, impossible, tempestuous, serene, thinly populated. I'd be smooth boulders carried by great rivers of ice, plopped down at random, and balanced precariously against the odds of gravity for thousands of years. I'd be spired mountains, crumbling ridgelines, and winds that literally make the water smoke. I'd be purple sunsets, bedrock that looks like marshmallows, and relentless green waves beating against the shore. I'd be dome-shaped islands with eider duck nests on the open tundra and puffin eggs concealed in the shadowed cracks between black rocks. I'd be clear streams flowing over pink granite, miles of imposing headlands, and icebergs of every conceivable shape making their way south from Greenland. I'd be Windy Tickle, Slam Bang Bay, Cape White Handkerchief, and Blow Me Down Mountain. I'd be sun one minute and rain like Ping-Pong balls the next, with rainbows that seem to span the world.

Person, place, or thing? The games we played as kids had such seemingly simple answers. How can a person be a place? How can a place not become part of a person? We remember a place not just for its beauty but for the way that beauty made us feel; those feelings are woven into the emotional tapestry we call self. The most special places are the ones that give texture to our dreams, that ground us, make us whole, remind us of what is real. When I think of Labrador, I not only see its landscape but feel a stirring within.

I was twenty-one in 1979 when I first journeyed to this isolated northeastern extension of mainland Canada. With five other Dartmouth students, four men and one woman, I sought adventure in the Torngat Mountains of northern Labrador. Anxious to prove myself, I stooped under a leg-numbing pack that weighed only forty pounds less than I did. There wasn't a peak we thought we couldn't scale, though we were turned back from several. We took our youth, our confidence, even the wildness of Labrador for granted. Summit photographs show us exuberantly displaying the flag of the Explorers Club, from whom we had received a junior explorers grant. What isn't as clearly recorded is how much we were learning—about ourselves, one another, and how to move through a hazardous, unfamiliar space. Jacques Cartier, exploring the north shore of the Gulf of St. Lawrence in 1534, described Labrador as "the land God gave to Cain. It is composed of stones and horrible rugged rock . . . there is nothing but moss and short, stunted shrubs." Yet for me, it was fertile enough so that I am still reaping seeds sowed there.

Ten years passed, a heady decade filled with Alaska, avalanches, wilderness rowing, and Doug, before I returned to Labrador. The two of us arrived in mid-June feeling battered and near paralysis. It had taken nine days, 6,237 miles of driving on an odometer that had already used up all available digits, and three ferries to reach this foggy, treeless brink of the continent. We had left one of our favorite corners of Alaska in shambles. The *Exxon Valdez* tanker had ruptured on Bligh Reef in March 1989, disgorging 11 million gallons of crude oil into the sea-otter-patrolled waters of Prince William Sound. Oil now blanketed quiet coves we knew well, and dead seabirds were still being recovered by the hundreds.

We entrusted Doug's rusting Volkswagen Rabbit to a local cod fisherman, who looked pleased when we told him that if we weren't back by the end of September, he could have the car. He seemed to think it a sure bet. We put in at Blanc Sablon on the Quebec-Labrador border and wound our way from the Strait of Belle Isle into the exposed Labrador Sea. This time I wasn't content to explore one fjord. I wanted the understanding that comes with context, the satisfaction of linking one place to another. We knew of no one who had tried to paddle the whole coast and had no idea if it was possible—as usual, the locals were assuring us it was not. Cape after cape, storm after storm, fjord after fjord, we scrabbled more than a thousand miles north until we reached Cape Chidley, the tip of Labrador, in mid-August. From there, with Baffin Island across Hudson Strait to the north and Ungava Bay to the west, we backtracked 385 paddle miles to Nain, the nearest Labrador village. Renegotiating exposed headlands we had managed to survive on the way north was not a welcome prospect, but familiarity also brought comfort and new dimensions. We took advantage of memorized bailout spots, lingered in places we had moved through too quickly, and found calm where there had been storm.

Chilled by a cold, southerly-flowing current, Labrador is a challenge to geographers trying to define the southern limit of the area described by the term *Arctic*. At roughly 52°N, the latitude of southern Labrador isn't much different from that of London, though this is hard to believe without a map in hand. Windy tundra sweeps to sea level. What little vegetation there is along the coast often doesn't bud until late June. The weather is like something out of a science fiction movie; with little notice, it takes on a life of its own.

One day in northern Labrador, Doug persuaded me into taking a lunch break in a nook the size of a picnic table. We'd barely started eating when we noticed a westerly breeze coming out of Bigelow Bight, a fjord we'd just traversed in complete calm. Two crackers later, I was climbing into my wind pants and parka. By the time I was slicing more salami with my back turned to the wind, the boats were beginning to get knocked around, so we slid them up onto the snow. In fifteen minutes, the winds in the center of the fjord were blowing near hurricane force, raising spumes of water. We were going to be in serious trouble as the tide rose unless we could figure a way up the short cliffs behind us.

It took several hours, most of our rope, intense climbing in rubber boots, four scraped shins, and two pulleys before we managed to suspend the boats from the cliffs so that they swayed like hanging victims. Then we hauled ourselves and our overnight gear up to the plateau above. A look around revealed the usual wandering caribou and tantalizing alpine hiking country but little sheltered terrain for the tent. Now what? We chose the lee side of a big boulder and set up the tent with every last stake and several hundred pounds of Labrador's abundant rocks.

That night I tried to escape to China, reading *Life and Death in Shanghai*, while the tent gyrated and bits of tundra blew under the fly. Then there was a terrific crack and our tent was down, flapping so wildly that we could barely hear each other. Doug managed to find the door, unzip it, and squirm outside to assess the damage while I sprawled across the floor, trying to keep the tent from shredding and blindly stuffing random belongings into bags. Doug returned on hands and knees long after I'd concluded he had blown away, and shouted into my ear that he'd found a cave, really a shallow overhang, about a quarter mile away. It was too windy to fix the poles and re-erect the tent. With Doug hanging on to me to keep my feet in contact with the ground, we stumbled to the spot in the late-summer darkness. We laid the tent on the ground like a bivouac sack, arranged our pads and sleeping bags inside, and climbed in.

Our lucky stars aligned, and the morning dawned calm. When we came out of our lair, cramped and cold, we saw that the top ledge of the overhang was lined with stout, evenly spaced rocks. Someone else, maybe a hundred, maybe a thousand, maybe three thousand years ago, had sheltered in this cave, blocking the entrance with caribou skins anchored by the rocks above.

Labrador scared us, battered us, awed us, spoke to us. It revived our hope in persisting wildness. Only a few hours' jet distance from Boston, we were able to travel a twenty-three-day stretch without seeing or hearing any signs of modern man. We encountered caribou who didn't know to fear people. Suspended in gentle quiet over perfectly clear green water, we spied on fish and forests of kelp that made us wish we had glass-bottomed boats. We ended the summer renewed, at peace, and married.

Four years later, in 1992, Doug almost killed himself. Teaching an avalanche workshop to professional patrollers at a ski area in California, he fell on glare ice, spun the length of a football field down a slope inclined like a ski jump, and crashed into a spruce tree at forty-five miles per hour, hitting it with four thousand pounds of impact pressure. He shattered seven ribs in eleven places and collapsed a lung, filling it with blood. Instead of spending the spring preparing for a trip to Norway as planned, we recuperated in the hospital and at home, happy just to hold each other. When summer came, we instinctively headed back to Labrador, a place we knew would help Doug heal. This time Doug's seventeen-year-old daughter, Sunna, accompanied us in *Porky*, an unsinkable dory-style rowing boat that is graceful on water but resembles an overweight, legless cow on land.

While most of my peers had children entering kindergarten, in the fourteen years since my first visit to Labrador I'd not only gained three stepdaughters but had seen two of them finish high school. I'd taught Sunna to drive and, in a moment of poetic justice for my mother, who had long battled my disregard for fashion, had even taken her to select an outfit for the prom. She had lived with us during the spring of her junior year, and had just spent a trying senior year as an exchange student in a smoggy Belgian steel town. Returning to Labrador with her felt like the perfect rowing stroke, our legacy to her, a chance not only to share country we loved but also to teach her what we knew about traveling through it without harming it or ourselves.

Red Bay is literally the end of the road that hopscotches via ferries from Maine to Nova Scotia to Newfoundland to southern Labrador. We'd planned to take the coastal steamer from there to Nain, the northernmost village, so that we would have weeks to paddle and to hike in the Torngat Mountains. But sheets of unbroken pack ice were delaying the coastal steamer indefinitely. Published schedules are a whimsy in Labrador's climate, and the locals were placing bets that the ferry wouldn't make it to Nain for a month, maybe six weeks. So the three of us launched in Red Bay, less than forty miles north of where Doug and I had started in 1989.

Red Bay would be as ordinary as any poor seaside village if not for a geographer rummaging in long-forgotten Spanish archives in the mid-1970s. She unearthed thousands of documents, including sixteenth-century wills and notarized contracts, referring to a port called "Butus" or "Buteres" in Terranova. Cached sailing instructions led archaeologists across the ocean to Red Bay. A bonanza of building remains and sunken ships were excavated, along with more than 140 skeletons, authenticating the area as the whaling capital of the world in the late 1500s. Before we even knew Red Bay's history, Doug had picked curved bits of red tile off the beaches and proclaimed them to be Basque; playing hooky from high school to spend his days in Boston museums had primed his archaeological instincts. In fact, the ceramic tiles had been brought over as ballast on Basque whaling ships and used for roofing, replaced on the return trip by the oil and baleen of right and bowhead whales.

When we stopped for lunch several hours out of Red Bay, Sunna mentioned that her tailbone was aching. This is not an uncommon rower's lament, but her comment caught my attention because she rarely complains. Named for the cheerful disposition she displayed even as an infant, Sunna has unusual enthusiasm, grit, and optimism. She was as young, immutably certain, and strong as I had been in 1979. I walked over to inspect her boat and discovered that her sliding seat was on the track backward. Disarmed by her self-assurance, I'd never thought to check the assembly of her rowing frame. It was a warning to assume less and to be more watchful.

In teaching Sunna, I began to learn what I knew. I was surprised by the scope of rowing tricks I'd nurtured and begun to take for granted—how to angle my boat into the waves, keep my hands loose in sloppy water, or navigate through shifting ice. Aware that the line between teaching and cloning can be fine, it seemed best to teach by example and let Sunna learn her own best ways by doing.

Sunna made Doug and me aware that we have systems for everything, many of which we had never verbalized or even thought about. When we attach the fly to the tent, for example, we always start at the same pole and move in opposite directions. We have set ways of hauling, tying, and packing the boats, and a similar order to most tasks around camp. Watching Sunna trying to master this routine was like having a mirror held in front of us. We looked efficient, competent, even anal. My friend Janis laughs when describing camping with us. "It's a trip," she says. "You just glance at each other and the tent goes up, or blink and there's dinner." Sometimes Doug and I angered Sunna by executing a decision before she realized that one had even been made. For years, a tiny nod toward shore had meant a beach break or campsite. We began adding words to the nod to ensure that Sunna was part of the process, transforming our private dialect into a common language.

Many of the gestures we use are intended to alert each other to the presence of wildlife without scaring it away or giving notice of our presence. Clawing the sky with one arm diagonally signifies bear. We used this symbol just four times in two Labrador summers, once for a polar bear with legs the size of telephone poles, stationed like a border guard on gray, striated rock near Labrador's northern tip. In the middle of a rising storm, it came into view as we were scouting for a place to camp, the first polar bear we'd ever seen in the wild. *No way in hell I'm camping near here,* I thought, and we squeezed another ten miles out of the weather. Another day, as we climbed a ridge on Whale Island, buffeted by seventy-mile-per-hour winds, my Viking partner remarked, "The only thing that could be worse about being stranded on this island would be being stranded with a polar bear." From the ridge, we spotted a lump on the flats below us that appeared to be a large and very dead polar bear. For twenty minutes, we strained to detect motion while Doug entertained thoughts of scientific investigation—a fantasy he had to abandon when the bear rolled over.

An upward curved motion of one arm signifies a breaching whale. In 1989, we'd seen as many as a hundred whales at a time along the coast north of Red Bay. They were mostly minkes, known locally as grumpuses, and sometimes a humpback or two. In a place named Bad Bay for its shoals, we were rounding a small point when fins began to serrate the water. A couple of boat lengths away, there was a wounded minke rolling over on its side, revealing a wide gash spewing blood into a reddening sea. Earlier in the morning, a fisherman had reported that he'd accidentally run over a whale, and we suspected this was the victim of his prop. We had read that whales will often protect an injured member of the pod but didn't perceive ourselves as a threat until whale missiles began to fling themselves at us from three directions.

Minke whales are mostly dark, with white patches. They are considered small whales, with lengths of roughly twenty feet, but small is relative. I had a whale six feet off my bow, two whales just off my left oar and a whale between me and Doug. The two whales next to me were spy-hopping, thrusting their heads six feet straight out of the water to periscope a better look at me. Seeking security in shallow water, I hung on the sloping back side of five-foot waves that were breaking on the rocks, just seaward of the curl, my right oar scraping barnacles and serving up foamy surf. It seemed a choice of shipwreck or skewering. My left oar was inches away from the whales at any given moment. Each phalanx of whales would stop abruptly a couple feet away, then dive out of view, only to be replaced immediately by yet another squad. I guessed that there were twenty whales on the team. What felt like a terrifyingly high-stakes game went on for a good fifteen minutes, until it dawned on us that if the whales wanted to hurt us, they could. We were being herded, not hunted, by an escort service with a plan. As soon as it was feasible, we landed and hiked back to the point to watch the whales, but they had moved offshore to cluster around the incapacitated animal.

It never occurred to us that we might need a symbol for sharks—that is, until Doug and I launched too soon after a storm, surfing the faces of still powerful swells and fishtailing in waves reverberating off of half-mile-high cliffs. As Doug careened into a trough, he saw a triangular black fin slicing through the water just ahead of him. Whatever the creature was, it was at least twenty feet long, and it was not swimming like a whale. Desperate not to ram it, Doug leaned hard on his paddle, braked the forward motion of his boat without flipping, and dug in four hard reverse strokes, propelling himself backward and uphill, something that is difficult to do without the help of fear. *"Shark!"* he yelled. I hadn't seen the fin, but just as Doug's warning reached me, my boat began to rise.

Though we have rehearsed many emergency procedures, shark levitation is not one of them. I instinctively snugged my oar handles together, grinding my knuckles in an attempt to balance the boat. There was barely a chance to register the marvel of flying before the next wave connected with the bottom of my boat. We later learned that the fin and four-foot-wide back probably belonged to a northern basking shark, which might have blown east from Greenland during the storm. With no teeth, basking sharks are limited to a diet of plankton, but that didn't stop Doug from mindlessly humming the theme song from *Jaws* for weeks.

We didn't see as many whales in 1992, because of thick sea ice. Still, Labrador's profusion of life meant a quick initiation into our sign language for Sunna. Stretching our necks in a bobbing motion indicates seals, which are common enough on the

Labrador coast so that we called attention to them only when they were especially close. Flapping arms, another symbol we used discriminately, indicates a particularly interesting bird or an unusual concentration of them. Contrary to common perception, birds migrate not so much to escape something harmful, like the cold, as to move toward a food source or something else beneficial. Our mid-June launch coincided with the return of winged migrants to the region, making us feel an intrinsic part of the life cycle accordioned into an Arctic summer.

In the early days of the season, we traveled much like a young duck family. Feeling vulnerable because of Doug's recent scrimmage with death, Sunna's relative inexperience, the ice, and Labrador's volatile weather, we made conservative "go" and "no go" decisions. It proved liberating to take a step away from the edge, where the margin between life and death might hang on the curling rim of a single wave, and to let go of expectations about how far we might travel.

Surrounded by bird lovers with binoculars pressed to their eyes, my best defense has been to claim that I hate all feathered creatures. But it is impossible not to notice the ease with which birds negotiate the very different mediums of water and sky. To swim, they rudder with webbed feet, tucking their necks and wings mostly out of the way. To fly, they must extend their necks and unfurl their wings, often retracting their feet like landing gear or towing them behind in their slipstream. Each day as we paddled, our three boats in close formation, murres would whiz by at shoulder height in search of food for their young while their mates sat watch at the nests. With their belly-flop landings, they looked like beginner pilots. Arctic loons typically did three flybys, reconnaissance loops to scrutinize the long-winged water creatures in rowing boats and the dragonfly in the yellow kayak. The best fliers were the fulmars and storm petrels, who waltzed past us with breathtaking elegance, making turns so steeply banked that their wing tips nearly grazed the surface of the sea.

Shadowed by moving curtains of wings, we watched the birds select their nesting spots, some on vertical cliffs, others, like Arctic terns, on exposed gravel beaches. One morning, Sunna commented that I reminded her of an Arctic tern. I was aghast. How could that be? Terns weigh only four ounces, but they are fiercely territorial. They routinely dive-bombed us whenever we strayed too close to their nests, sometimes scoring our scalps in one of their sonic swoops. Their battle cry, a bickering, shrill *Killllllllllllllll-Killllllll*, ratchets even the best nerves. Sunna tried to assuage my horror: "Terns fly here all the way from Antarctica. I mean, like them, you are incredibly strong, protective, and loyal." "And don't forget," I replied in my sternest stepmother voice, "revengeful."

Within a couple of weeks, we began to spot eggs in the nests, sometimes as many as seven speckled green common eider eggs within a carefully arranged scoop of grass and downy feathers. Frantic squawks alerted us to raids on gull eggs by foxes or winged predators like skuas. Sometimes we came upon empty nests and bits of shell. Unlike many other birds, female eiders do not lay more eggs if the first ones are destroyed. When threatened, they flatten their chunky brown bodies over the eggs and into the tundra, utterly motionless, willing themselves unseen. They are beautiful, bravely sacrificial, stoic. "Sunna," I asked, "are you sure I'm not like an eider duck?"

On a walk up a rounded knob one clear afternoon, we came upon a newly hatched duckling still slickly wet, its shell in two uneven pieces beside it. Another egg rocked back and forth, powered by vigorous Morse-code-like taps that were rapidly enlarging a hole in the shell. We retreated hastily so that the parents, who had flown off at our intrusion, would return.

Through the eyes of the birds, Sunna, Doug, and I must have appeared a family of odd ducks. Certainly, we had some identifying marks in common—two legs, two arms, brown callused hands, short beaks. Sunna's blond hair could have been interpreted as that of a juvenile in a species of brown-haired adults; her pleasant chirp resembled that of a songbird. The variation in our plumage must have been mystifying, though, especially given the rapid alteration in our outer colors in response to frequent weather changes. Our habitat could be described as wide-ranging; we showed a propensity for landing on sand beaches or smooth rock ramps and then sprawling in sun-warmed pockets of flowering tundra. We loved high perches, especially the spines of mountains. Actually, we routinely appear odd ducks even to humans. Sunna can find delight lying on her stomach for hours on a cold beach, arranging small rocks in Stonehenge fashion. One village boy we'd met in 1989 could not be convinced that Doug was not my father. The truth is that none of us aspires to act like all the other ducks anyway.

Though maternally wired friends watch anxiously as I lumber into middle age, to date I haven't regretted not having children of my own, although I enjoy playing with theirs. My nesting instinct seems to have self-arrested after I built my house. Perhaps my decision is rooted in the kinship I feel with the overloaded boat we call Earth. Part of the irony of loving the natural world is understanding that it would be better off without human presence.

I feel privileged, however, to have witnessed the birth of my friend Natalie's baby. Attending class as Natalie's birth coach, I trundled off to a corner with all the fathers when the instructor asked us to brainstorm ways to help during labor. We used a marker to record suggestions such as "drive the car," "say 'Yes, dear,'" and "get ice chips" on a piece of butcher paper. But I doubt anyone is ever ready for a train wreck. There were life-threatening emergencies, hot towels wrapped in garbage bags, laughter, and extraordinary grace and bravery before the crown of Dash's dark head emerged at the end of a long weekend. Natalie is envious that I saw more of the birth than she did. "You remember so much," she says, "that it is more real for you than for me." What is starkly real to me is the mental and physical toughness labor requires. People exclaim about the hardship of the journeys Doug and I take, but I believe they are well within range for anyone who has ever had a baby.

We treasure Labrador for the few times we had to use our symbol for people, an upside-down peace sign made with two wiggling fingers. The sparse population along the southern coast consists mainly of "settlers," the descendants of fishermen attracted from Europe several centuries ago by fish of such legendary abundance that nets weren't even needed to scoop them out of the water. Though the fish are mostly gone, the settlers are still looking for them.

"Hello, me chil'ren. Fuurst, we t'ought ye was swor'fish and den we saw ye was y'rself."

It was 1989, and Doug and I, only a few days into our trip, traded furtive glances, each hoping to find a glimmer of comprehension in the other's eyes. Newfoundlander is workingman's English, arrested in another century by the isolation of Newfoundland (locally pronounced New-fin-LAN) and Labrador (Lab-ra-DOOR). It is a brogue as thick as honey, seasoned by the salt of the ocean. To an outsider's untuned ear, it sounds like Latin spoken backward through a mouthful of sand.

We'd been bucking through whitecaps, crossing a three-mile-wide channel that was not in a gentle mood. Focused on angling my boat so that I didn't keep getting doused by spray, I noticed that some waves looked more solid than others, some had fins, and a few even appeared to be geysering. Just as I realized that we were in the midst of a large group of spouting minke whales, a wooden skiff emerged from an island and gunned straight for us, as if purposefully adding to the melee. Its motor slowed only when our heads emerged from the troughs of the waves and the disappointed fishermen inside saw that we were not swordfish. They stood regarding us, their hair the color of clouds, in black waterproofs and patched woolen sweaters knit by their wives. Men of the sea and lifetime boatbuilders, they had never before seen craft like ours.

"Var ye goin, Skipper?"

"Doon the Labra*door*? Ye'll be rate harty. Ar ye Merikin?"

" 'Tis durty vedder."

"Come fer braffus. Wid the new tad, if y'r lucks in, sar, it'll be mawr cam."

By now, we had discerned that "tad" was tide and "cam" was calm. Accepting what we guessed and hoped was an invitation for breakfast, we asked our hosts if they had any difficulty under-standing us. "Nay," they replied, "ye tawks jus lake the peeples on TV."

As the fishermen sped toward home and more tranquil waters, we followed more slowly as they'd directed, through a "tickle," a narrow channel between two islands, and into a circle of eager arms reaching down to secure us to a log wharf. Several families, with kids ranging from floor-level infants to ceiling-height teenagers, crowded into a plywood cabin behind us, filling the shadowed fringes of the room. We were more than visitors, we were live entertainment.

Doug's name in Newfoundlander is "Dog." He was usually hailed as "sar." In this country, the "b'ys" (men) traditionally talk to men, and women are quiet. That freed me to focus on dispatching bread and jam. The conversation ebbed and flowed around fishing. Our hosts had decided not to set any nets that morning—the whales would churn right through them. The day before, six nets had caught only two fish, and more often than not, a day's work would yield no fish. They bemoaned the disappearance of the cod, once their mainstay, decimated by indiscriminate pillaging of the seas by offshore trawlers. The men were accustomed to spend winters at the head of relatively sheltered, forested bays, and to shift out to the coast in summer to earn their livelihood, as had their grandfathers and great-grandfathers before them. Now they fretted about no longer being able to support their families.

In 1992, we turned into the same tickle bearing chocolate bars as gifts for the Cape Charles families who had befriended us. This time the water was full of icebergs—"hoice," as the locals would have said—but the houses were empty, looking even more ramshackle in their abandonment. There was no reason for our friends to shift out to the coast. An order from the Canadian government to close the cod fishery indefinitely in Newfoundland and Labrador was expected any day, a belated attempt to allow depleted stocks to rejuvenate and an end to a little-regulated way of life that had dominated this coast for more than two hundred years. More than nineteen thousand people would find themselves without work. From conversations with other fishermen in similar straits, we knew their options. For now, they were eligible for unemployment compensation. Later there might be government retraining programs. Strong, scarred hands accustomed to handling nets would have to mesh together new lives.

Too often our upside-down peace sign seemed an appropriate comment on the failure of people to be responsible stewards of the land and sea. One day, we rounded the blind curve of an island and came upon several settler families perched on a smooth slab of granite, cheerfully having a barbecue in the fog. The women, with bikini tops exposing chubby acres of pale skin, laughed that the sun really had been shining minutes before. They stuffed us with chicken, fish, caribou, hot dogs, coleslaw, potato salad, and cookies. Sunna's grasp of Newfoundlander wasn't any better than ours, but her smile broadcast universally. Kids crowded around her, fascinated by a map of Canada and Alaska spread across her lap. All but a few of the older ones had never been off the Labrador coast, even to Newfoundland, and they had little sense of where they lived in relation to the rest of the world. When the families piled into their skiffs to head back to Fishing Ships Harbor three miles away, they left all their garbage—cigarette butts in puddles, bottles, torn paper wrappings, aluminum foil. To them, this rock was their birthright, the ocean their dump. To us they were a paradox, like the oncologist who smokes or the peace lover who carries a concealed weapon. It seemed unfathomable that parents who displayed such obvious love toward their children could be so disrespectful of their surroundings. We stayed behind to make amends, cleaning up as best we could.

If we taught Sunna nothing else, we wanted her to know how to move through the country without leaving a sign that she had been there. This is not only a conservation imperative but an art form, the best hope for allowing whoever visits the same spot after us to experience the thrill of being in a place that feels wild and unspoiled. True wilderness may no longer exist in our bordered world, making the places where wildlife abounds and people are scarce, where the patterns and rhythms of nature are still dominant, all the more precious. The host of tricks we use to limit our impact includes camping on gravel rather than less durable vegetation, taking time in the morning to rough up the flattened pads where the tents have been. On particularly alluring beaches, we try to minimize or even to erase the footprints we leave above the tideline. Many Native groups traditionally have a different ethic for the land, which they see as an extension of their home. Some see fire rings or heaps of discarded cans as welcome signposts. One Inupiaq man on the North Slope told Doug, "We like to leave our mark so that the land seems less lonely to us."

As we continued to gain degrees of latitude, we cheered baby gulls testing their wings, and steered clear of duck families on marine outings, the ducklings strung in a ragged line, churning their feet like windup toys. If they were separated in surf or blown out to sea by strong winds, they'd likely die, as did a marooned duckling Doug tried to warm in his hands. As the weeks added weight and strength to their bodies, we saw them venturing beyond the shadow of the shoreline. Sometimes, in the fog, the last to flee us were the almost full-size young gulls, their youth betrayed by their fearless curiosity and gray feathers.

Both Sunna and I steered off of Doug whenever we could, for, in his kayak, he had the only pair of eyes facing forward. Sunna is definitely her father's daughter, with the same propensity for ramming icebergs with enough brute strength to bend the aluminum riggers supporting her oarlocks. Ancestors of these bergs are famous for dispatching more formidable ships than ours; the *Titanic* was only the best-known of a long list of victims. Doug, however, was not a completely trustworthy guide. Subject to visual obstructions and lapses in concentration, he was also not above deliberate deviousness. Early one morning, I saw a smirk flash across his face and turned for my own view. Sunna, humming as she rowed, was in a world of her own. I asked if her shoulders were loose—she had a habit of hunching them, restricting the flow of her stroke. "Yeah," she said, "I feel good." I asked again, and received the same response, this time with a tinge of annoyance. "Well, I'm just checking," I said, "because you're about to smack an iceberg." She whipped her head around and yelped at the sight of a tower of ice the size of a French cathedral. Thrusting her oar handles into her ribs and dragging the blades to stop the forward motion of her boat, she missed impact by inches, coming to rest in water tinted eerily green by the ice. As the trip progressed, she began to rely on us less and to trust herself more.

Our sixteenth day, June 30, found us two hundred miles from our starting point, marooned on Cape Porcupine. My scribbled journal entry reads: "Going nowhere fast." And for July 1: "Still here. Big crashing waves." There are ditto marks for the second, third, and fourth of July, which was decidedly not Independence Day. Storms sucked the words out of us; our energy was inversely proportional to that of the weather. In nature's perpetual quest for equilibrium, the rising bog outside began to infiltrate our tent floor. Doug and I hibernated, seeing Sunna mostly at meals. I worried that she would decide she hated camping and, by extension, us. But characteristically, she took the wet, the wind, and the enforced captivity in stride. She spent hours with Doug in the rain kneading dough for bread, donating the heat of her body to help it rise.

The headland where we were camped was the only rock for almost fifty miles that had resisted the battering of time. On both sides lay curving expanses of white sand beach, named Furdurstrandir—"the wonderful beach"—by the Vikings, the first of whom, Bjarni Herjolfson, sailed along the coast in 986 A.D. The beach didn't look that wonderful on close inspection. It was pockmarked by bomb casings and shrapnel, souvenirs of low-level practice strafing runs from Goose Bay, the nearby military air base that played a strategic role in World War II.

On July 5, the three of us stood studying wave sets, anxious to be released from Cape Porcupine. The last three waves in each set of seven appeared to be the annihilators. Offshore, the water looked reasonable, if we could only get off the beach. It would be Sunna's first serious surf exit. I asked if she was scared; her light-hearted negative reply should have been a clue. She didn't yet know enough about surf to be afraid.

Our plan was to push each boat off just after the last big wave in a set, then row as if we were on fire to clear the line of break-ers. We were sending Sunna out first, not because she was the most expendable (as she later snappily accused us), but so that Doug and I together could give her a good push. But in our haste to take advantage of a particularly favorable wave set, we shoved her out before she was ready, without any of us double-checking her gear. She might have been able to recover from falling off the sliding seat if her oarlocks hadn't been turned backward, trap-ping her oars at an awkward downhill pitch and making it impos-sible for them to clear the waves. At first, it was comical, but stuck in the surf zone, Sunna was swamped by incoming waves while we yelled anxious instructions she couldn't hear. By the time she escaped the breakers, *Porky* was full of water and Sunna was soaked. Though well-intentioned, we had interfered more than we had helped. Even the best mother ducks must let their young swim.

Somewhere after Cape Porcupine, I stopped coaching Sunna on her rowing stroke. Already I was having to row a little harder than at the beginning of the trip to match her pace. It struck me that in a few weeks I'd been able to teach her what had taken me at least five years to figure out. I've never seen myself row except upside down, in a reflection. But when I watched Sunna, she looked exactly the way I felt. It was as if we were partners in an intricately choreographed waltz, mirroring each other's movements and timing, mimicking slight nuances in the flow of our bodies. Whatever else she needed to learn she would teach herself.

The country grew steeper and taller. On hot days, shimmering mirages flattened pointed peaks into buttes and made gulls look as though they were sitting atop mountains. Sheer granite faces, the kind that make climbers and national park planners drool like teething babies, loomed out of the sea so often as to be commonplace. We began to flash peace symbols over our heads more frequently, our sign for caribou. Not wanting to startle them when we first landed on a beach, we'd bend at the waist, lower our heads, and pretend that we were grazing along the water's edge. Sometimes, in our enthusiasm, we'd hold discarded, weather-whitened antlers or ski poles over our heads as props. As long as our movements were gentle, the caribou seemed to accept us as two-legged creatures with old or metal antlers. If we failed to fool them, they'd sprint away in a clatter of hooves.

Names on the map like Snug Harbor and Black Tickle gradually gave way to Inuktitut terms. We knew the translations of some—*tikkegatsuk* means point, *kogukoluk* is a little brook—and envied the familiarity with the landscape that the names implied. On the outer coast, north of the inlet that reaches more than a hundred miles inland to Goose Bay, there are five main villages where the Canadian government in the 1950s autocratically consolidated groups of Innu (Indian) and Inuit who had been scattered along the coast.

Doug and I remembered the Naskapi (Innu) village of Davis Inlet from our 1989 visit for the dock graffiti that said "Fucken Eskimo" and for angry demands by residents that the government move their village to a new site where non-Innu would not be welcome. We'd stayed with a white Newfoundlander teacher, his Naskapi wife, and their three children in their house on "Halfbreed Hill" while our thirty-year-old host spoke of unbearable tension in the village and confided that he drank sixty-three ounces of whiskey a week. Jaco, an old Naskapi man living in a canvas tent near the water, had volunteered to watch our boats. Otherwise, he said, they would be vandalized and pushed back into the ocean. He pointed out the high school with plywood-covered windows as an example of recent trouble.

We'd been in the village at the same time as a boatload of Smithsonian anthropologists and archaeologists who had been working along the north coast for a couple of decades. One of them gave a talk in the community center, a slide show unlike any I'd ever seen. Thick blue cigarette smoke filled the room, collecting in stringy clouds near the ceiling. The scientist stood front and center, lecturing quietly, while children ran in circles and people milled about. No one appeared attentive as the village chief translated the talk from English into Naskapi, yet the room was abuzz in native tongue as the audience recognized places and people in the slides. Many of the photographs had been taken by American explorer William Cabot in the first decade of the century, when he'd traveled into the country with nomadic bands of Naskapi in search of caribou. He'd first made contact by waiting for the Naskapi to emerge from the interior to trade furs at a small post in Davis Inlet. Cabot's slides showed the great-grandfathers and great-grandmothers of those in the room at their hunting camps, dressed in skin clothing standing in front of the tepee-shaped tents. A couple of the babies slung across their mothers' chests were now elders, stretching gnarled fingers and squinting toward the hazy screen.

This time, we skipped Davis Inlet and pushed on to Nain. We arrived on July 20, after thirty-six days and 650 miles, beating the coastal ferry, the *Taverner*, into town by at least two ice-troubled weeks. We had nothing but good memories of this old Moravian mission town where four years before, an ample, exuberant woman we'd only just met had thrown a wedding shower for us. The men, including the ten brothers in her settler family, crammed into the kitchen, a quart of whiskey per man. Meanwhile Sarah and her female friends sequestered me in the living room, plying me with unsolicited marriage advice and playing country-and-western love songs at top volume. Even now, the phone rings every few years at four in the morning. When I hear vaguely familiar crooning in the background, I know the caller is Sarah.

But in Nain this year, our boats were broken into by thieves, something that had never happened anywhere, and important things were taken—our tent, Sunna's tent poles, Doug's prescription sunglasses. The Mountie to whom we reported the robbery said he had a pretty good idea of the culprits, as he had just passed some nine-year-old Inuit on the street who looked as if they had "eaten a canary." He called us at Sarah's an hour later and asked Doug to accompany him to the house where one suspect lived. Doug still hates describing what he saw.

The mother had a face that obviously had been used as a punching bag, and Doug was astonished to learn later that she was only thirty-five. Her kids were clustered nearby, all of them marked by the ragged look of neglect. Most of the outside boards of the house had been pulled off, and inside the trim was gone. There was no furniture except for a three-legged stool and some cardboard boxes. During the winter, the family had run out of fuel oil, so they'd dragged in a half-barrel stove and burned the wood around them, staining the already filthy green walls with smoke. When the pipes froze, the children had begun to use the back room as a toilet, defecating on the floor until the stench was vile enough to penetrate the parents' alcoholic stupor. Without raising her eyes or saying a word, the woman roughly pushed her son out the door to collect his accomplices and show Doug where they had thrown our gear.

We left Nain provisioned with food for six weeks, which was the likely window of time before the weather shut us down for the season. In writing about northern Labrador, I feel as though I should change names and details, as if to protect the innocent. I could make the waterfalls shorter, the pinnacles less dramatic, the water murkier, the natural gardens of sculpted rocks and small pools more mundane. I could omit the chiseled bowls and broad plateaus of the mountains. I could muffle the voices of the past, pretending that we found just a few tent rings and mounded rock graves, and I could make them only hundreds of years old instead of as much as seven thousand. I could make us less alone, less free to wind in and out of uninhabited fjords, less enchanted.

One element I needn't tamper with is the weather—the saucer-shaped wind clouds stacked five high that sent small boats fleeing toward the beach and disappeared as soon as a camp suitable for hurricanes had been erected. Or the calm transformed into sixty-mile-per-hour winds in one five-second moan. Or the squall that turned into a six-day storm, sending confused geese skittering backward over our heads while we rolled two-hundred-pound rocks into a windbreak.

Paddling into northern Labrador's mountains is like walking into a restaurant of great repute and, instead of ordering off the menu, asking the chef to surprise you with choices of his own. The hors d'oeuvre might be a pile of stone chips next to a flat rock where an Inuk man of long ago sat making a scraper or spear point, the mound of pebbles nearby most likely collected by one of his playing children. Entrees could include a glistening cave big enough to be used as an echo chamber by a floating family of three, or a summit view uninterrupted by anything but other peaks lining the blue, iceberg-dotted fjord far below. Dessert might be blueberries picked from the yellowing tundra on Fenstone Tickle Island by frozen, juice-stained fingers. Inevitably, dinner will end before you know it, and you'll find yourself anxious for the next day, so you can feast again.

One still morning in the Torngat Mountains, Doug woke me gently with a kiss and whispered, "We're surrounded. Listen." With concentration, I could discern a kind of murmuring, a subtle sigh of barely audible nudges and breaths. The nearby tundra visible through the sliver of open tent door looked as though it had sprouted velvety stalks overnight. Lying in a close circle around the tent, as if clustered around a campfire, were a group of fifteen caribou. There were males bearing magnificent, multipronged racks, females with long legs tucked underneath them, and the season's babies, with unscarred brown pelts, puffs of white on their chests, and button-sized black noses. Anxious not to spook them, we lay quietly enchanted until they wandered away to graze. Another afternoon, Sunna decided she wanted to sneak up on a lone caribou. As she crept slowly over a slight rise on hands and knees, the caribou decided he was curious about her, and began to circle around until he was almost close enough to nudge her from behind with his antlers.

On day sixty-six, we landed on an island, pulling in to a perfect nook of a beach. We settled in, draped our wet clothing on a sun-warmed rock wall, cooked a huge meal, and lingered, anticipating spending the next day climbing a mountain that jutted straight from the sea. After dinner, Sunna and I went for a walk along the tundra, paralleling a narrow channel on the north side of Saglek Fjord. No more than a quarter mile from camp, I pointed to an off-white object ahead and said, "Does that look like a polar bear to you?" Sunna, with a confidence I haven't felt since I was seventeen, replied, "No, it's too big. It's definitely a rock." Old enough to feel a prickle of déjà vu, I thought it prudent to return to the boats for binoculars. Minutes later, concealed by a boulder and squinting hard toward the object in question, I whispered, "I still can't tell for sure, but it looks like a rock." Sunna, taking her turn with the binoculars, proclaimed, "Yeah, it's definitely a rock." But Doug and I have a maxim when teaching people to evaluate avalanche hazard—seek bull's-eye data that does the most to eliminate your uncertainty. So we wriggled closer on our bellies, doing our best caterpillar imitations, repeating almost the same conversation more than once. Suddenly, the binoculars froze onto Sunna's eyeballs and she whispered an almost inaudible, "Uh-oh. It's moving." The rock had a head, the rock was a polar bear, the head was the size of a bushel basket, and the polar bear was at least ten feet long and not far from where we intended to sleep.

We hastened to break the news to Doug and analyze our options. We could move camp in the dark to a location that probably wouldn't be much more secure, or, my preference, make Sunna stand guard all night while we slept. Or we could all go to sleep, banking on the probability that when the bear awoke, it would hunt upwind, away from our camp. We were tired after fighting wind and swell for every inch of the day's thirty-mile gain. We chose the last alternative. Sunna, placing her usual, sometimes disconcertingly total trust in our logic and experience, promptly crawled into her tent and fell asleep. Doug and I also turned in, but only after he uncased and double-checked the 12-gauge shotgun, a weapon so undersized against so much bear that it could merely offer last-resort defense at appallingly short range.

Several things did not go according to plan. First, either despite or because of our experience, neither Doug nor I could fall asleep. Second, in the middle of the night, the wind died, replaced by a dangerous stillness in which our scent would be much more detectable. We decided that we'd take turns lying awake listening for big footsteps while the other slept. I selflessly volunteered for the first shift, but Doug soon perceived a problem when he was awakened by the loud, familiar sound of a buzz saw, only inches from his ear. I promised to be more vigilant, and struggled like a trucker to stay conscious for the next hour. On his shift, Doug heard what sounded like a one-winged bird trying to take off but proved to be a skinny fox scratching himself. I was dreaming restlessly (presumably about bears) when Doug accidentally bumped me, startling me into a "Hey, bear!" that should have commanded the attention of all the fauna on the island. Doug muzzled me, and shortly thereafter the three of us made a chilly, predawn, mercifully uneventful exodus from the island.

As we took our cue from the birds and rowed south through mountains of diminishing size, it was impossible not to wonder what Labrador would await Sunna's return in a decade or more. In the fourteen years between my first and last visits, coastal Labrador had seen the cod fishery closed, new roads and offshore oil fields developed, and helicopter traffic increased. A few years hence, the world's greatest nickel deposit would be discovered near Nain, a mother lode worth an estimated $10 billion.

Our first night back in Nain, we slept fitfully in Sarah's hot house. In the middle of the night, Doug sat up, disturbed. I draped my arm around him, asking what was wrong. "Look," he said, pointing to a shaft of light tunneling into the attic's next room, "something is very strange." I reminded him that the trip was over. "Oh," he murmured, "I thought we were in the tent."

We would scatter soon, us back to Anchorage and avalanche work, Sunna to college in Seattle, where she'd row crew. Within a couple years, she would migrate to Fairbanks, where she would finish her degree, work as an environmental educator, row the length of the Yukon River with a friend, and build herself a cabin with Doug's help.

In the meantime, the *Taverner* took us south, along with Inuit families, sullen Naskapi, disgruntled fishermen, a few other tourists, and a huge amount of cargo ranging from toilet bowls to rusting trucks to mangy dogs. For six days, we rattled in our cabin near the boiler room, where the Holy Bible was strategically mounted on the wall on top of the barf bags and next to the life jackets. A sub-Arctic version of a Mexican banana boat, the *Taverner* makes whistle stops at sea to hoist or lower passengers and pulls into ports big and small for stays of unannounced duration.

Trying to exercise our atrophying legs in one village, Sunna and I made the mistake of being more than five minutes away from the boat when the five-minute whistle sounded. The gangplank was up when we returned at a fast trot, but Doug had persuaded the crew not to throw off the lines. Out of breath and already contrite, we were motioned sternly on deck by the first mate. With a glint in his eye and a thick Newfoundlander accent, he said, "I want to tell you a little story."

The story went like this: A man was bringing his bride home in a horse-drawn buggy. When the horse stumbled on the rocky road, the man snarled, "That's once." A short distance later, the horse lost his footing again and the man grunted, "That's twice." When the horse slipped a third time, the man climbed down from the buggy, drew his pistol, and shot the horse dead. His horrified bride cried, "You brute, how could you do such a thing?" Her husband turned to her and said, "That's once." The mate turned to Sunna and me. "There's two of youse, so that's twice," he said, then he put his hands in his pockets and ambled away. Our laughter floated skyward, lost in the clamor of gulls wheeling above the ship's wide wake.

Most technology, on balance, has improved things. I think that sitting

in an air-conditioned room watching C-SPAN on a color television set

beats being next to a primitive fireplace outside of a cave.

—Newt Gingrich

Wilderness without its animals is dead—dead scenery.

Animals without wilderness are a closed book.

—Lois Crisler, *Arctic Wild*

8

The Devil in the Violin:
Alaskans in Norway

ON THE WALL of our kitchen, amid a bright sea of images, hangs a sepia portrait of a man with piercing eyes, a square forehead, a sharply ridged, slightly curving nose, and a gray beard that reaches almost to the second button on his shirt. It is hard to know if he is smiling, as his full mustache conceals his lips, but I suspect he is not. A stamp on the back shows that the photograph was taken in Cooperstown, North Dakota, over a century ago.

Our Norway saga began in part with this man, Tollef Olsen Nordhaugen. He left Norway in 1858, at the age of twenty-one, forfeiting his right as eldest son to inherit the family farm in Lismarka, near Lillehammer. Instead, the rolling fields went to the next brother in line, Johannes. Tollef and Johannes both look familiar. Either of them could be Doug's twin.

Tollef's descendants have a variety of explanations for his exodus. The juiciest is that he was forbidden to play the violin by his sternly religious mother, who thought it an instrument of the devil. Whatever the reason, we know that in 1858 he traveled by ship to Quebec and then by train to Chicago and Milwaukee, with little more than his violin and his Bible in hand. He wrote his first letter back to Norway on November 1.

> I've only been here a short time but I've already seen much that you there at home could never have imagined . . . After six weeks and two days we came happily to Quebec. None of the ship's passengers were dead, neither were any born. While we anchored in Quebec, I went many times into the city and walked alone through the streets, but could not perceive anywhere what was talked about at home—that they would walk around with stones in their coat pockets and a kind of a walking stick with which they would attack and slaughter each other, so this is a sheer lie . . . There is no nation on the whole earth which is so indifferent as to how things are as the American . . . On my trip up through the country I saw many black people or Negroes and many of them had also been slaves . . . I have also seen two Indians or "wilds" . . . and a group who call themselves Methodist . . .

In Wisconsin, Tollef helped to invent the rotary snowplow, but family lore has his co-inventor, a rascally Swede named Olson, pocketing the profits. Tollef married a woman descended from the first white child believed to have been born in Wisconsin, then homesteaded in Dakota Territory and fathered nine children. The sixth, Josie, was born in 1881. As a youngster, she once hid from approaching Indians under the belly of a cow she was retrieving from the fields; even as an old woman she remembered their hilarity when they discovered her. She also described blizzards so strong that snow drifted up to the second stories of houses anchored into the plains, and children were sent out to do their chores with ropes around their waists. Josie staked her own homestead at seventeen and rescued her younger siblings from the orphanage to which they'd been sent by Tollef when their mother died, supporting the household by teaching school.

Another photo on the kitchen wall shows a man holding a Norwegian flag and standing on a hill covered with lush grass and yellow wildflowers. This is Josie's grandson, Doug. His eyes are lost in the shadow created by a dark blue seaman's cap, and all but his cheeks, nose, and lower lip are covered in beard. Though he cannot read his great-grandfather's letter in the original, he has long been proud of his Norwegian heritage, wearing T-shirts proclaiming, "Ya sure, ya betcha, I'm a Norwegian," and holding together the rusting bumper of his car with a bright green sticker that boasts "Norvegen speling champyun." Minus a Bible or violin, he also had left home at a young age, seeking greater personal freedom. But like Uncle Al, who had to know where the Yukon River came from, Doug had long felt the tug of his family headwaters on the far side of the Atlantic. And so in 1995 he proposed that we row the length of Norway from Sweden to Russia, a distance of about twenty-five hundred miles.

As part of our preparation, it seemed a good idea to learn some Norwegian. Soon finding myself at least a week ahead of Doug in *Norwegian in Ten Minutes a Day*, I volunteered to drill him on numbers. He did great until he got to two. I gave him a hint by pointing to my toe (same pronunciation), whereupon Doug slapped his knee and exultantly declared *"ni"* (Norwegian for nine), highlighting either his poor grasp of anatomy or his lack of language proficiency. He did, however, display an affinity for the number six (*sex*) and perfect recall for catchy words for which he would never find uses, like *fartsmåler* (speedometer). Ultimately, surrounded by Norwegians who shamed us with their fluent English, we ended up speaking our less than perfect Norwegian mainly to each other.

We began our trip, inauspiciously, without boats. When we arrived in Gothenburg, Sweden, in late April, after two calendar days of jet travel, the shipping company whose name was on our paperwork had never heard of the two brand-new rowing boats we'd crated and shipped from Alaska several months before, didn't care, and couldn't suggest anyone else we might call. Enter Tanase, a hero disguised as a Romanian sailor who had jumped ship in Sweden twenty-six years earlier. We met him while milling about at the gate in Copenhagen waiting for a rescheduled flight, attracted like hummingbirds to his red sweater with an emblem of crossed oars. He turned out not to be a rower; no doubt he now selects his clothes more carefully. But he was in the shipping industry himself, and he was just returning from a business trip to Singapore. Tanase made a few more fruitless calls for us from the Gothenburg airport, then, incensed by the runaround we were getting, slammed down the receiver and began dragging us and our two cartloads of gear toward the line of cabs, insisting that we come home with him.

Gothenburg, headquarters of Volvo, sprawls for miles, each of which was celebrated by a happy tick of the taxi's meter while my tired brain strained to divide by six, converting currency. By the time we reached Tanase's house, the tab in U.S. dollars had topped three digits. Tanase wouldn't take the new Swedish kronor we thrust into his hands. Instead, he introduced us to his surprised but gracious wife, who bustled into the kitchen to prepare pork chops and fried eggs.

We would have preferred to sleep until we had rejoined the living, but Tanase was obsessed. From his home office, he made strings of phone calls, switching effortlessly between rapid-fire

Romanian, Swedish, and English while we exchanged increasingly frustrated faxes with the freight forwarder in Alaska, who insisted that our boats were where they were not. Our luck changed after six hours of effort, when a receptionist in Stockholm remembered that, during lunch several days before, a friend who worked for a different company had mentioned something about two canoes that had arrived for two Canadians. Most Europeans attach Alaska to Canada, a fact we eventually stopped disputing. As for the distinction between rowing boats and canoes—by then, we would have settled for anything that would float.

We decided it would be easier to row from Gothenburg than arrange further logistics to move the boats a hundred or so miles north to the border. We contacted Bengt, a friend of a Norwegian colleague, who proved that being an avalanche specialist is like belonging to an international fraternity with chapters throughout the world. Though he did not know us, Bengt took time off from work to pick us up at Tanase's and guide us through the formidable bureaucracy necessary to claim our belongings.

The boats were more or less intact, though one crate had been smashed, rats had gnawed into the boxes of gear we had also shipped, and a large waterproof sack of granola had been stolen by someone who must like breakfast more than I do. Bengt's Volvo had a roof rack, enabling him to deliver us, with boats and baggage, to waterside, where we had a fighting chance of regaining our self-sufficiency. He left us on the beach to unpack, assemble, and repair ad infinitum, but returned early in the evening with his wife, Gudrun, and their two small sons, bearing a picnic of hot homemade blackberry lemonade and elaborate cakes. Just as we launched, cold rain turned to colder sleet. The boys waved goodbye with little blue-and-yellow Swedish flags plucked from the tops of the devoured pastries, splashing after us into the water like puppies.

The west coast of Sweden looks like parts of Labrador, only with aromatic bakeries every few miles, quaint villages all painted red, dressed-up families commuting to church in varnished wooden skiffs, and a turreted castle called Marstrand set amid pink granite knobs and narrow channels flecked with pansies. A week of rowing brought us to the Norwegian border, where little changed except the flags and the colors of the summer houses, which were still empty for the season. Soon, open groves of trees and small sand beaches gave way to the wide maw of Oslo Fjord, a crossing we had to make unless we detoured far inland toward Norway's biggest city.

Twelve miles is a respectable crossing under any circumstances, and this one was complicated by pervasive fog and large commercial vessels plying a heavily trafficked corridor. We plotted a strategy that had worked for us before. In the evening, a time when the winds often diminish, we'd cross from the eastern shore to Rauer, an island about four miles out. There, we'd land, climb a hill, pull out our binoculars, and scout toward the far shore. If conditions were good, we'd keep rowing. If they were poor or our energy was flagging, we'd wait.

We were hungry when we landed on the island, so we decided to cook dinner before we climbed the hill. We'd barely had time to put on extra clothes when two camouflage-colored military jeeps screeched onto the sand, spilling red-cheeked soldiers with big black guns at their sides.

"*Forbudt, forbudt,*" they cried in their most forbidding twenty-year-old voices.

We apologized and explained that we didn't speak Norwegian.

"Oh," said their lieutenant crisply. "You must leave at once."

We asked if we could just climb the hill, which, we now noticed, was misshapen by artillery and bunkers.

"No, you must leave now."

"Can we just cook and eat something before we go?"

"No."

"Okay," said Doug, "but if the water is too rough, we are coming back."

At this, the lieutenant looked unhappy. Shifting his gun, he picked up his radio importantly to call his commanding officer. *Jabber, jabber, jabber, forbudt, ja, ja, ya-hoo-da-hoo-da-hoo, jabber, jabber, ja, ja, ja.* My stomach grumbling, I tried to imagine what he was saying. "There are two Americans here disguised as hungry rowers who are trying to steal our national secrets." I took advantage of the long conversation to munch the contents of my snack bag, not knowing when I'd eat again. Finally, the lieutenant reported, "You can return if you need to but you will have to spend the night in jail." He looked a little disappointed that he couldn't immediately confiscate our chocolate bars and scuttle our boats.

It was after eight o'clock at night and we'd already rowed almost thirty miles, but we rounded the corner and sat off the tip of the island, our boats bouncing about in two-foot chop, as we sniffed the wind. Just then a fisherman in a classic wooden boat came by, cheering us with a double-handed victory wave, in a rare Norwegian show of enthusiasm. Conditions weren't perfect, but with the brig as our less enticing choice, we went for it.

We were beat and starving when we reached the far side. The first island had yellow *"Forbudt"* military signs all over it. So did the second. "Screw it," Doug said by the time we reached the third island and discovered it to be similarly posted. "Who will care? We're going to leave early in the morning anyway." But just as we were drawing close to the beach, a gray Navy destroyer pulled around the corner, only two hundred yards away, and we froze like guilty deer. Perhaps there was a region-wide alert about the suspicious rowers in stealth boats. We made ourselves keep straggling along until, just shy of the day's forty-mile mark, we located a beach that was not *forbudt*, and gladly granted ourselves unconditional permission to sleep.

The next day, we let tailwinds strong enough to break my rigger push us into the nearby town of Tønsberg, where we were to meet Erik, the solicitous Norwegian friend who had hooked us up with Bengt. Erik and his wife, Gerd, had driven two hours from Oslo for this rendezvous. Within minutes, we found ourselves perched with crossed legs on a couch in the home of Gerd's aunt and uncle, surreptitiously rearranging our wind-disheveled hair as we sipped tea from delicate demitasse cups and tried not to stare at all the little sandwiches arranged in front of us or eat all the cake. Though this was Doug's first "tea" in Norway, he recognized the front room with its embroidered chairs, the fuss over special guests, the use of the best plates and silver, even the Norwegian names for each kind of cookie, for the ritual had survived transplant to North Dakota intact.

We went to Oslo with Erik and Gerd for a few more days of pampering, visiting the Norwegian Geotechnical Institute, where Erik and his colleagues worked to manage Norway's *snøskred* (avalanche) problems. It was May 8, and at noon, along with the rest of the nation, we observed two minutes of silence commemorating the end of the country's occupation by Germany during World War II.

A mere half century hasn't come close to healing the scars left by the war on the land and its inhabitants. Virtually every headland guarding the entrance to a major fjord is riddled with bunkers and gun emplacements. Some, as we discovered and became better at anticipating, have been commandeered by the Norwegian military. Many are honeycombed with miles of tunnels and chambers chiseled into the rock by prisoners of war under German direction. Rusty barbed wire still lines much of the less populated shoreline; in places it has been pulled into great gnarled heaps. In the village of Hamningberg, we slept in a rare square-beamed log structure built in the 1700s. Few old buildings survived along the northernmost coast, because Nazi occupation forces, fleeing as Russian liberators approached in the fall of 1944, began a scorched-earth policy, burning whole towns and farms in vengeful fury. Our trip's end point, Kirkenes, near what was once the Finnish border but is now Russian as a result of the war, was among the most heavily bombed villages in Europe.

Those Norwegians we met old enough to have a memory of the war stiffened at the mention of anything German, though they bristled slightly less about today's massive influx of German tourist revenue. Most hated the idea of Norway's ever joining the European Community, fearful that such union might erode their self-sufficiency and apoplectic at the prospect of enabling Germans to own pieces of their fjords or mountains. The war had also fueled Norway's resentment of its old rival, Sweden, whose neutrality allowed the Germans to roll unhindered into Norway, although this bitterness was tempered by gratitude for Sweden's generous recovery help after the war.

The Norwegians are a strong, stoic people so serious about never again compromising their self-sufficiency that they willingly build noxious aluminum smelting plants next to nature preserves and oil refineries in the middle of blue fjords. In our conversations with locals, it was rare not to hear the comment "You must love the nature very much." The way Norwegians said it, as though nature were an abstraction, an entity separate from ourselves, always gave me pause.

The massive emigration that occurred between 1850 and 1880, of which Tollef was a part, gave Minnesota more residents of Norwegian descent than remained in Norway. Conformity and honesty are valued above all else in this small, prosperous country, where people are educated and medicated for free in exchange for high taxes, including a 100 percent luxury tax on alcohol and gasoline. Describing his travels in Norway and Sweden, Bill Bryson writes, in *Neither Here Nor There*:

> It's as if the inhabitants are determined to squeeze all the pleasure out of life. They have the highest income tax rates, the highest VAT, the harshest drinking laws, the dreariest bars, the dullest restaurants, and television that is like two weeks in Nebraska. Everything costs a fortune. Even the purchase of a bar of chocolate leaves you staring in dismay at your change and anything larger than that brings tears of pain to your eyes.

The ethic of national honesty is staggering. I have little doubt that we could have left our loaded boats onshore for six months and they would have remained untouched. At train stations, passengers purchase tickets from metal boxes on the platform, though the chance of these tickets being checked upon boarding is about equal to Doug's odds of breaking a champagne glass by singing. At trip's end, after 128 days and 2,468 miles of effort, I was determined to actually enter Russia, so I let my boat drift six whole feet past the Grense-Jakobselv border marker in the wide river mouth before turning around. Norwegians who witnessed this blasphemy seemed to expect that I'd march straight to the guard tower and volunteer the requisite fine, rumored to be five hundred dollars. No doubt my failure to turn myself in confirmed the worst they'd suspected of Americans.

Norwegians have an isolated people's wariness of outsiders. The villages were such quiet places that we imagined we could hear the potatoes growing in the small, manicured yards and the curtains moving as apparitions snuck careful peeks at us, grandfather clocks ticking steadily behind them in immaculate parlors. We heard that when the Winter Olympics came to Norway in 1994 (prompting Doug to buy our first television set, so that he could see his ancestral town of Lillehammer), promoters had been so concerned that dour-faced Norwegians would promulgate a poor image that they'd initiated a campaign to teach Norwegians to smile at people they didn't know. A year after the hugely successful Olympics, the Norwegians seemed due for a refresher.

One morning, we caught up with an old fisherman rowing at a sedate pace in a wooden dinghy. Obviously intrigued by our long oars and sliding seats, he studied the boats intently whenever he thought we weren't watching, but if we looked toward him or waved, he'd ignore us. Sometimes, in cities, we'd have a crowd of twenty on a dock observing every move we made, even photographing us from a variety of angles as if we were zoo creatures. If we tried to joke, or ask questions, or engage them in simple conversation, most would continue to stare silently, drop their eyes to the ground, or melt further away. Maybe, like us, they just needed more sunshine that summer. Once when Doug asked an Inuk in Canada why our waves of greeting were often not returned, he answered, "Probably because they do not know you." Norwegians would undoubtedly have given the same logical answer.

Doug, who likes to blend into a crowd, began to take it personally that onlookers consistently giggled and even laughed outright when they saw him. Was it his unruly beard, not neatly mowed like those of Scandinavian men, or his spandex shorts, or even his great-looking legs? Finally, he asked a wharfside sailor. "I don't know," the man said gravely. "Maybe it is because they think you are a prophet."

Hints of Norway's cultural ancestry are sprinkled liberally about the coast like trail markers. We usually found signs of the Vikings—big obelisk-like rock cairns, burial mounds, or square sod house foundations—when we were waiting for the weather. Obviously, they had hovered in the lee of the same capes more than a thousand years before us. We shared Lindesnes, the country's southernmost point, with them while the sea beyond sheltered reefs raged. In the intervening years, it had also become home to Norway's oldest lighthouse, a wealth of German bunkers, and a restaurant that offered a Sunday smorgasbord of legendary proportions.

If you want to see Norwegians at their most serious, ask them about rounding the southwest coast from Lindesnes to Stavanger, which is completely open to the oil-rich North Sea. Methodically, authoritatively, and with a minimum of intonation, they will describe waves that top the tallest lighthouses and leave you with no doubt that you will die. Twisted fragments of vessels strewn along the shore lend credibility to their stories.

Of course, we had to try it anyway. Gulping dread, we edged out of protected waters before dawn, ready to turn around at the slightest provocation. But offshore winds had a stranglehold upon the ocean, beating the swell down and sending the waves toward Britain. With the cage open and the dragon slumbering, we knew we must row until we dropped, and we did—along the endless solid-rock fences that Norwegians seem to build as a national pastime, past boringly flat farm country. The occasional concrete breakwater cradling small fishing harbors gave us the chance to stretch and to visit with the few fishermen outgoing enough to actually want to talk to us.

Only one cloud darkened our fantasy. We couldn't breathe. We were choked by industrial stench, along with fumes from nearby fields that had recently been fertilized with cow and sheep manure. I'd row for ten strokes and then take just the tiniest, shallowest, mouth-only inhalation, gaining enough oxygen for maybe half my brain cells. If I'd had extra breath, I would have laughed at the irony of dying from asphyxiation when, by all rights, we should have drowned.

Fifty-two straight miles, a sleepless night on a beach covered knee-deep in rotting seaweed that smelled like dog shit, and another half day of the same kind of marathon drudgery brought us within sight of the coast's biggest oil town, Stavanger. It struck me as a possible symptom of insanity that we had worked overtime to reach a bunch of smokestacks, but I was too weary to pursue this painful line of questioning. We stopped short of town at a beachside campground, where we treated ourselves to greasy shoe-leather hamburgers for twenty-two dollars and watched a blond boy of about seven purchase three ice-cream cones, put them carefully into the pocket of his baggy pants, climb onto his bicycle, and pedal away.

Two days later, on May 27, I scraped bottom. If the highs and lows of any journey were plotted, they would be erratic in size and spacing, like the electrocardiogram of an intensive-care heart patient. But in Haugesund, not too far from Haraldhaugen, where the first king of Norway was buried in 872, I flat-lined. I was sick of noise; sick of bridges, pleasure boats, hydrofoils, and cargo ships; sick of foul-smelling air, cigarette smoke, and flatlands; sick of stone walls; sick of being viewed with suspicion; sick of sheep and their poop; desperate for wild country and mountains. By the time we found a place to land I was in complete arrest. I lay on my back wilting in the sun while an almost equally discouraged Doug was driven to the grocery store by the gas plant manager. I revived in stages—a little with fresh bananas and a cold orange soda proffered by Doug, a bit more when another local confided, unprompted, that this was the boring, noisy, stinky part of Norway.

Thankfully, the country did start to become intriguingly steeper. On May 30, we reached Bergen, where most tourists visit the famed medieval fish market or ride the cable car to the top of the mountain above town. But not us. We spent the day in the hospital.

Our saga began when we went to the police station to pick up the resident's permits we'd applied for months before by calling the Norwegian consulate in San Francisco. Over the phone, a woman had politely informed me that rowing the whole coast of Norway, which would require a longer stay than the conventional three-month tourist visa allowed, wasn't a good enough reason to qualify for the permit. "You need a purpose," she said, reminding me of my father. I'd mumbled something about wanting to compare Norwegian avalanche terrain to that of Alaska, given similar snow climates, and that had gained us enough credibility to continue the process.

But now, as we watched the rubber stamp meet the paper, Doug asked for a translation of the three typewritten pages we'd just been handed as a formality. The number one rule for travelers embroiled in foreign bureaucracy is never, never to ask any questions. A corollary is never to ask a Norwegian to read the rules. For there on page three, close to the bottom of the exhaustive list of instructions, was the stipulation that all foreigners must be tested for tuberculosis. Our newly stamped passports were whisked back across the counter, and off we went to the hospital. Eight waiting room hours later, we were pronounced fit enough to have already rowed 675 miles, though not before two nurses and a doctor came running toward the waiting room pushing a wheelchair, asking, "Mr. Fesler, do you know you have broken ribs?" Doug's chest X ray looked as if a bull had gotten loose within his rib cage, a legacy of his close encounter with the tree three years before.

North of Bergen, we began catching more frequent glimpses of the Norway of postcard fame. Still, sometimes we started out looking for a *konditori* (bakery) and found an oil rig instead. Or we pulled into what would have been a charming town if we didn't have to first tie our boats up next to a slimy pipe dumping sewage into the harbor.

June 4 was Ascension Day, a national holiday in Norway. It also happened to be my birthday. The next day we camped in a waterfall-rimmed natural amphitheater named Vingen. There we found petroglyphs left as much as four thousand years before the Ascension of Christ the Norwegians had just finished celebrating. Figures of fat-bellied, deerlike animals, sometimes striped, sometimes antlered, covered almost every granite ledge and boulder. The flat rock next to our tent was covered with squiggly and straight lines of more recent vintage, rune characters that persisted in Scandinavia into the Middle Ages. We bounced our voices off the tall rockfaces that walled this beachless fjord and listened as they resonated with a power and mystique we couldn't have generated on our own. Inspired, we later rowed about fourteen miles out of our way, in gale-force beam winds and sideways rain, to view the first known petroglyph of a skier, rumored to be four thousand years old. Shivering and soaked, we felt like fools when we found it chipped into a rock outcrop. The petroglyph was tiny, and it looked like a bunny in a boat.

After Vingen, we again tested Norwegian honesty and the rumors of Russian sailors stealing what they could find (especially old tires, and women's lingerie off clotheslines), by leaving our boats unattended for several days as we toured into the mountains with another avalanche friend named Krister. I could feel the eyes of the Norwegian consulate smiling proudly upon us as we studied path after avalanche path, some barreling down onto a road that the Germans had ordered all available civilians to shovel in March 1943. Passing green farms, quiet lakes, and the first blossoming apple trees Doug had seen in twenty-nine years, we literally drove back to the Norway of my memory. I'd thought I recalled little of my family's visit to Norway when I was seven, except for falling into cold water and the ensuing trauma of having to change my pants in front of strangers, but standing in front of the fractured ice of the Briksdal Glacier, I flashed back to a windy picnic along-side blue icebergs, my father slicing cheese with his pocketknife, and the novelty of making snowballs in summer.

In the friendly haven of Krister's house, we finally ate lamb, de-liciously sweet revenge for too many nights of sleep-interrupting bleating. Talk centered on the Stadlandet Peninsula, known as the Stad, the next killer cape awaiting us. According to Krister, in the eight hundred miles we'd traversed, including Lindesnes and the southwest coast, we'd only been skirmishing in the minor leagues. An important maxim for rowers and other travelers: Any obstacle, no matter how formidable, becomes insignificant once it has been surpassed. The Stad was evidently so bad that there was a plan to blast a tunnel for small boats, most of which now only dare round it in convoys. With the familiar smell of intimidation upon us, we returned to the coast, where we found our underwear un-molested by the Russians.

After two days of waiting where the Vikings had and sleeping with malodorous sheep, we were around the Stad, out of the North Sea and into the Norwegian Sea. We'd started at 5:30 in the morning, in light wind and gentle swell. Hour after hour, we kept plugging, into bigger swells and more confused water, until by 10 a.m. we were back in a protected channel, chatting with a classically handsome Norwegian on a beach while his two-year-old son amused himself by loading rocks into the family car.

The cape was the geographical twin of the Alaska Peninsula in southwest Alaska, where we'd rowed the summer before, especially the Kupreanof Peninsula, another of nature's long, crooked fingers into the open ocean. Both have cutaway cliffs, ragged scree slopes, the kind of tundra crags that might hide trolls, and few bailout spots. On the end of the Kupreanof, we'd seen thirteen brown bears and a reef covered with bellowing sea lions. But on the Stad, when we heard a deep throbbing, we'd already been conditioned not to expect bears or sea lions. We turned to see a several-hundred-foot black cargo ship changing course to get a better look at the kamikaze rowers. Along the Alaska Peninsula, we'd encountered 119 brown bears in eighty-nine days, all of them well fed and mild-mannered toward us. In Norway, our closest animal encounters were with the twelve hungry sheep marooned on an island who thought the bags I was pulling out of my boat were feed sacks and with the ten cows who surrounded our tent one morning, licking salt from the fly. There was also the shaking, bawling, hypothermic sheep that I rescued from drowning with the blade of my oar, summoning up the requisite compassion with effort after weeks of camping amid prodigious sheep shit.

On July 4, one of the few summer days that is not a holiday in Norway, we reached the magic 66.3°N latitude line. Actually, we'd encountered a so-called Arctic Circle one and a half miles south of the real one, a metal globe set into concrete and conveniently located on an island surrounded by deep water. We'd just surmised what it was—and who it was for—when the *Canberra*, a big white cruise ship out of London, came around the corner spewing black smoke. Hundreds of people stood on the inland side of the ship, taking flash photographs of what must have been, from their perspective, a barely discernible marker on a flat gray island, and two floating yellow and red specks (our boats), while the *Canberra* sounded its horn in a long triumphant toot.

8 July 1995. Dear Turi, Lahde, and Sunna: Jill and I are sitting in our tent on a little island north of the Arctic Circle (near Bodø) waiting for the wind to die . . . I just took a Norwegian bath, washing my hair outside fully clothed, with the hood of my rain parka tucked in. Jill was braver and stripped to the waist, now she's paying the piper, shivering next to me. This is day 71—we've rowed 1521 miles, with probably around a thousand left to go. Norway has a great variety of landscapes— fjords, granite walls, narrow channels, spires, snowy peaks, sand beaches, waterfalls, and green pastures. But we always have the feeling that everything has been discovered once, twice, hundreds, maybe thousands of times before. We need a few more secrets. We miss bears in the night. Mostly we see sheep (even in nature preserves!) and cows and salmon farms, though on a good day, we might come across a land otter or mink, a seal, and a couple of deer . . .

Just as Tollef's first letter home contradicted common lore, the content of Doug's letters to his daughters wasn't what either of us had expected. In 2,468 miles, we never saw a whale except for a skeleton. Most Norwegians, defiant nonmembers of the International Whaling Commission, were defensive about this, saying that we were in the wrong places or that our timing was off. But there is no question that whales used to frequent these waters, just as they still abound in similar habitats in Alaska. When we rowed in Alaska's Prince William Sound the following spring, we observed more wildlife in the first hour out of Whittier's small boat harbor than we saw during five months in Norway.

Much of Norway's built environment has an aesthetic that many of Alaska's towns, big and small, sadly lack. We live on the outskirts of Anchorage, a place John McPhee describes in *Coming into the Country* as "that part of any city where the city has burst its seams and extruded Colonel Sanders." He continues: "Anchorage is sometimes excused in the name of pioneering. Build now, civilize later. But Anchorage is not a frontier town. It is virtually unrelated to its environment. It has come in on the wind, an American spore. A large cookie cutter brought down on El Paso could lift something like Anchorage into the air." Alaska could learn much from Norway about building good habitat for people, communities where the buildings fit their surroundings and exude charm, where there is a social and economic center, where it is possible to get to the store by bike or foot or boat as well as by car.

Still, even the undeniably beautiful portions of the Norwegian coast that send visitors from more developed, congested parts of Europe into raptures seemed sterile to us. In almost every one of our scenic photographs, I can tell you what has been edited out—a house or boat just to the left, a power line, bridge, tunnel, or road to the right. Rowing the coast was like walking into a kitchen hungry and reaching for a perfect red apple, anticipating sweetness, only to find that the apple is made of wood. The experience frightened us to the marrow. It made us realize that, like the perpetually grazing sheep, centuries of human habitation have nibbled away not only at the earth but at our perception of what constitutes nature. When we do not miss what is absent because we have never known it to be there, we will have lost our baseline for recognizing what is truly wild. In its domestication, nature will have become just another human fabrication.

Already many of the wild lands set aside for "preservation" around the world have become recreational refuges for people more than places of shelter and sustenance for the flora and fauna. An anomaly is the McNeil River State Game Sanctuary at the northern end of the Alaska Peninsula, where visitors are limited to ten a day and are made to adhere to a routine, so that the bears have come to know where and when to expect them. In turn, the bears have been obliging, allowing visitors to watch them eyeball to eyeball, unprotected by fences, as they leap and pounce for fish, nurse their cubs in the afternoon sun, sleep, stroll, and play. To see bears and people interact without fear or bias is inspiring. As bear biologist Charles Jonkle has said: "If people can learn to live with bears, there's a good possibility that we can learn to live with other people. In short, to live with ourselves . . . With them we have to go through a process wherein we learn to trust them and learn to accept the small amount of risk. Perhaps we can accommodate bears. And develop a philosophy that we can share the earth."

We'd visited the McNeil River sanctuary in the summer of 1994, during a rowing trip along the roughly thousand-mile length of the Alaska Peninsula. After portaging in a truck over the Chigmit Mountains into Iliamna Lake, Alaska's largest lake, and following the outflow into western Alaska's Bristol Bay, we stopped in a village store. There, we first heard of the murders of Nicole Simpson and Ron Goldman and the subsequent indictment of ex–football player O. J. Simpson. In *Newsweek*, a jury selection consultant hired by the Simpson defense team was quoted on the challenge of finding impartial jurors: "Unless they've been living in a cave for the last month and a half, they know a lot about the case. If they don't know anything, I'd have to wonder what they'd been doing in their lives." That night, I wrote in my journal: "Unless she has watched nine bears feed on a whale carcass or paddled for months without ever landing on a beach with human footprints, I'd have to wonder if she understands the dangers of a human-centric world not only for other forms of life but for ourselves."

Traveling has renewed our appreciation for Alaska's abundant wildlife and vast, relatively inaccessible wild areas. Still, the "Norwegianification" of Alaska is occurring, one project at a time, with each road, each bridge, each new house built where none has been before. In recent years, Alaska has built a new road into Prince William Sound, studied the feasibility of expanding the road system throughout the state, promoted wilderness races and ecotourism in remote areas, and built a rocket complex in prime bear habitat on Kodiak Island. Sometimes, as in Norway, development is driven by the exigencies of war or by princely oil revenues. But however persuasive the rationale, these projects have a cumulative impact that may be underestimated until it has rippled irreversibly.

Alaska has laudatory conservation measures in place, but even within its federal wildlife refuges, the acreage of private lands exceeds that of the entire refuge system in the rest of the United States. Most of these lands are controlled by corporations created when the U.S. government settled land claims with Alaska's indigenous peoples. These regional and village corporations need to promote development to survive. Though protected areas will likely remain intact longest, the hope that they will be able to sustain themselves as islands is like expecting the passengers in seats 3A, 22D, and 44F on a jumbo jet to survive, suspended at thirty thousand feet, as the plane around them disintegrates. Ultimately, the future of the bears at McNeil River lies far outside the boundaries of the sanctuary, within the landscape of human reason.

In Norway, we noticed that Europeans often interacted with each other in much the same way we did with Alaska Peninsula bears. Standing on a scenic viewpoint, they would tend to ignore the other visitors, as if deliberately creating a bubble of personal space. If forced to shuffle around one another, they would politely leave as much room as possible and avoid direct contact, averting their eyes. In Alaska, meeting another group of paddlers used to be an occasion to socialize. But now it is not uncommon for two groups of paddlers camped on opposite ends of a beach to adopt the same avoidance behavior. As development shrinks the open spaces and technology makes the remaining spaces more accessible, this may become a standard coping mechanism. We will have replaced the privilege of solitude with isolation.

On August 15 we sipped champagne with two new friends, Ole and Anne, on Nordkapp, at 71°10′21″N. Billed as the northernmost point in Europe by advertising geniuses who attract around 275,000 visitors a year to this private park at an entrance fee of about twenty dollars a head, Nordkapp is not the northernmost point on the mainland. In fact, it is not on the mainland at all, but on an island called Magerøya. On the same island, roughly a mile and a half to the west of Nordkapp, there is another, lower-lying point that juts further north. But Nordkapp is as far north as it is possible to drive and, like the fake Arctic Circle, has been made into a major tourist attraction. We'd triumphantly rounded the plateau-topped cliff more than a week before, capping a fifty-nine-mile day, while the sky on the horizon gleamed yellow, then orange, then pink, and fulmars streamed overhead. We could have skipped it altogether, as it is on the outer shore of Magerøya, but we were not immune to the marketing hoopla or to the prodding of Norwegians who, with the Stad and other notorious obstacles behind us, were now insisting that this was the truly impossible cape.

We'd found Ole and Anne—or, more precisely, Ole had found us—the morning after we'd swung around Nordkapp into one of the few protected bays. From Trollholmen, the little island he and Anne alone inhabit, Ole had noticed us slowly cruising the main shoreline. A month earlier, we would have been shocked if a one-handed, fifty-four-year-old Norwegian fisherman had hailed us boisterously from the end of his wharf, but as we'd traveled north, we'd found the country less developed and less populated, and its people more outgoing. Not that there were many people around—a good number were vacationing along the southern coast, in the shuttered summer houses that had been ghostly empty in the spring. Within minutes, our boats were installed on the lawn next to the potatoless potato patch where Ole had offered to store them while we rented a car and drove back to Tromsø to meet my parents for a weeklong vacation. (My poor parents, exceeding normal limits of devotion by personally resupplying us north of the Arctic Circle, had little idea of what they were in for. On the phone, my mother had asked, "Are you sure I really need to bring a raincoat?")

Upon our return, Ole briefed us like prizefighters preparing for the final round in a championship bout with the coast stretching to the east. It would require a series of long, carefully timed leaps from one peninsula to another. Usually the information we are able to garner isn't tailored for boats as small and underpowered as ours, or is laughably useless. Not far from the end of our trip, a man, impressed with the distance we had rowed, asked, "Do you know that the water comes up?"—as if somehow we could have traveled the ocean for months and remained oblivious to tides. He also corrected us, "No, Russia is that way," when we cut south to follow the coast rather than heading straight east across open water. But with laserlike precision, Ole used our maps to peg every possible bailout spot, some less than ten feet wide.

He extracted a promise to send a postcard as soon as we made it to the border and safely to Kirkenes.

It took nineteen days of rowing and hibernating to travel from Nordkapp to the Russian border and back to Kirkenes, where, inadvertently but appropriately, we ended up camped on a gravel beach below the "Psykiatrik Sykehus." It was September 3. We were tired, more than ready to go home, desperate for liberation from the tyranny of the weather. There's an axiom that "bad weather always looks worse out the window," but that has to have been written by someone who didn't spend five months outside in rain and waves, tantalized by snug-looking houses harboring luxuriously warm, safe, and dry inhabitants.

On the final stretch across the northernmost coast, near Hamningberg, we negotiated a minefield of breaking twenty-foot swells, against wind and current so strong that my position relative to a lighthouse didn't change for ten minutes. While we were still in the worst of it, a seventy-five-year-old fisherman named Edvald waved us in toward a landable beach behind a rotting pier. At one time, Hamningberg was home to about seven hundred, but now its summer-only population consisted of about twenty elderly souls, most of whom rushed to the water to greet us, saying we were "very important people in Hamningberg today." Warming up in his living room, we asked Edvald if he had thought we needed rescue when he spotted us off the point. "No," he said. "I figured that anyone who could row in that sea would be able to make it to tea."

Edvald posed a question we fielded often in Norway: "What has been the hardest part of your journey?" With an exposed corner of the North Sea, an assembly line of infamous capes, and a summer rainier and colder than even the oldest, most stoic Norwegians could recall, the list of obvious answers was long. We'd come to think of 1995 as "the summer of small potatoes"—

everyone lamented the pathetic specimens of the national staple that their gardens had produced. But because it was a question we found difficult to answer honestly without explaining that what we hadn't found—wildness—had been hardest on us psychologically, Doug usually replied, "Figuring out how to use Norwegian washing machines." These excruciatingly small-chambered devices have byzantine operating instructions that reduce normally intelligent foreigners to near-naked zombies, hypnotized into witnessing the torture of their clothes as they interminably spin to the right, stop, spin to the left, stop, and spin right again.

Waiting at the post office in Kirkenes was a reply to Doug's letter from John Haugen, the great-grandson of Johannes, Tollef's brother, inviting us to visit the family still living on a portion of the original Nordhaugen farm. We took the coastal steamer south to Tromsø, arranged to ship our boats to Spitsbergen, an island northwest of northern Norway, where we'd try to find them the following summer, flew to Oslo, and took the train north to Lillehammer. As the train pulled into the station, we spotted a man on the crowded platform who looked uncannily like Doug. Later we discovered that John and Doug were the same age and had many of the same interests, including wood carving. Walking confidently to John, Doug extended his hand and asked, "Have you been waiting long?" "Only about a hundred and thirty-seven years," answered John.

I have felt the pain that arises from a recognition of beauty, pain we hold when we remember what we are connected to and the delicacy of our relations.

—Terry Tempest Williams, *An Unspoken Hunger*

9

A Whale of a Day in Svalbard

WE SPENT MUCH OF OUR TIME at the end of the Norway trip plotting the quickest way home. Our boats, which had performed so laudably, now felt like chains preventing us from leaping onto the next plane. We didn't want to sell them, and anyway, it was illegal to do so. Shipping them back to the United States would have cost close to what they were worth. Our most expedient option was to take up a Norwegian friend on her offer to get the boats a ride on a supply ship to a meteorological station on Bjørnøya, a tiny rock frozen into the Arctic Ocean for much of the year. From Bjørnøya, Monica was sure, they would be able to hitch a ride the rest of the distance to Spitsbergen the following July on the deck of a passing coast guard vessel. The only problem was that the little we'd heard about Spitsbergen did not make it sound like an enticing place to row.

Stretching north of the 80° parallel, roughly three hundred

miles east of Greenland and five hundred miles northwest of northern Norway, Spitsbergen is the largest in a group of islands collectively called Svalbard. The islands are first recorded in Icelandic annals from 1194, which report the discovery of *Svalbardr fundinn*, "the land of cold coasts." Administered by Norway since 1925, the islands are nearly obscured on model globes by the metal fastener that grips the North Pole. The only reason they are not completely encased by sea ice, as are most areas of similar latitude, is that the surrounding waters are warmed by the last of the Caribbean Gulf Stream current that threads its way up the Norwegian coast. Still, thick pans of drifting ice often clog the coast, rendering it impassable even to boats with motors and thicker hulls than ours.

Svalbard is known for having more polar bears than just about any other Arctic locale. Our Norwegian informants would pause for dramatic effect, then say in a tone reserved to describe ax murderers, "You know about the polar bears, don't you?" The picture they painted was of bloodthirsty, meat-starved predators behind every rock. We had less experience with polar bears than with their darker-haired cousins, so we were particularly vulnerable to the follow-up comment, usually delivered with an all-knowing sneer: "Polar bears are different, you know. They stalk anything that moves."

The limited reading we had done, a daunting history of Spitsbergen from 1506 to the nineteenth century called *No Man's Land*, was also less than encouraging:

It is known that the Muscovy Company tried to bribe men by the offer of great rewards to winter in Spitsbergen, but in vain. Then the Company obtained some criminals condemned to death, who were promised a reprieve, on condition that they should spend a whole year in Spitsbergen. They were to be well supplied with food and other necessaries and to be generously rewarded on their return after the year. The men were shipped to the north, but when the time came for them to be left behind, the horror of the place was so heavy upon them "that they preferred to return home and be hanged rather than stay on those desolate shores."

On the beach in Kirkenes, we weighed our options. We had thought it impossible for Norwegians to be any graver, but they frowned themselves into near-corpses warning us not to try circumnavigating the island, a distance of about eight hundred miles. By all accounts, the North Sea, the Stad, and Nordkapp were rowers' nursery school compared to Spitsbergen. But as Doug remarked: "If we'd died every time we were told we would, we'd be mummified by now." My father, who had read *No Man's Land* with alarm before giving it to us, said he could think of no earthly reason why anyone in their right mind would row in Svalbard, though I suspect he had an inkling we would decide to go. Contrary to what our families believe, it was not only desperation that attracted us to Spitsbergen. The same wild cards that could kill us also appealed to us.

When we returned to Alaska, we called John Bauman, a friend we had been planning to paddle with the following summer in Greenland. "Sure, I'll go to *Sbalvard*," he answered without hesitation, mispronouncing the name in the clipped Wisconsin twang that has survived almost twenty years of living in Alaska. John is an exceptional character in a small body, a secret weapon so humble and unassuming that few would suspect how many difficult climbing and sea kayaking trips he has accomplished. We knew he had a penchant for paddling around islands in his kayak, having already circumnavigated Iceland, Kodiak, the Aleutians, Tasmania, and Fiji.

In July 1996, the three of us, compos mentis by at least our own judgment, set off for Spitsbergen. Our goal was to circumnavigate the island in a clockwise direction from Longyearbyen, the largest (population fifteen hundred) of a handful of research and coal-mining settlements on the west coast. It didn't really matter to any of us whether we made it all the way around, as long as we enjoyed the country and didn't get devoured along the way.

Literally loaded for bear, with sixty days of food and a shotgun per person, we left Longyearbyen on July 15. After paying thirty dollars for the privilege of staying in a mandatory campground alongside drunk Germans singing hunting songs and a huge British group planning to study "the fragile Arctic," we were eager to leave town. We'd return seven weeks later, having circled the island and experienced a day so vibrant that at times I wanted to drop to my knees in order to make even more solid contact with the earth, and to shout my gratitude for the epiphany of being in this place, at this moment.

Not that the days leading up to the tenth of August were ordinary. We rowed under crenellated cliffs vibrating with birds and alongside the pointed, snowy mountains for which Spitsbergen is named. Groups of sixty or more blinking beluga whales swam gently between our boats, and bearded seals tailed us like private detectives. Orange-beaked puffins made us laugh aloud as they flashed by with their feet held stiffly behind them, like flying nuns on vital church business. There were so many caribou that John said he felt as though he were in a petting zoo. The ground was almost without vegetation, patterned with ice-formed polygons and striped by rocks sorted by size. One evening we entertained ourselves by using the low sunlight to make pictograms with our bodies, projecting our oversized shadows onto the broad face of a fractured glacier streaming into the sea.

Only the polar bears were missing. We saw none for the first nineteen days, as we slipped through the alpine country of the northwest coast and traversed the flatter north end of the island, where I could imagine the curving horizon tugging downward into the apex of the North Pole, less than seven hundred miles away. Even as we began to descend the east coast, rumored kingdom of the bears, we found no prints or scat. On the evening of August 2, however, the wind intensified after a day of iceberg dodging, forcing us to camp on the side of a steep promontory. We didn't have good visibility, and we knew that polar bears favor such exposed places, but we didn't have a choice. The only campsite we could find was a tight, rocky beach with barely enough room for one tent.

After dinner, John and I hiked a lunar, rubbled landscape to reconnoiter tall, curving towers of rust-brown basalt, remnants of a volcanic age. I returned to camp to read, while John kept exercising his atrophying kayaker legs. I'd barely snuggled in next to Doug before John came back at a trot, reporting that he'd seen a polar bear a half mile away. With the wind blowing and no immediate option of moving to a better spot, this couldn't have been a more unwelcome bulletin. I went to sleep in the center of the tent with my feet curled up, feeling reasonably secure with a man and a gun on either side of me. Thinking that three shotguns in one tent was overkill, I left mine in my boat, a decision that nearly cost me Doug in the morning.

Doug was up first and took advantage of leisure time to make bread and heat water for a much-needed sponge bath. My first thought upon waking was that I might not be the only creature pulled to my feet by the aroma of fresh bread. John and I climbed back up the ridge to scout for the bear, without success. All of us scanned over our shoulders every few minutes; we've found that if we spot bears early and give them advance notice of our trespass, they usually avoid us. They are no more eager for trouble than we are.

Approaching Doug, who had his shirt off, his eyes squeezed shut, and suds in his hair, I caught a slight, stealthy movement out of half an eye. I looked up, stepped back, and said quietly but firmly to John and Doug, "You guys, there's a polar bear right here." In tense situations, I get so calm that I sound as if I am on Quaaludes. From my unruffled tone, John and Doug expected to see a polar bear in the distance, instead of on a boulder just forty feet—one jump—above Doug.

We judged him to be the polar bear equivalent of a teenager with an attitude—about three years old, cocksure, and very curious. Not good news for us. He had probably never seen humans before, and we, unfortunately, were not in a position to be positive ambassadors for our species. Doug tried moving parallel to the bear to reach his gun, which he'd left leaning against a boulder, but abandoned that attempt when the bear responded by crouching and hissing aggressively, strings of spit spraying from his yellow teeth. So Doug, shirtless, dripping wet, and goose-pimpled with cold, was reduced to throwing baseball-sized rocks and reasoning with the bear: "Go away, we don't want to mess with you." Meanwhile, I had retreated to my boat and was vehemently shaking my gun out of its waterproof case, repeating my most intimidating "Hey, bear!" calls like a medicinal mantra.

John already had his gun in hand, and he quickly pumped a cracker shell into the empty chamber. A cracker shell is a combination of firecracker and flare. The noise doesn't make much of an impression on polar bears routinely exposed to thundering, shifting ice, but the orange smoke can be another story. Cracker shells are difficult to shoot because they are light and easily deflected by the wind. As with flares, the cardinal rule is never to overshoot, an error you might have the luxury of making only once, as the likely result would be to scare the bear toward you.

John's first cracker shell was right on target, dropping in front of the bear's nose. The bear was startled but didn't retreat even a step. John fired another cracker shell, again with perfect placement. This one didn't seem to faze the bear either, although he kept swaying his head, trying to catch our scent, which was getting stronger by the second. At this point, it was a tough call. John could resort to the more deadly slugs that we keep loaded in the magazine, but none of us wanted to harm the bear, which was only doing what bears are supposed to do. But Doug especially was horribly vulnerable if the bear chose to charge or jump.

I would shoot a bear to protect Doug. But I would also be dishonest not to recognize that, in doing so, I'd be helping to destroy the very wildness I had intruded upon. Some wilderness travelers argue that carrying a gun makes people less resourceful, more likely to take the easy way out by shooting. A wily seventy-two-year-old friend of ours, skiing solo across the Northwest Passage, was being followed by a polar bear. Alone, without a gun, and far from help, our friend went into his tent, cooked some frozen fish, loaded it with Tylenol and Advil, and laid it in his tracks. He never saw the bear again.

Trying to give the bear one last chance, John fired a third cracker shell and, sweet relief, the bear darted back into the boulders. We kept looking for him, but he didn't return. After that we shifted into full polar bear alert, attempting to camp only in flat spots with long views in all directions and erecting a trip-wire system around camp, as if we were movie stars and it was our compound. Our system was relatively simple. We'd pound four ski poles into the ground and guy them with extra tent stakes so that they formed a rough square, with the corners about fifty feet from the tents. Then we unspooled two strands of 125-pound-test halibut line, and threaded one of them through rings taped to the top of each ski pole, and the other through rings at mid-pole. On the end of each of these lines, in opposite corners, we attached personal alert alarms about the size of pagers, the kind that are most commonly used to protect the purses of city dwellers. Each alarm had a lanyard hooked to a pin which, when pulled out, emitted a shrill signal. To prevent breezes from constantly setting off the alarm, we tensioned the pins with rubber bands so that they would pull out only under a more concerted force—for example, a bear walking into the line. The idea was not that the alarm would scare the bear, but that it would wake us up in time to greet and forewarn our visitors. It worked well, especially for John, who routinely slept through it while Doug and I leapt out of our sleeping bags and ran naked to reset the alarm. Usually the culprit was a gust of wind.

By August 10, we had descended roughly four-fifths of the way down the uninhabited east coast, our favorite stretch for its other-worldly isolation, its montage-like light, and a wild beauty even more acutely felt than seen. We had landed on only one beach with human footprints. The morning dawned atypically calm, with a temperature of 40°F. We woke early, roused by sunshine, a meteorological phenomenon never to be taken for granted in the High Arctic—particularly in Spitsbergen, where 39°F water breeds luxuriant fog. At breakfast, we noticed the same radio-collared polar bear sow and cub we'd seen the night before when they had skirted the lagoon behind camp and climbed four hundred feet straight up a mountain. Mama had seemingly effortlessly pawed a deep pit in the rocky ground, then lay in the hollow to nurse her cub. The pair were now perched on another high bench down the beach, where the sow had an unimpeded view of all that moved within her turf, including us.

The fog slid back over us as we set off to cross in front of our first tidewater glacier of the day, a groaning ice front called Jemelianovbreen. Occasionally, we'd catch sight of a chiseled peak in the background or a snowfield that appeared suspended in the sky. We needed a compass bearing to keep our boats on course, but our minds were free to wander as they pleased. Mine flew with the pink-footed barnacle geese we startled as they fed around undercut edges of icebergs, and dove deep underwater with the black-and-white murres seeking food.

After an hour of rowing, I began searching more frequently over my shoulder, anticipating land. Each look revealed only a wall of gray. In time, the murk began to take on more depth; a little brown emerged, then some black, until I could dimly make out steep scree slopes leaning back from the edge of the sea. A strange shape high above the water caught my attention, teasing my imagination. I kept trying to study it, snatching glances over my shoulder, wrestling with the image the way a dog might with a chew toy. Using a technique I learned when searching from the air for a missing person or a downed plane, I let my eyes be drawn to the thing that didn't look like everything else. I even blinked hard a few times, thinking I might have something caught in my eye, before I gathered the nerve to speak up. "Is that a whale above my head?" I asked in my sanest, most level tone of voice. John and Doug laughed and didn't look. Then they made me repeat the question a few times, thinking they had misheard me, before they finally raised their own eyes upward.

If you've never seen a whale above your head, you might not appreciate the confusion. The visibility was so sketchy that even Doug, resting in his boat next to mine, looked more like a fire hydrant on a pedestal than himself. Moreover, I am so accustomed to making up stories to amuse myself during long days that it can be difficult to know in mid-reverie whether my mind is processing fact or fiction. And of course we are not supposed to see whales on mountains. But emerging sunshine confirmed that there was indeed a whale hanging from the side of a mountain, embedded to its belly in riveleted black ice. Its tail hung perpendicular to the water, at least fifty feet above sea level, and its front section was even higher. The whale was intact, with a two-pronged tail and enough leathery flesh to attract the attention of gulls. We couldn't see its head because, as we discovered later, it didn't have one. Taking into account the curve of its body, it was roughly twenty-five feet long. And yes, to answer the question my sister Dale asked, it was dead.

Closer inspection would have required crampons, helmets, and suits of armor to negotiate the ice and protect us from continual rockfall, which had pulverized the whale's light brown hide so completely that it appeared to have hair. So we floated for quite a while, gawking, alternately effusive and quiet. Rocks bombarded the water around us, the feeding gulls ignored us, the whale of unidentified species stayed in place. Only two plausible theories occurred to us. One was that this was a modern-day whale that had been pushed up by pressure-ridged pack ice or a frightfully big storm wave, like the computer-generated monsters in the movie *The Perfect Storm.* It seemed to be too far up the mountain for that, however. The other, more intriguing conjecture was that this was an ancient whale, hundreds or thousands of years old, that was just now melting out of remnant ice from a glacier that had receded about a half mile around the corner.

All along the northern and northeastern coast, we'd been finding huge whale skulls, twenty-foot-long jawbones, thin curving ribs, broad shoulder blades, flat disks, and propeller-shaped vertebrae strewn over old beaches at an elevation of 80 to 120 feet above current sea level. Doug, after examining the perfectly preserved, honeycombed bones and estimating the rate at which the ground had rebounded since it was bowed concave by sheets of ice, guessed that these bones were eight to nine thousand years old. John and I had humored him by nodding our heads, but we noted that the bones weren't even slightly rotted. It never occurred to either of us that Doug could be right. When we returned home, a friend unearthed a report by scientists who had dated whalebones found at about the 100-foot elevation in northeastern Spitsbergen. Their conclusions as to the age of the bone concurred with Doug's. Maybe the hanging whale was from the same era.

Anticipating that our whale tale might not be deemed credible, we snapped photos at a film-depleting pace. We were reluctant to leave, certain that anything else we might see on this trip would be anticlimactic. Only when our chilling bodies demanded motion did we pry ourselves away.

After about half an hour, John noticed an iceberg that was moving incongruously fast. The first time I turned to look, I saw a motorized pancake with thick yellow fur and an anvil-shaped head. On second glance, it revealed itself to be a swimming polar bear with alert ears and a black nose cutting the water. As we drew closer, the bear dog-paddled away at half our speed, impressing us with its lack of both fear and aggression. In keeping with all the tracks on the beach and bears we'd seen, the bear was headed north, away from us and back to thicker pack ice. We would have been content to spend the day rowing in circles around him, but not wanting to harass him, we continued on.

Before lunch, we had already paddled past five sparkling glaciers, each framed by Alp-like peaks and offset by blue sky. Lunch was a leisurely affair. John and I roasted spread-eagled in the sun, relishing still air and rare temperatures that had topped the 50°F mark while Doug baked flat, delicious loaves of bread. When I sat up to smear butter on mine, my eyes were drawn several miles ahead. Plump, saucer-shaped lenticular clouds were pouring off the edge of a mesa ridge. The winds associated with these telltale clouds were so strong that they were dispersing the water of a formidable waterfall; little more than mist was hitting the ground fifteen hundred feet below. Other clues as to what we were in for included ominously grinding ice out to sea and a gentle but rising swell. We had the option of camping right where we were, but the day was beautiful, the water still flat, the country captivating. And we were mere humans with bloated stomachs making a bad tactical decision.

We'd slid past another glacier and were pulling close to a section of cliffs when offshore winds of sixty miles per hour slammed us, blasting us sideways. As long as we hugged the coast, rough water wasn't a problem, though a hundred yards further out, the sea was agitated into a froth more white than green. Even with feathered oars, Doug and I were doing shuddering bench presses just to get our oars forward against the most intense gusts. It was like trying to knit in the middle of a typhoon. Helped by rhythm and technique, I usually paddled faster than Doug or John, but in this battle of brute strength, they clearly had more power, and I began to fall behind. My mantra, in between gulps for air, was *"Puuuullll."*

One minute I was worrying about catching up, the next the wind was pushing and holding my boat against a pebbled turquoise iceberg the size of a large motor home, forcing the port side and one oar under the ice. The boat was listing so severely that gravity was barely holding me inside and my nose was pressed close to the ice, which smelled like death. I had seen the iceberg several hundred feet before I hit, but I had badly misjudged the wind-driven sideslip of my boat. Doug stopped rowing, letting the wind blow him back toward me, certain that the only way I could escape was to somehow climb over the high side of my boat without upsetting it and jump into the water. Now my mantra was a rapid-fire *"Shit, shit, shit."* In a rush of unequivocal fear, I reacted intuitively, knowing my fate would be decided in seconds. Maneuvering my one remaining, sharply canted oar like a gondolier and using the weight of my body, I was able to pivot around the end of the iceberg and kick off of it with one leg. Then the wind shunted me free.

Weariness replaced adrenaline, and we inched our way in tiny increments toward the theoretical safety of a sand beach. When we reached it, Doug nosed his boat onshore and climbed out to check the camping possibilities. I stayed in my boat and treaded water nearby, fascinated by thousands of winged snails fluttering like fairies just below the surface. Simultaneously, we spotted a polar bear sleeping three boat lengths away from Doug. Without delay, Doug tiptoed back to his boat and pushed off as noiselessly as he could. As we rowed past the bear, he rolled over, stout ivory-colored legs in the air, scratched his broad fuzzy belly, and padded purposefully down to the water. When John paused to take photographs, the bear slid silently into the ocean and began swimming after him. Determined not to be lunch, John stuffed his camera between his legs and focused on paddling. Probably because the bear was even more discouraged than we were by what were now headwinds, the pursuit was short-lived.

We'd hoped to find a place to camp before the next glacier, but there was another bear standing where the smooth bulge of ice sloped down to the beach. He tried to hide from us by pulling in his trademark elongated neck and bending his knees. Profiled on the ice ramp, it was the comical equivalent of trying to hide in the middle of an empty four-lane highway. So we found ourselves in the dangerous position of hugging close to the face of a tidewater glacier in order to keep from getting blown to sea. We were well aware that glaciers shed ice frequently and without warning, and given that we've taught thousands of people how to recognize and avoid avalanche hazard, it would be an especially embarrassing way for us to die. If we were unlucky enough to be hit directly, even a basketball-sized piece of ice calving off the equivalent of a ten-story building could kill us.

The day's mileage tallied twenty-seven by the time we reached a possible camping spot with a landable beach, no bears, and good visibility for any that might approach. In the spirit of the day, there was a catch—a teeming, pungent bird rookery. An unfathomable population of black-and-white birds known in these parts as Brunnich's guillemots, or thick-billed murres in North American birdspeak, crowded onto barely discernible ledges in the cliffs, creating the wild kingdom equivalent of a teeming high-rise. We happened to arrive during the few days when the season's crop of fledglings make their one-time migration from the perch where they were born to the sea that will sustain them.

The problem with this rookery was that the cliffs were set back a half mile from the water, and thousands of the palm-size rookie fliers were taking shorter than necessary trajectories and crash-landing at the bottom of the cliffs, bouncing on their sides, their heads, their bottoms, and only occasionally on their feet. Their faithful fathers, aware that the babies could not yet fly without the aid of gravity, landed almost as violently right next to them. Having done their work up on the cliffs, the mothers had already flown to sea. Smeared with dirt and blood, the surviving father-baby pairs picked themselves up, fluffed their feathers, and waddled very much like penguins toward the water, braving a gauntlet of predatory skuas and glaucous gulls. The half mile of flat ground was littered with fresh bones and feathers, testimony to the many birds who hadn't succeeded.

Too tired to muscle against more wind, we made camp. As I was cooking dinner, John and Doug discovered that the high-pitched alarm on our polar bear trip-wire system sounded much like the murres already at sea. When they mischievously bleeped it, the pilgrimaging birds would abruptly change direction and stream into our compound. Between mouthfuls of chili, we cheered jubilantly as pairs of battered survivors trooped past us and dropped into the water. A tall order, to learn to fly and swim in the same day. Doug worried that, given the blistering winds, the young would find themselves far out to sea before they knew much about staying afloat.

Doug and I made special love that night, a keening for the murres that didn't make it to the water, a celebration of the bears, a wonderment at the whale, a precious understanding of the ephemerality of the being called "us." We were joyous and sad, afraid and free, humble and bold, vulnerable and strong. We were the ribbon of foam along a wave-pounded beach, a fragile connection between land and sea, here and there, now and another splinter of time. The last conscious thought I had before drifting into sleep was that the birds were still clamorous, and our campsite still protected from the winds by the rock ramparts above.

Violent change awoke us at two in the morning. The migration had subsided and the winds that had been barreling over our heads at cliff level intensified, swooped to lower elevations, and nailed our tents. John, whose tent had a higher profile than ours, thought it wise to abandon ship. While I held our tent down by lying diagonally across the floor and Doug piled additional rocks on the guylines, John dismantled his tent and passed gear in to me, stowing what he didn't immediately need inside our vestibule. Wedged together, the three of us tried to recapture our dreams, hoping we wouldn't awake to the sound of tearing nylon.

Morning brought fog instead of wind and sluggish, aching bodies. One downy-soft baby bird, still warm to the touch, had died next to Doug's boat, only yards from the tideline. Few of the birds that had crowded the water near shore could be seen or heard. In packing his gear, John couldn't find his tent. We searched in vain for the waterproof blue sack. In the scramble of the night, it must have been overlooked and whisked away by the wind. By now, it was probably miles offshore with the birds. John was quiet, trying to be a good sport, but angry at himself and discouraged by the prospect of the next few weeks without privacy. With wind-bludgeoned arms that had barely been able to help us get dressed, we set off in thick fog. Ten or fifteen minutes later, with visibility virtually limited to the ends of our boats, we came upon a dark blob floating in our path. Defying impossible odds, it proved to be John's tent.

We reached the southern tip of Spitsbergen on August 17. An opaque blue sea quilted with kiwi-green and icy-white patches stretched around us. In typical Viking fashion, Doug proclaimed this "one of the easiest trips we've ever been on." Two minutes later, we heard the all-too-familiar roar of headwinds. We fought them, along with the thickest ice of the trip, for the next 175 miles back to Longyearbyen.

Back in town, we reported the hanging whale to scientists at the Norwegian Polar Institute, circling the location on a map. Initially skeptical, they grew excited enough to send a helicopter with a biologist aboard across the island to take samples for radiocarbon dating. Two years later, a scientific reprint entitled "Carcass of a bowhead whale (*Balaena mysticetus*) found in the lateral moraine of the Jemelianovbreen glacier, eastern Svalbard" arrived in the mail. The study suggested that the whale had lived during the last part of the cold period known as the Little Ice Age, between 1535 and 1660. Presumably, the whale washed up on the beach or into shallow water after its death and was incorporated into an advancing glacier. I read the paper with a smile. Our whale had lived in Shakespeare's time.

Experience is not what happens to a man; it is what a man does with what happens to him.

—Aldous Huxley, *Texts and Pretexts*

Much as I object to such things, I did on this trip have some small "adventures"—but fortunately they illustrate a favorite thesis: that most adventures are a sign of incompetence which may consist either in bad craftsmanship or an insufficient knowledge of local conditions.

—Vilhjalmur Stefansson, *An Ethnologist in the Arctic*

10

Reflections from a Hard Seat

BEACHCOMBING along the northwest coast of Spitsbergen, John found a crystal ball. Actually, it was an old glass fishing float the size of a basketball and the color of smoked quartz, a rare find among smaller green glass floats. On windy days, when we couldn't quite decide whether it was safe to travel, the three of us would place our chapped hands upon it and mutter incantations, waiting for a sign to tell us "go" or "no go." But one cold morning, after surviving untold journeys at sea, our crystal ball cracked. We were left worriedly scratching our heads, wondering what troubles lay in store for us.

Toward the end of our Spitsbergen circumnavigation, John started itching with "back to the barn" syndrome. He was anxious about his ill father and missed his wife. Lying alone in his tent for days at a time, in a bay ominously named Stormbutka, was not what he wanted to be doing. Thus far, when the three of us had stood on the beach debating whether conditions were doable, we had reached similar conclusions. Now, when waves were assailing the gravel, Doug and I would conclude, "What's the point?" or "It's not worth it," while John would say, "It doesn't look great, but I think we can make it." The three of us never argued. If it felt all right to compromise, Doug and I would agree to go. If not, we cooked pancakes in the sunshine until it started to snow, or we went for a walk.

One marginal morning, to avoid larger ocean waves, we decided to thread an inside route through a reef awash in surf. In retrospect, the words of Irish dramatist John Millington Synge seem the best summation: "A man who is not afraid of the sea will soon be drownded . . . for he will be going out on a day he shouldn't. But we do be afraid of the sea, and we only do be drownded now and again."

John was in the lead, trying to follow the sketchy route we had identified from shore. I was about fifty feet behind him and Doug kept a similar distance from me, to give one another maneuvering room. Looking over my shoulder, I could see nothing but white foam, a scene worthy of Winslow Homer—and one I'd rather view on the wall of my living room than from a little boat. But John seemed to be moving confidently ahead, so instead of trying to pick a route, I focused on him, mirroring his zigzags. Doug, in turn, was steering off me. Our strategy was working until an incoming wave hurled John broadside toward shore, like a bowling pin. Left to lead the way backward through the center of an essentially unknown rapid, I bashed my way through the rest of the reef. John and Doug arrived minutes later, water dripping from their beards. With little discussion, we headed for shore, paddling a turbulent course so narrow that I had six-foot waves breaking over rocks off one oar and gnashing ice swirling around the other. My boat would hang for a moment on the bigger waves, suspended two-thirds in the air like a diving board.

On the beach later that afternoon, as we watched the ocean do battle while caribou grazed calmly around our tents and two silver-furred foxes skirmished in the boulders, John said quietly, "You better take me out of the loop. I don't think I'm making good decisions. I'm letting my wishes get in the way."

When Doug first started teaching people how to travel safely in the mountains, he focused on the physical parameters that make avalanches possible—the terrain, the snowpack, the weather. But without people, there is no hazard. When dealing with objective hazards, the subjective thinking our society values—*How do I feel? What do I want?*—can kill, because Nature doesn't care about the answers. Our assumptions, schedules, goals, and abilities make no difference to an unstable slope or a stormy ocean. Before long, Doug pioneered a new approach to avalanche education, emphasizing the importance of what he termed the "human factor" in allowing accidents to happen. In the outdoors, biased judgments are at the root of most trouble—maybe our ego is at stake, or we are aggressively eager, or we're suffering from tunnel vision. We might be bolstered by Kodak courage, or pressured by peers, or afraid of approaching darkness. Perhaps we're tired, or not communicating well, or in denial that something bad could happen, or complacent because nothing bad has ever happened before. Maybe we're worried about being back at work on Monday. So what? An analogy we use when teaching is that few of us would choose to cross a busy city street without first looking both ways and listening for the traffic. But if we attempt to negotiate any wild place on our own terms, without heeding Nature's clues, we might as well be donning blinders and earplugs. When in the mountains, we have to think like an avalanche.

The terms *hazard* and *risk*, though often used interchangeably, are not the same. Hazard takes into account the exposure to potential danger—the angle of the slope, the size of the waves, the intensity of the storm—as well as the probability of an event occurring. Risk is the hazard multiplied by the consequences—in other words, what might happen if something goes wrong. Given the same snow instability, skiing on a slope with a cliff below it involves potentially greater consequences and, thus, greater risk. The risk of paddling in Spitsbergen, where the water is frigid and help far away, is inherently higher than paddling in the same marginal conditions along a lifeguard-patrolled section of warm California coast.

At our wedding, embarrassed by toasts to our bravery, Doug stood up and declared, "You know, the most dangerous thing we've done for years is try to drive around here." Most of the guests thought he was joking, but I knew he was not. In the outdoors, our own decisions primarily determine our safety; on New York streets, we are at the mercy of other people. Doug and I have learned to make good decisions through experience, which has often been gained as a result of bad decisions. Close friends have died making the same mistakes in similar situations. The process of learning to make sound judgments is the most dramatic journey we have ever undertaken. Along the way, we have amassed an extensive "geography of fear."

One of us only need mention Smith Bay for the other to remember with dread a combat crossing along Alaska's north coast, where a wide scoop in the shoreline necessitated a jump of at least sixteen miles. Paddling from a leeward to a windward shore is a setup for trouble, because as the winds work a greater surface area, the waves increase in size and power. From the back side, these waves can look misleadingly benign. The brisk northeasterly tailwinds that had pushed us an exhilarating nine miles an hour the day before were blowing again. But we were restless from being tentbound for much of the week, and we thought we could make it.

Within a hundred feet of the shore, cat's paws—the diamond-shaped ripples that are the first step in the genesis of any wave—began to ruffle the surface of the water. In less than an hour, we were angling through the three-to-four-foot seas we had anticipated. But the ocean has a way of exceeding our expectations. As the fetch increased and the depth of the ocean bottom decreased, the waves grew disproportionately, some cresting at heights of ten, even twelve feet. Instead of making a beeline for land, we had to cut a wider angle to keep our sterns into the waves, which lengthened the crossing to twenty-two miles.

There were no good answers to the "what-if" questions. Water at 30°F is so cold it burns. We couldn't expect to swim more than a few minutes, assuming we survived the first gasp of immersion. With land far away in any direction, we were entirely dependent on our skills. It was no different from crossing a high wire without a net except that no one was watching. The effort took more than three stomach-clenched hours. We took each wave as it came, concentrating on climbing up and sashaying down without swinging broadside, a precursor to flipping or swamping. With an open cockpit, I faced greater danger of swamping than Doug, but at least I could see the waves coming; in his kayak, he was being assaulted from behind. When we were within reach of the far shore, my concentration wavered for a fraction of a second, enough for a wave to plunge down my neck, coursing all the way into my boots. Shivering, I lined up with the incoming waves and joined them in crashing onto the beach. They instantly began to seep back to sea, but I didn't plan to leave land until the ocean granted us clear permission.

As we gained skills over the years, Doug and I also gained confidence in our ability to handle potential hazard. With greater confidence, we more readily put ourselves in situations with diminished margins of safety, ensnaring ourselves in another kind of trap.

Our "experience" marooned us on Flet Island in 1994. The day began with calm, sunny weather, nice by normal standards, and exceptional for the Alaska Peninsula. Pavlof Volcano, an eight-thousand-foot snow cone, was out in full glory. We knew that noon was late to begin an eight-mile crossing of a wide, low-lying bay notorious for funneling winds between the Bering Sea on the west side of the Peninsula and the Pacific Ocean to the east. But the day was beautiful and . . .

About four miles from shore Doug pulled his Viking routine, announcing how perfect conditions were. Moments later, we noticed a very gentle, wide swell, really just a slight undulation of the surface. We didn't have to speculate long about its cause; the first few puffs of headwind arrived within minutes. In our early paddling years, they would have been enough to send us scurrying back to shore. Instead, we let ourselves be swayed by our disinclination to backtrack, our hope that the winds wouldn't pick up much, and our previous success in outdueling headwinds. Disinclination, hope, and confidence, however, have no influence over how hard the wind is going to blow. The message we chose to ignore was delivered by the swells.

Ten minutes later, the winds were blasting thirty-five miles an hour against us, buffeting our backs. Within a half hour, gusts were stinging us with spray, humming in our ears, and pushing us backward unless we leaned into them with bold strokes. The waves whipped up to five feet—steep and closely spaced, they felt personal, aggressive, indifferent to our fate. On the far shore, now only a tantalizing two or three miles away, waves reached to room height before their tops blew off in spumes of white smoke. The wind there was around sixty to eighty miles per hour, more than hurricane force. We still could have turned around and had a delightfully fast ride back to the shore from which we had started. Just ahead, though, lay a tiny vertical lump of black lava reef that didn't deserve the distinction of being called an island. With a nod, Doug and I decided to hide in its living-room-size lee and see if the winds would abate. Grabbing hold of some kelp rooted to the sea floor, we hunkered down in our boats and gobbled energy food.

Despite our plan, the wind continued to build until even the route back looked ferocious. Initially, the reef had appeared unlandable, but as the winds approached a shriek and the waves wrapped around even the lee side of the reef, we let go of the kelp, scrutinized the rocks, and began to see possibilities where none had been before.

We studied one lava ledge with special intensity. Its edge was about six feet above the waterline, but if we timed our landing with a high swell, it looked like we could get washed onto a relatively level surface made up of wickedly sharp nubbins, the volcanic equivalent of razor blades. If our timing was wrong—well, best not to think about that. Both of us made it intact, on carefully picked waves about five minutes apart, though we sacrificed our shins in the tussle to keep the boats from getting sucked back out to sea.

We secured the boats out of reach of the waves and took a look around. The island rose about fifty feet above sea level, a narrow, precipitous mesa reached by a series of sheer, irregular ledges. There was just about no flat surface or vegetation anywhere, save for some bird-fertilized grass that clung like a Mohawk haircut to the top of the mesa, which was guarded by nesting puffins and auks. The whole area above mean high tide couldn't have been larger than a basketball court.

Normally, we are reluctant to alter the landscape, but survival changes the rules. Doug went to work with our rock hammer, ingeniously and noisily creating a reasonable tent pad out of an unreasonable gully. Though the tent clung to the gully at a 20° angle, inside there were two stretcherlike, almost level sleeping places. Using all fours and occasionally my teeth, I made repeated climbs, hauling our cooking gear and food up to a two-foot-wide ledge, which became the kitchen. Ten feet above that, I found a perfect reading nook, no wider than three feet, with a straight-on view of Pavlof if it happened to live up to its reputation as one of Alaska's most active volcanoes and erupt. We clambered around our campsite feeling like modern Anasazi. Anyone flying overhead would have thought us in dire need of rescue. Though chagrined by our stupidity, we were quite content in our self-sufficiency.

The wind blew for five straight days and nights. At first, we didn't move around much, for fear of disturbing the birds or the seal rookery operating at full tilt near the waterline. Almost every low-lying rock was covered by basking seals and their babies. Initially, they leapt into the water at the slightest provocation but they came to accept us as part of the surroundings, barely blinking when we squatted only a few feet away. The seals' rhythm became our own. We joined them in napping on the rocks in the hottest part of the day, raising our heads to investigate the commotion when we heard accentuated groaning, barking, or splashing. Our principal concern was that we were running out of fresh water. The bags we had brought with us were nearly empty and there was no place to resupply on the tiny island. One night Doug literally dreamed up a way to make a desalinator out of our pressure cooker and some rubber tubing. But just as we were about to construct a prototype, the winds released us. We left Flet Island and, in less than an hour, did what we'd been hoping to do for days—finished the crossing to the mainland on a calm sea.

Most of our close calls along the ocean have occurred when small failures to prepare adequately, to anticipate conditions, to pay attention to critical clues, or to choose the right timing compounded quickly. On the first day of our 1989 Labrador trip, for example, we inadvertently packed our compasses among the twenty-nine sacks of gear and food wedged in our boats. But hey, we'd been stuck in a small car for more than a week, it was a blue-sky day, and we were anxious to get on the water. Doug couldn't fit all his gear into his boat, so he strapped two heavy bags to the deck of his kayak, one in front of him and the other aft. This made the boat top-heavy, but Doug was a skilled paddler, and the water was calm. We discovered later that Point Amour is infamous for lethal conditions at tide changes. Numerous vessels have met their demise there, including a coastal ferry and a warship. But hey, we were experienced, and we didn't take time to check with the locals.

The fog descended in minutes; wind and waves followed soon after. With neither vision nor compasses, we had to rely on our ears to follow the shoreline. When the sound of surf receded, we knew that we were entering the mouth of Forteau Bay. We could have camped in the bay, but we were managing fine, so we cut blindly across it, navigating toward the foghorn of a lighthouse on Point Amour, four miles away. The wind notched up five miles an hour at a time and the foghorn's moan grew ominously louder, but it did not occur to our singularly focused minds that lighthouses are generally constructed to warn of navigational hazards—until we steered right onto a buried reef, amidst a changing tide and winds that had grown vigorous enough to knock us sideways.

The result was a melee, with riptide waves ten, twelve, and fourteen feet high charging toward us from different directions. Neither of our boats was very responsive—they were fully loaded, and we hadn't paddled for nine months—but Doug, in the top-heavy kayak, was especially vulnerable. He'd lay his paddle blade flat on the water on one side to keep from capsizing, a defensive maneuver known as a brace. Then he'd have to react instantly on the other side as a gust or a wave threatened from another direction. He describes it as like being in a boxing ring with a gang of heavily muscled opponents throwing punches from all sides. At the foamy crest of one breaking wave, the wind blasted the paddle out of Doug's left hand, tipping his boat completely perpendicular to the water, and submerging one shoulder. For an instant, I could see only the bottom of the hull.

We were lucky. Doug did not flip. He popped open his spray skirt, grabbed the gear bag off his foredeck and jammed it between his legs to make his kayak more stable, then resealed the cockpit. Though we were close to land, it was clear that to save ourselves we had to head out to sea, into disconcertingly thicker fog and deeper water where the waves would be less chaotic. As the sound of the foghorn receded and the riptide began to subside after about a half mile, we pulled a gentle U-turn and groped our way back into Forteau Bay.

For the unlucky, such a moment gets chalked up not as experience but as a fatal mistake. On our return from Greenland almost a decade later, we learned that a woman who had been paddling Greenland's east coast that same summer had capsized and died. Her paddling partner, a short distance ahead, heard her scream, looked back and saw her in the water, but was unable to turn around in the craggy seas. As the wind and waves pushed him away from her, she yelled for his assistance, pleading with him not to leave her. I flashed back to Doug on the verge of flipping. I tried to take the image a step further, to put him in the water, to imagine the ugly side of risk and the impossibility of helping him. The exercise was much like when, as a kid, I'd lie on my bed with closed eyes, determined to clear my mind of all thoughts, but all I could ever think about was trying to think about nothing. In my mind's eye, I could not make myself row away from Doug. He is more than my partner, he is part of my soul.

Nature is indifferent to such choices. Both the mountains and the ocean, with constantly changing conditions, demand that we take nothing for granted. In these environments, evaluating potential hazard isn't an event so much as a continual process of vigilance. Our own close calls, along with years of investigating avalanche accidents and retrieving bodies, have made the consequences of poor decisions hauntingly clear.

In the winter, Doug and I respond to avalanche rescue missions wearing two hats. One is as "technical experts" who are called to the scene to ensure that the site is safe for searchers; the other is as volunteer members of the Alaska Mountain Rescue Group. The label "avalanche expert" makes me nervous. Once, I heard a legendary Swiss avalanche worker tell a story at an international symposium about watching his son get caught and battered in an avalanche on a slope he had deemed safe. "So you see," the old man admonished the audience. "The avalanche, it does not know you are an expert." I've developed a corollary to brandish at Doug when trouble inevitably follows one of his Viking proclamations. "So you see," I say, in not my nicest voice, "the ocean, it knows you are a fool."

One gorgeous day in March 1999, cloudless sky offset three-thousand-foot mountains sparkling with more than three feet of new snow. Knowing that it was also a perfect day for an avalanche massacre, I had reorganized my rescue pack before breakfast and stored it near the door. When we got the call that snowmachiners had been caught in an avalanche at a popular recreational area south of Anchorage, we knew before we arrived at the accident site that we'd almost certainly be unburying the dead. People still alive when trapped under the snow are literally drowning; their chance of survival drops to less than 50 percent after a half hour.

Avalanches are not random events. Most victims trigger the slide that catches them. Usually, it is their weight on or near steep slopes that causes the problem. The best clue of all to potential snow instability is avalanches on similar slopes. When the fish are running, we go fishing. When one avalanche has run, there are likely to be others.

That spectacular Sunday, snowmachines were buzzing across the flats on the west side of a mile-wide valley called Turnagain Pass while others played highmark, testing the brawn of the machines and skill of the drivers by riding as high as possible up the mountainsides. Highmarking is an inherently risky game because it involves approaching millions of pounds of snow from the bottom. About 2 p.m., a large avalanche released near the north end of the pass. But most of the snowmachiners either didn't see or pay much attention to it, or to a smaller one to the south that ran sometime around 3:30. They continued riding on the slope between these two avalanches.

At 4 p.m., the inevitable happened. A large avalanche, seven feet thick and a half mile wide, cut loose, almost connecting the two previous fractures. Within moments, the descending snow built a powder cloud that accelerated to more than a hundred miles an hour, rising at least 150 feet into the air. Skiers on the east side of the road watched in horror as snowmachiners scrambled to escape. Given the speed of the avalanche, they barely appeared to be moving, though most had their machines open full throttle. One snowmachiner later described how he spent most of his ride airborne, hurtling across five-foot blocks of tumbling snow. When the avalanche came to rest, there was a terrible silence. Everyone knew that people were buried, but no one knew how many.

Both skiers and snowmachiners hurried to the rescue. They found some riders with cuts and bruises, some still wet with the dust of the powder blast, one man buried to his knees digging himself out. Several snowmachines looked as though they had been dropped off a skyscraper. Here and there, handlebars and crumpled windshields protruded from the snow. Very quickly, five snowmachines were uncovered for which there were no riders.

Several people used cell phones to dial 911. In response, the Alaska State Troopers, responsible for rescues, dispatched a patrol car from Girdwood, twenty-five miles away. Fire departments, rescue groups, and ski patrols were also called; most rescuers, including us, had to drive an hour and a half from Anchorage. Once the Troopers arrived at the parking lot, still a couple of miles from the accident site, they struggled to bring order to the chaos, trying to discern how many people were unaccounted for and who was out in the field searching. It wasn't until the lot was ordered cleared, unclaimed trucks and trailers counted, and witnesses of various parties interviewed that a clearer picture began to emerge. There were at least six victims. That first night, two of them were found.

The next morning, Doug and I flew back to Turnagain Pass by helicopter, evaluated the site as safe for rescuers, interviewed witnesses, and figured out the most likely places to search. Over the next few days, what began as a rescue effort became a recovery mission and took on a life of its own. The governor made a visit to the command center, declaring a state emergency so that the National Guard could be called out. Snowmachines ferried searchers, food, and gear to the scene, rescue dogs sniffed the debris, magnetometers and radar detectors were brought in without result, and a videotape of the avalanche taken by a teenager was enhanced by computer specialists to help determine where the victims were last seen. Reporters and cameramen were everywhere.

I was in charge of the lower site, where as many as 250 people, most probing the snow with long metal rods, were searching for three buried men. Probing is a crude method—it is how people looked for avalanche victims in the Alps three hundred years ago—but it is still the primary means of finding a completely buried person who is not wearing a transmitting rescue beacon. Doug directed roughly 150 people higher in the avalanche path, looking for the snowmachiner who had been near the top of the slope when it released. Each probe line of twelve or fourteen people worked elbow to elbow for hours, moving uphill twenty-eight inches at a time.

On Monday, two more men were uncovered in the lower path. By Tuesday, despite the effort of almost 350 volunteers for over twelve hours, neither of the remaining victims was found. Debriefing, planning, and driving took up our after-search hours, so it was midnight before Doug and I fell into bed, and only four in the morning when we stumbled toward the shower.

By Wednesday, the weather, which had already been poor, grew increasingly inclement, with strong winds and horizontal snow. Searchers retreated inside their hoods and probed with bowed heads. I could squeeze water out of my gloves. Radio traffic was constant. At one point, exhausted from limited, fitful sleep and the pressure of making incessant rapid-fire decisions, I called myself on the radio—"Jill, this is Jill"—providing a moment of unintentional comic relief. Early Thursday, after finding five of six victims, we had to suspend the search because of the continuing blizzard and increasing avalanche hazard.

By the time Doug stopped counting in 1980, he had helped recover more than a hundred bodies—victims of car and plane crashes, drownings, falls, hypothermia—the list is too long. He has responded to forty-five avalanche fatalities occurring in twenty-seven separate accidents over the last twenty-seven years.

I have never counted, but the number of bodies I've helped find is greater than my age, probably more than double.

Sometimes in bed, in the middle of the night—particularly after digging a dead friend out of an avalanche or talking with a shell-shocked wife—the faces of other victims wind through our heads in a grainy succession of images. Some portion of this unwanted mental movie is usually narrated by the paraphrased words of an ex-Vietcong soldier-poet—"A bullet fired, for whatever reason, is, first, a bullet to the heart of a mother." I've learned to try not to look at the faces of those I dig out of the snow because I know that I'll never forget them. But it is impossible to block out painful snapshots—the wedding ring on the frozen, extended hand of the newlywed; the distress on a father's face as he identifies the young man in the yellow body bag; the anger of a brother that the search is not proceeding faster; the obituary photographs in the newspaper.

Recovering the bodies of avalanche victims has taken a spiritual toll, especially when we have spent our careers chipping away at a metaphorical iceberg, trying to prevent accidents. Every time we look up, the iceberg appears larger than ever, and we wonder if we have accomplished anything. It seemed to grow to overwhelming proportions in the weeks following the Turnagain Pass accident, when we had barely wrapped up one rescue mission and dried our gear before there was a call-out for another.

On April 3, an hour before eight friends were due at the house for dinner, we were called to search for a snowmachiner buried in a slide about a hundred miles northeast of Anchorage in the Chugach Mountains. I had just enough time to scribble a note to our guests to have the party without us before the State Trooper helicopter landed at the top of our driveway. We returned home at five in the morning to find the dishes washed and a few leftover brownies.

Less than two weeks later, I dragged home after a twelve-hour day with a film crew making an avalanche documentary to find not Doug waiting with a much-anticipated dinner, but an empty, disheveled house and another hastily written note. Doug had responded to a large avalanche in Cordova, roughly 150 miles east of Anchorage, where an equipment operator for a hydroelectric project was buried. The only way in or out of Cordova is by plane or boat; Alaska Airlines held the jet while Doug raced to the airport. I'd been home long enough to unbuckle only one boot when the phone rang. The ex-husband of one of my best friends had committed suicide that afternoon. I spent most of the night at her house, helpless to ease the pain twisting her twelve-year-old daughter's face or to penetrate the shock of the teenage son who had found his father. By now, I had almost total laryngitis, a fitting physical manifestation of my despair.

The next day, the phone rang again. I would have raged aloud if I'd had a voice. Seven more snowmachiners had been caught in an avalanche near Denali National Park, about 150 miles north of Anchorage. Six had been found alive, one man was still missing. I slapped a note that read "Avalanche, Cantwell" on top of the one Doug had left me and sped downtown to meet the Trooper helicopter.

Within three hours of flying north, I found myself alone on yet another thick pyramid of avalanche rubble with a snowmachiner named Bill while he shouted the name of his friend K.J., who lay buried somewhere under our feet. It certainly wasn't the end he had envisioned to a day of riding and highmarking. Bill and I had been dropped off by helicopter just at dark, twenty-five miles from the nearest road, in a valley too steep-walled to allow communication with the outside world. Other searchers were supposed to be snowmachining in, dependent upon my word sent back with the pilot that the route was safe.

As we probed, I thought about how we are all blinded by our needs, experiences, and assumptions. Bill and his companions may have been misled by the joy of a spring day in beautiful country, by a false sense of security inspired by their large number, by their snowmachining skills. My friend's ex-husband appeared to have been so blinded by his depression that he could not see any other options or the awful ripple effect of his death. We live our lives as a series of actions and reactions, with great capacity to cause joy and sorrow to others.

By midnight the other searchers still hadn't arrived at the site. Surmising that they were waiting until daylight, Bill and I spent two more exhausting hours excavating one of the six snowmachines that had been buried in cementlike snow so that we could ride out to the road. I remain grateful for the journey that night, a reminder of the magic of life in a month of weight and sadness. I felt a tremendous bond to Bill, a stranger I was unlikely to have ever known in everyday life or to see again. We were tied by the tragedy of his friend, by shared experience, by our aloneness. I'd be startled if he didn't feel the same bond to me. We rode through steep canyons, through dense trees, across slippery river ice, under a star-filled night sky animated by pulsating curtains of northern lights. My arms were wrapped tightly around Bill's waist to keep from getting bounced off the machine, but no matter the need, the contact felt right. I thought about the coincidence of circumstance that had brought me to this moment, about Doug, who had no idea that I was riding through rugged, five-thousand-foot mountains with a man whose last name I didn't even know. Though he was in a different mountain range, hundreds of miles away, I sensed Doug's absolute trust that I would know enough to keep myself and others alive and took comfort in having the same faith in him.

Bill and I reached the Alaska State Troopers' station at Cantwell, a tiny town on a dark, isolated road, at three in the morning. Bill's hands were cramped from gripping the handlebars, and my spine and hip were locked so stiffly from too many bumps in the trail that I dismounted with a straight leg, like a rusty tin soldier in snow pants. At first light, Bill and I flew back to the scene. With twenty-two searchers, we found the buried man's snowmachine under seven feet of snow, after noticing telltale drops of oil brought up by the probes. A short time later, at 9:30 a.m., we found K.J. buried eleven feet deep. He had died instantly. The whole group worked together to move tons of snow, shoveling successive tiers until the site resembled a quarry. As we neared K.J.'s face, I suggested to Bill that he might want to climb out of the hole and let us finish digging, explaining that I'd found greater peace remembering my friends as they looked when they were alive. He thanked me and went over to sit on the snow a short distance away.

After we'd zippered K.J.—friend to many in the group, husband, and father of one—into a vinyl body bag, someone commented softly, "You know, it sounds terrible but I just keep thinking that I'm glad it isn't me." Most of the heads in the group nodded in gentle assent, and a few of us reassured him out loud. The finality of death is the ultimate reminder of the potential of life. Human bonds are another.

K.J. and another snowmachiner, the Cordova equipment operator, two snowboarders, a hiker, and a mountaineer we knew were killed in six separate avalanche accidents after Turnagain Pass. In all, Alaska had thirteen avalanche fatalities in less than two months, compared to the state's typical annual average of three or four. Twelve men, one woman. Women rarely get killed in avalanches. When I try to explain at our workshops that this may have something to do with women's enhanced ability to communicate and to resist peer pressure, I'm usually playfully heckled into silence by the male participants. Doug advises students to travel with a good woman—and to listen to her.

Those weeks left us physically sick, exhausted, emotionally bruised. I wanted to do little but sleep. News of the rampage shooting at Columbine High School in Littleton, Colorado, and "ethnic cleansing" in Kosovo deepened our gloom. We have noticed a cumulative toxic effect of too many body recoveries and grieving relatives. Sometimes we want to flee snow country and our obligation to it. The night we return from a mission, we are as likely to fight as to make love, using each other as targets for our frustration. It is easier to argue than to talk about the blood-soaked snow or the grimace on our dead friend's face. The unconsidered words I sling toward Doug are a poor disguise for the terrible fragility I am feeling. But the impact is not entirely negative. We have had the opportunity to learn from the misjudgments of others, and we have been imbued with determination to use our time wisely, to cause as little pain as possible to others, to pay attention, to live and love with few regrets.

Avalanche accidents are no longer a mystery to me, but they are harder to bear. The longer I have been involved with them, the better I understand that they don't need to happen—and the more acutely I feel the pain of the friends and relatives left behind. Avalanches happen in certain places, at certain times, for particular reasons. The clues we need are almost always apparent if we know how to look for them and are willing to listen to the message. Too often, the victims themselves recognized the clues but ignored them.

At the same time, I have become less judgmental. We all have select areas of expertise. Months before the spring 1999 avalanche nightmare, I had missed a melanoma on Doug's back that was as obvious to the dermatologist who saved his life as critical indicators of snow instability are to me. Hindsight has repeatedly shown that we humans have a tendency to underestimate hazard, or to overestimate our ability to deal with it. Over the years, Doug and I have found that people with risk-taking attitudes generally filter data about potential hazard and draw unrealistically optimistic conclusions that lead them to push the fine line finer. Skiers with a "ski to die" attitude probably will. Those who are conservative by nature use the same information to justify their conservative approach. Almost any human activity involves risk, but often people don't understand the risks they are taking until they are faced with the consequences.

The dermatologist also told Doug that since the advent of good sunscreen, the incidence of skin cancer has actually increased. Thinking that they are protected, people are not decreasing their exposure to ultraviolet rays. Many outdoor recreationists arm themselves with safety talismans—avalanche beacons, radios, cell phones, and more. Though these things may make travelers feel safer, they don't generally reduce the hazard.

The thrill and challenge of risk can be seductive, and may be heightened by other factors, like competition for limited sponsorship or a craving for recognition. This is fine as long as the static doesn't become so intense that it obscures judgment. Doug and I attempt to define our goals clearly, because they influence the level of risk we are willing to assume and become the yardstick by which we judge each trip's success. For us, the increased reward of greater wildness often justifies greater exposure and thinner margins of safety. We are not averse to taking risks, but we have become increasingly discriminating.

Through intimidation and experience, we have learned something about where the edge between hazard and consequences lies. In turn, we have gained a better understanding of where to find the survivable middle. As we've become better able to handle and more comfortable with hazard, we've made a conscious decision to take a step back from its crumbly edge. We don't want to be like the carpenter who has grown so casual that forty years into his career he cuts off his finger with a table saw. We also came to understand that if we continued to push the line, the uncompromising law of probability would catch up with us.

We have long since internalized the same decision-making strategy we developed to teach backcountry travelers how to evaluate avalanche hazard. Our priority is to gather and integrate bull's-eye data that does the most to eliminate our uncertainty about our chances of success versus our chances of getting too scared or killed. To help take the subjectivity out of our "go" or "no go" decisions, we assign each critical piece of information a hazard level that can be thought of as a green, yellow, or red light. Red lights say stop, danger, a hazardous situation exists; green lights indicate the opposite. Yellow lights mean be cautious, there is potential hazard, too much uncertainty, or conditions are changing. For example, we can travel red-light terrain along exposed coasts if the bull's-eye sea and weather variables are green lights.

The ocean has taught us to build fluidity into our decision making so that we are less likely to back ourselves into dead-end channels. We travel with more food than we think we need and don't file an expected itinerary. This buys time—days and even weeks—to sit on the beach and wait for the right conditions. In Spitsbergen, where the police required us to list a return date, we added six weeks to what we thought was realistic to ensure that worries about being the subjects of a costly rescue (which we'd have to pay for) didn't force us into making bad decisions.

We, or at least I, always say that we will *try* to paddle from point A to point B rather than state the plan categorically. No self-respecting Koyukon would do otherwise. This not only leaves us more mental latitude but also makes it easier to turn around without feeling like weak-kneed failures in the eyes of the public or friends or family. Paddling exposed coasts requires being part meteorologist, part hibernating bear, part cheerleader (for when the waiting grows demoralizing), and part rabbit (for when conditions get good). My father would add "and part crazy," but I think he's wrong.

We live by our habits—they might just save us from misjudgments. Even small habits matter, like always paddling close enough together to communicate easily and tying both boats down in case we happen to be wrong about how high the tide will rise. We rely on each other and any partners to do exactly what has been promised: dependability equals safety. This principle has carried over to other facets of my life, making me a zealot about meeting deadlines and obligations and causing me to lose an inordinate amount of trust in people who fail to do the same.

We try hard not to second-guess ourselves. It is easier to know when we have made the wrong decision than to know we've made the right one, because the terrors of rough water are unequivocal feedback. Playing "could have, should have, if only" was a bad habit of mine. In our early days, it was not uncommon for us to make a "no go" decision, climb into the cozy tent, decide conditions weren't too bad, break down camp, pack the boats, and then before launching decide that it was "no go" after all. In our worst moments, we have set up and taken down the tent as many as three times without actually moving anywhere. Now, if we've made a decision based on data, we stick with it. If the data has changed, we reevaluate. Probably our most important pact is that if one of us wants to go and the other disagrees, we heed the more conservative opinion.

It seems a good sign that we return home from most trips with fewer adventure stories than before. But still my mother worries. One spring, having exhausted all conceivable questions about our contingencies for wind, rough seas, medical emergencies, bad ice conditions, and bears, she asked, "How will you know if a tsunami is coming?" All we could do was look at her truly apologetically and mumble something about fate.

In a place where distant peaks sometimes appear inverted above the horizon, where you could

walk for hours toward a hill you guessed was a mile way, where the sun rises at all points of the

compass and sometimes casts pale ghosts of itself, nothing would or could ever be certain . . .

Slowly I learned to let go. The Inupiat had always moved within these eddying currents of

time, space, and light; to them insubstantiality wasn't a question, but a fact of life.

—Nick Jans, *The Last Light Breaking*

11

Searching for Open Water: Greenland

MY MOTHER has always worried about me. No matter how much I cajole and reassure her, she worries whenever we are beyond the comforting reach of telephone or mail. My father says she is exuberant the first week after I call to confirm we are still afloat, tolerable the second, irritable the third, and impossible by the fourth. I've come to realize that Doug and I don't go on trips by ourselves; our families and friends are with us, and the decisions we make ripple far beyond the shores within view. At least we only have to carry food for two.

The table didn't turn the spring of 1997, it flipped over violently, splintering into thousands of jagged pieces. I stood by my mother's head in a New York City hospital room crammed with doctors and nurses and crash carts. Hovering by the door were a dark-suited rabbi and a priest, each willing to claim domain that had purposely been left unspecified on my mother's admission forms. I had been allowed to infiltrate the room only because, at the first sign of crisis, my customary outer calm had come clanging down around me like the metal gates that protect urban storefronts.

Mom's eyes were rolling, like rudderless boats on a sea of fear. She didn't yet understand that she couldn't talk because she had a breathing tube jammed down her throat, that she couldn't move because both her arms and legs were strapped to the bed. "It's okay, Mom. It's okay," I repeated, stroking her cool forehead, summoning a sincerity I didn't feel. In hospital vernacular, my mother had just coded. Or, as I explained to my frighteningly flushed father, who came rushing into the room, Mom had stopped breathing. The immediate cause appeared to be a pulmonary embolism—a blood clot. No one had any idea of what more serious bodily failing might have precipitated it.

So this is how it is going to go, I remember thinking when my parents had first called to tell me that my mother had cancer. The phone call came on a Thursday in late March, right before dinner. In a voice that didn't sound like her own, my mother said, "They've found a big mass in my abdomen. It is probably malignant." Only later did she disclose that the doctor had said that she had no more than three months to live.

My mother had brought me into the world, nurturing me with unflagging loyalty and kindness. Now it appeared to be my job to help her leave. Dropping everything that had seconds before been occupying me fully, I made plans to scramble east for a protracted stay. I arrived at the Anchorage airport well before departure time, bringing along the seventeen-foot blue-and-purple rowing boat Doug and I had rejected years earlier as too flimsy for Arctic trips. When asked for the number of checked bags, I casually answered "three," as if this were something I did routinely, and helpfully showed the airline agent where to attach the tags to the fiberglass boat and wooden oars taking up most of the floor space in the check-in area. "We're going to have to charge you seventy-five dollars for oversized luggage," she said apologetically, and I tried not to grin.

The ensuing weeks were a blur of discouraging choices. Which hospital? Which doctor? Pain. Surgery. Respiratory arrest. Chemotherapy. More surgery. Instinctively, I took my cue from rowing, trying to handle each new crisis a stroke at a time. Like rounding a cape, I told myself, sleepless and scared in the middle of the night. Don't think about the icy surf, the cliffs, the "what-ifs." Take it one stroke, one mile, one hour at a time. Be patient, let events evolve, take things as they come. You're not in charge. Breathe, find a rhythm, stay loose, balance the boat, keep pulling.

The five-by-three-inch memo book I carry with me to help my wandering writer's mind capture migrating ideas is the only record I have of those weeks. Scribbled on the first pages are questions for doctors, then doses of medication, followed by more questions and abbreviated answers. The anguished notes I dimly recall making in the waiting room during my mother's surgery remark that rich people get cancer. And old people. And young. Ugly. Beautiful. Nineteen floors of cancer in a single building. A turbaned, well-dressed Arab family clustered in one corner; out-side, their shining white limousines could be seen pulled up in front of the "No Standing" signs. To reach the cars, you had to penetrate clouds of cigarette smoke generated by a knot of nurses on break and patients hooked to IVs puffing just outside the main entrance. Even sheiks get cancer. And nurses who work in cancer hospitals. It was the children who reduced my mother to tears. While waiting during pre-op rounds the day before, I had stood to block her view of the bald six-year-old boy in the wheelchair. But, of course, she had seen right through me.

The surgery went better than expected, said the doctor, his

red-streaked eyes so hollowed that it looked as if he'd been wearing swim goggles. We clung to life rafts of hope. But we were foundering again by the next morning when Mom stopped breathing. Inside the intensive-care unit, it was impossible to tell night from day. We'd entered a foreign land, where people spoke in muted tones and jargon, where bodily fluids and orifices were no longer private geography, where impending tragedy seemed to have laid claim to the territory.

As my father, sisters, and I stood shifts, days went by with the usual names—Tuesday, Wednesday, Thursday, Friday—but they had more hours in them than normal. Mom, anxious to understand her new reality, scratched one-word questions on a child's sketch pad. By the weekend, she was freed from the breathing tube and we were released back upstairs to a room with plate-glass windows that were like portholes into a world of light. In my notebook, I began to make preparations for the transition back outside. There are notations about arranging for home health care, medical supplies, oxygen, and rails for the bathroom. Most encouraging, there are grocery lists and crude directions to preferred stores.

Leaving the hospital with Mom hobbled by the surgery and still riddled with cancer felt like driving an unfamiliar mountain road on a moonless night. It was an act of faith simply to keep going, to assume that the upcoming switchbacks were navigable or even that there was a road beyond the headlights. I had no choice but to focus on what lay directly ahead: making Mom less uncomfortable, fielding phone calls, taking care of only the most necessary chores.

At my mother's urging, I began to steal at least an hour every day to row. Being back aboard a boat I could control was like discovering a becalmed island in the middle of a hurricane. Some days I barely had the wherewithal to row around the corner before I collapsed against my backrest to soak in sun. On inspired mornings, Tracy Chapman in my ears, I cruised beyond *Ikky Kid*'s old haunts, about twelve miles round trip to a lighthouse named Execution Rock. During the American Revolution, the British were rumored to have tied rebel soldiers to the gray, sloping granite below tideline there. At least, I thought, the soldiers would have known their fate as they waited for the ocean to rise around them. The moments of glide on those long rows—the instant after the oars had left the water and before the boat began to decelerate—were tremendously calming. In those moments, I had nothing to do but be.

Sometimes, as I launched, a shadow by the window of my parents' bedroom betrayed that my mother was standing in her nightgown watching me leave. I would take a few extra seconds to center myself, making sure that my first strokes were especially elegant and strong. "It only took you four strokes to reach the island today," my mother would say with pride when I returned, and I'd know that my wake of hope had reached her.

The trip to Greenland that Doug and I had been planning had dropped off the radar with the phone call in March. But as Mom grew stronger, her legendary powers of persuasion returned, and each day she lobbied harder for us to resurrect the trip. And so, on July 1, after a week of racing through only the most necessary logistics, we found ourselves flying from Anchorage to Kangerlussuaq, where we would begin rowing northward along Greenland's west coast.

We'd had a vague notion of spending three seasons attempting to row all of Greenland's navigable coast, which, roughly speaking, means much of the west and less than half of the very sparsely populated east coast. The rest is barricaded by ice. By the time we launched, we had dispensed with any agenda for the first summer beyond rowing as far north as possible before scrounging a place to store the boats. We bolted our boats together at the far end of Søndre Strømfjord, a long arm to the open sea, still surprised to find ourselves flanked by horned mountains and waterfalls rather than pale green hospital walls. If we'd had musical accompaniment, it would have been the triumphant score from *The Sound of Music*.

For the first few days, my body and spirit felt as though they were regenerating with every stroke. But in our haste, we'd overlooked one essential, the mental preparation that is the cornerstone of any journey. Rowing trips require a certain adjustment period to relax into a different pace, to weave a web of connectedness in surroundings much bigger than we are. Even on several-week forays, it may never happen.

The further we drew from a telephone, the greater my emotional turmoil. How could I even have contemplated such physical and mental separation? Mom would never leave me if I was so sick. My imagination stayed in New York, working overtime to concoct worst-case scenarios. On the day I knew my mother was receiving chemotherapy, I tracked the process through a six-hour time change, picturing each small step in the routine. I couldn't find a way to feel present. For ten miserable days, I was crabby, easily frustrated, unengaged. Sometimes I could hardly see for the tears that flooded without warning. Nothing Doug said could comfort me; at thirty-nine years old, I wanted my mother. Finally, we reached a tiny village where Doug stood with the boats in a sludge of seal guts, rusty chain, whiskey bottles, and dog shit while I plugged coins into a prehistoric pay phone, trying to decipher incomprehensible Greenlandic instructions. Only when I was able to confirm that all was well could I begin to be where I was.

For a connoisseur of ice, Greenland is paradise. Expecting a single three-letter word to describe sea ice along with the glacial icebergs spawned by the vast frozen sheet that covers much of Greenland's interior is like saying "flower" and assuming the word conveys an appreciation for the vast spectrum of shapes, colors, and fragrances. We thought we already knew most of what there was to know about paddling through glacial icebergs, but Greenland's colossal specimens taught us otherwise. They were different from the well-traveled sentinels that had drifted from Greenland all the way to Labrador, where they'd first cast a spell of enchantment over me in 1979. Bathed in light and color, their shapes were a carnival for the imagination. We saw dripping ice-cream cones, walled fortresses with arched doorways, three-masted schooners, old-fashioned radiators, and spectacularly smooth luge runs. Sometimes, we'd see one-eyed dragons, with fluted feathers and spiked topknots. They boomed when they calved, and growled as the water slopped against their emerald-green cantilevered edges.

Our Greenland trips will always be linked with my mother's cancer, and not just because of the timing. Attempting to row in water that is mostly frozen is an exercise in humility, a study in the limits of human vulnerability, patience, and desire. It is also an efficient way to brutalize the human spine.

Jakobshavns Icefjord in Disko Bay, which we reached about a month into the trip, was the highlight of the first summer. The locals call this fjord Kangia, or "ice stream." It gives unequivocal visual definition to the word *unnavigable*. Hulking ice firmly grounded in shallow water and wedged against the shore blocked our route, so we landed to climb to a vantage point. At the top of a 320-foot hill, we were still looking up toward the tops of the bigger bergs. Given the rule of thumb that four-fifths of an iceberg's height and seven-eighths of its mass can lie underwater, some of these bergs would dwarf even Chicago's 1,454-foot Sears Tower. Jammed shoulder to shoulder, these giants entirely filled a fjord more than four miles wide and fifteen miles long.

The source of the ice stream is a glacier fed by the Greenland Ice Sheet. Like a down escalator on overdrive, the glacier delivers more than eighty feet of its heavily crevassed forward wall to the ocean daily. It is thought to be responsible for about a tenth of the floating ice in Greenland, calving roughly 20 million tons of ice each day—enough to supply New York City with drinking water for a year. Newly created icebergs then begin to journey out the long fjord, pushed along by nearly continual calving behind them. At the seaward end of the fjord, a former glacial moraine about 850 feet below sea level extends across the mouth, snagging the keels of the larger bergs and preventing their escape. Pressure builds behind this bottleneck as more and more ice is dumped into the fjord, relieved every few weeks when larger tides help float the blockading bergs up and over the sill. Sailing directions for this coast warn sternly that these outpourings of ice are often explosive and can be accompanied by enormous surge waves hazardous to small boaters.

I would have had difficulty fathoming how it was possible for a single glacier to be so prolific if I hadn't spent three months inside the ice sheet itself in the early 1980s. The ice sheet, a smooth, almost featureless dome, covers roughly 90 percent of the island, with so much weight that the underlying bedrock sags almost twelve hundred feet below sea level. It is the Northern Hemisphere's largest remnant of the last Ice Age, harboring tens of thousands of years of compacted snow in a mass more than 1,500 miles long, 450 miles wide, and up to 11,000 feet thick. If you've ever wondered what Vermont looked like fifteen thousand years ago, take an excursion to Greenland.

When I worked with the Greenland Ice Sheet Project, I lived in a white canvas tent in a world so flat, so white, and so lifeless that the rare sighting of a mosquito, likely a stowaway from the coast brought in on the supply plane, could become the focal point of animated dinner conversation. A quarter mile away was the program's logistical headquarters, a *Star Wars*–like radar station on stilts where I'd ski or walk for meals, showers, and ferociously competitive Ping-Pong. Each day, dressed like the Michelin Man, I'd leave the snow surface behind and descend with other scientists and technicians from the United States, Iceland, Denmark, Switzerland, and Japan into a labyrinth of tunnels built into the ice. There was a drilling chamber, an ice storage vault, and various laboratories, all connected by long hallways wallpapered with feathered crystals condensed from our accumulated breath. Our mission was to finish drilling a continuous core through the ice sheet, a project that had already taken years of effort, and to tease from the compressed layers of time a story that might hint of changes in climate and atmospheric conditions.

My work station was literally at the seventy-yard line. The old Astroturf from the University of Nebraska's football stadium had made the trip north in a C-130 cargo plane on skis to remedy the problem of slippery tunnel floors. My job, as one of the stratigraphers, was to log notable physical characteristics of each two-meter core as soon after it was extracted as possible and before precious bits of it were parceled out for further study. When the season began, the core was at 900 meters. After a hotly contested lottery to guess the date, time, and thickness at which we'd reach bedrock, we touched bottom at 2,035 meters, or 6,675 feet. That means that, over a period of months, I scrutinized roughly

113,500 centimeters of core with the same intensity with which teenagers hunt for new pimples. I was cross-eyed even before we poisoned ourselves at the celebration party by putting tiny fragments of ancient ice in our drinks, not realizing that they were tainted with drilling fluid.

How old is almost 1.4 vertical miles of ice? That's been the multi-million-dollar question. Dating of ice cores is relatively straightforward back to the limits of radiocarbon analysis, about twenty-five thousand years. Beyond that, scientists rely in part upon glacier dynamics modeling—in other words, estimates of how long it would take a piece of ice to flow from point A to point B. By conservative evaluations, the ice at the bottom of the core drilled at Dye 3 predated the last Ice Age, the Wisconsin glaciation, which began about 100,000 years ago. It could well be 130,000 years old.

For verification, reference horizons found in a core, such as highly acidic layers of volcanic origin, are correlated to those in other cores and cross-checked with historical events. When Julius Caesar died, Roman poet Virgil wrote that "the Sun felt pity for Rome, as it covered its beaming face by darkness, and the impious generation feared an eternal night." Indeed, it is probable that the skies did dim over Rome after Caesar was killed in 44 B.C., for the cores show that around 50 B.C., a major volcanic event took place somewhere in the Northern Hemisphere. Likewise, another acidity peak in the cores circa 1388 B.C. seems to represent the Thera eruption in the Aegean Sea, which exterminated the Minoan society.

In the fall of 1981, I left Greenland for England to begin graduate school. Though I was beginning to suspect there was more to life than ice bubbles, I wrote a master's thesis on ice cores as indicators of environmental change. Ice core data has been at the center of the battle about global warming—with scientists using the same data, showing dramatic fluctuations in temperature and carbon dioxide levels, to vigorously refute or support the theory that human activities are resulting in climate change. Whatever its causes and long-term significance, it is indisputable that much of the Arctic and sub-Arctic has warmed by about 5°F in the last thirty years, compared to a global average of 1°F over the past century. Most Northern Hemisphere glaciers are in rapid retreat. Doug and I had heard that Greenland's tidewater glaciers were dumping ice at dramatic rates, contributing to a rise in worldwide sea levels. Standing on the hill at the south side of Jakobshavns Icefjord trying to plot a route north, we needed no convincing.

The only option was to skirt the outside of the submerged moraine blocking the ice stream. That meant rowing more than ten miles to make a six-mile crossing and praying that the light offshore breeze wouldn't intensify. Whether this route was doable depended too much on luck for our comfort. We would have to squeeze between bergs bigger than aircraft carriers, knowing that, inviting as they appear, etched into cerulean sky and mirrored on still water, to come much closer than three times their height is potentially suicidal. When we didn't have a choice, we'd play Russian roulette, stealing by them one at a time, rowing as fast as we could through their cold, dark shadows.

It doesn't take two avalanche consultants to deduce that leaning towers of ice are likely to peel off, but we'd also routinely witnessed square, seemingly stable bergs roll and cleave apart without warning. When this happened, a wall of water laced with ice would explode outward, traveling hundreds of feet in seconds, creating a devastating wave for small boaters unfortunate enough to be too close. This wave would sometimes climb thirty or forty feet up the sides of adjacent bergs, inciting them to roll and break, filling the water with newly created bergy bits crackling so loudly that they sounded like fire. To date, we'd been in deep water and far enough away so that by the time the wave reached us, it had mellowed to a heaving swell.

We needed no urging to keep our distance from the big bergs, but often it was impossible to know what lay under their proverbial tips. Once, we'd thought we were a conservative quarter mile from a nondescript berg when it calved from an unseen underwater shelf less than half that distance from us. From still water, a missile with a rounded nose cone the size of a grain elevator rocketed at least two hundred feet into the air before raining fragments back into the ocean.

We rowed around the blockade at the mouth of Kangia as though we were sneaking around a yard full of hungry, snarling guard dogs, but there was no attack. When we reached Illulisat, the village on the north shore, two plain wooden coffins were quietly being loaded into a truck. Two Greenlandic fishermen had been knocked out of their skiff and drowned by the surge wave from a self-destructing berg a couple days before.

By mid-August, it was time to return to New York, where my mother would be undergoing more surgery. After 750 miles of rowing, we let the ruckus of hundreds of barking dogs guide us through dense fog into Uummannaq, a picturesque village of small houses clinging to an island of sheer rock where we hoped to stash the boats so that we could continue north the following year. Earlier in the summer, I had left a message to that effect for a woman who had taken a kayaking workshop from us seven years before when she was an exchange student in Fairbanks. The irony of white people teaching a Greenlander to kayak in Alaska was not lost on any of us. Laila had returned to become Greenland's first woman helicopter pilot, and we wondered if it was she who had buzzed overhead in a big Sikorsky as we bounced through choppy seas early in the trip. (We hadn't wanted to wave too energetically lest it was a stranger who might think us in need of rescue.)

It turned out it had been Laila, and she'd even written a response that never caught up with us. But less than five minutes after we arrived in Uummannaq, while we were unloading our gear in the rain, a Toyota Land Cruiser pulled up and its driver walked toward us. He extended his hand and introduced himself as Peter Fleischer, Laila's father. In good English, he said that he didn't speak much English, but that his son would be along in a few minutes. He had a place for us to keep our boats and asked us to be guests at his house. When we asked him how he had known of our arrival, he answered, "I think the word in English is *spies*."

We had some misgivings about committing ourselves to return to Greenland. In forty days, we had seen country as beautiful as any that exists. But for each fiery red slope, dark basalt cliff, and pure white ice tower, there was a shocking display of human waste. Garbage spilled out of the villages and drifted into almost every remote corner, breaking the magic of even the quietest cove. We came to dread landing because we knew it meant breaching the flotsam line of plastic containers, bottles, sanitary pads, diapers, and the bright yellow "honey bucket" bags once containing human excrement that were so ubiquitous that they could double as Greenland's national flower. How could Greenland's meager population—fewer than sixty thousand souls—generate so much rubbish? With the pressure of tourism, this is beginning to change. Destination towns like Uummannaq are relatively clean; the biggest problem stems from the smaller villages, with less European influence and a Native culture more accustomed to biodegradable refuse than to the permanence of plastic. In deciding to continue the following summer, we reasoned that the coast must be more pristine to the north, where villages are more widely scattered.

My mother's surgery went well, and she began another round of chemotherapy. In October, I resumed life in Anchorage, though Mom and I talked by phone two or three times a day. By November, she felt well enough to travel, something she'd thought she would never do again. Wearing a wig and taking frequent naps, she helped Dad uphold a tradition, taking a grandchild to London. By December, her hair had begun to grow back in a duckling's fuzz. She was heartened by her returning strength, but she says it is impossible to be confident that you will truly be healthy again once you have been so ill. She describes a special wariness that makes it difficult to take even the smallest things for granted.

In May, the whole family gathered in Nantucket to celebrate her seventieth birthday, and in June, Doug and I flew back to Uummannaq by helicopter, because it was too early in the season for ships to navigate the north Greenland coast. Some people might have thought that a clue, but we were pleased just to see patches of open water in the fjord. Our plan was to unearth our boats from the basement where they'd overwintered, spend a few days patching the iceberg dents from the summer before, and then work our way north as we could, when we could. There was no hurry; we relished the unscheduled time, and it was pointless to arrive at the edge of Melville Bay, the ice rower's equivalent of Mount Everest, much before August 1. We weren't sure how committed we were to pushing through to the north side of the bay where we could return from Thule, the U.S. air base, but thought we would take a look.

Melville Bay is not really a bay at all, just a broad bight on the northwest coast that scoops inland. There are villages on its fringes, but most of its shore is uninhabited. The maps are daunting. More than a hundred miles of coastline is essentially tide-water glacier, broken only occasionally by nubbins of recently exposed land. Over the ice sheet, the map says *Ikke Opmalt*, which means "unexplored." Melville Bay is often plugged by both sea ice and a prodigious amount of glacier ice. It has a notorious history as a wrecking yard for boats. In 1830, so many whalers and sealers were crushed by ice there that at one point almost a thousand men were camped on the frozen sea. Out of three summers, its inshore waters might be navigable one summer—or none at all.

A mere few degrees Fahrenheit separate an ocean we can paddle on from one that stops us in our tracks. Saltwater begins to freeze at just over 28°F. It progresses from a stew of individual crystals to thicker slush, to a bendable layer that, when it thickens and whitens, is called first-year ice. Any ice that survives a summer of melt, in the process becoming bluer, denser, and less salty, is known as multiyear ice. Typically, this ice thickens to ten or twelve feet. More generally, any sea ice not fixed to the land is termed pack ice. Sometimes a band of reflected grayish-white light on the horizon, a shimmering mirage called ice blink, betrays the presence of sea ice before it can be seen.

Pieces of pack ice, called pans or floes, move in response to wind, though to frustrated small boaters they often appear to be going nowhere. In contrast, glacier icebergs, which are essentially large centerboards, are driven primarily by current. For us, the biggest difference between glacier and pack ice was that we could sometimes stand, walk, or even camp on the latter, though that might well mean ending up somewhere we hadn't intended to go.

Only a few days out of Uummannaq, our bodies were tired. It felt as if there were a balled fist in the small of my back, and my wrist and elbows were strained. My stomach muscles hadn't yet readjusted to doing the equivalent of thousands of sit-ups a day. If I focused on it, I could feel my pulse in the blood-filled blisters of my right hand. The fjord we needed to cross was still mostly ice-covered; in our search for liquid water we'd been forced further out of the widening bay than we liked. From camp, we climbed a ridge to scout across to a large island named Illorsuit. We'd have to weave through tightly packed floes studded with supertanker bergs for the first few miles, but then it appeared to be mostly open water.

A twenty-two-mile Arctic crossing is no joke, particularly at the beginning of a trip, when our boats are heavy and our bodies unhoned. If all went well, it would take at least five or six hours. We prepared like warriors—packing extra snack food into the cockpits, monitoring the weather for the slightest whisper of unrest, taking more time than usual for our ritual goodbye kiss, tugging on our bike gloves—before pushing off at 6:15 in the evening. June is the season of the midnight sun, so daylight was not a problem, and our internal clocks were still in international traveler's limbo. I tried not to pay much attention to the pit in my stomach.

Weaving through the ice near shore was fun. More perfect water for rowing has yet to be invented. It was creamy, with mystical lighting and gemlike refractions. Icebergs emerged from low-hanging tongues of fog, backlit and majestic. It took more than forty-five minutes to row out to our first landmark, a turreted glacial iceberg the size of the Tower of London, which was further offshore than we'd guessed. Clearly, it would require time to remember the measure of this country. Reaching much thicker pack ice, we wiggled right and left through connecting leads of open water, looking over our shoulders on almost every stroke. I felt strong and confident—if there were an Olympic ice-rowing competition, this could have been my moment of glory.

The ice eased into smaller bits, the air came alive with the bergy seltzer hiss of melting bubbles releasing ancient air. And then, open gray water. That's when the exposure hit. We were a long way from nowhere. Land was more than ten miles away in any direction, further than that in most. The wind was awakening the surface of the water, chilling one shoulder and cheek. How much stronger would it get? What were we doing out here?

I didn't let myself watch the clock too much, part of the mind-control game I've learned to play. One hour down. Go for two, I told myself. Two hours. Three hours. We should be over halfway. Okay, bring on four. Sixty minutes in an hour. Try not to look at Doug—he will look as vulnerable and tired as I am. Steer off the mountain behind us. Count snow gullies, not strokes. Make a mental photograph of the crenellated, Mongolian-looking slopes. To distract my mind from the danger, focus on flowing, on finding a rhythm, without increasing power. Think of house projects that need doing. Don't look at the waves, they're increasing and beginning to lick at the edges of my boat; don't think about my seized-up back. Make promises to whatever higher powers are out there that if we get through this, I'll never make another mistake in my life. Come up with a new song to sing, another memory to replay, someone else to think about. Shit, a cold wave just slopped in over my feet. Wiggle my toes, stay warm.

We took brief breaks, inhaled chocolate, adjusted clothing. I kept my dark glacier glasses on. Sometimes my eyes reveal too much of what I am thinking; if Doug senses my hesitations, it makes them seem more real. The weather was relatively mellow, yet I was rowing with more clothes on than normal—over two lightweight polypropylene shirts, I had on a vest, pile jacket, and a Gore-Tex parka. In the distance, I could see the heart-shaped mountain for which Uummannaq was named. The sun was painting an inland cliff pumpkin orange.

Pull past the dimpled iceberg, don't look at my watch until I reach the next one. Try to draw even with the steep ribbon of fissured glacier off to the left. At 10:48 I can see flat pack ice over my shoulder. The red cliffs of the island are definitely the closer shore now. We should reach land in maybe an hour, by 11:30. Go for the ice, keep moving. Years ago, I started reciting simple mantras in moments of need, unaware that this was common practice in Native cultures, where boatmen might chant in unison or sing to take themselves out of their bodies, escaping from physical or mental stress. My mantras don't look like much on paper, mostly one-liners like "smooth and easy," but they can keep me occupied for hours if I am tired or afraid enough.

I'm really exhausted and slowing a bit, but I still answer "fine" whenever Doug asks how I am doing, and he does the same. It occurs to me that even when my mother was very sick, she always said she was fine. I remember the nurses asking her to rate the quality of her pain on a scale from one to ten, with one being negligible pain and ten intense agony, a perfect score like in the Olympics. It all seemed so subjective. How was she supposed to know what a ten was if she hadn't tested out one through nine? How could she judge pain in isolation from fear? I try to refocus my thoughts, because there isn't much point in listening to my pain now. If I don't keep rowing, I could die. But geology and history are beyond my numbed brain. I feel like I'm playing an old record where the needle keeps getting stuck in a groove, creating a hum of static. Neither Doug nor I have energy for much conversation. Breaks are for eating, lying back against my clothes bag, and slipping the seat under my hamstrings to allow my broken butt to decompress.

We draw nearer to the ice. Damn, it is solid, cutting us off four or five miles from shore. We are like cornered rats in a maze, edging around the frozen sheet, trying to find a route, a flaw. This is a country of illusions. What looks like open water is ice. And some-times the opposite. But now, the shoreline in every direction appears rimmed by ice. We are cold, in a bad spot, trapped. If I let myself, I could be very scared. But whining no longer gets me anywhere, so I don't waste energy. I am too preoccupied to moni-tor time. An ominous grinding, a low rumble really, comes from the direction of Uummannaq. Is it moving ice? Deteriorating weather? I long for quiet.

Midnight. Still no route. Why do we do this to ourselves? Part of me thinks we should head back across the fjord, but this is too grim an option to contemplate. It would take at least four hours. Doug says he is too spent, and he is worried about the building wind. We could camp on the ice, but this is risky given the wind direction. We could wake up far out to sea, on our way to Canada. I explore a branch of lead perpendicular to the one we've been following. I row a little ways up it, then a little further, standing up in my boat trying to see if it is viable, willing it to let us through. Doug joins me. Resting our oars on deck, we pry with ski poles through increasingly narrow, irregular passages until we are only a couple hundred yards from the next major lead. Doug rams his bow up on the ice and steps out. I don't want to be there. The ice looks thin, with puddles all over it—I keep expecting Doug to plunge through to a quick, gasping death. Confident that the ice is sufficiently strong, he draws on his ice-jumping days as a boy, probing the surface ahead with a spare canoe paddle. Two plates of wind-driven ice collide, and the edges near us begin to grind upward into a small pressure ridge. Floating, I am in the way. Our channel has closed behind us. Reluctantly, I "land."

We push, pull, slide the boats across rough ice. Eventually, I become more comfortable. My legs stop jackhammering. I take Doug's mantras for my own: "Step on white ice only, move fluidly, don't stand in one place, pretend you are walking on rice paper."

One boat, then the next, we leapfrog toward open water. It would be fun, if only we could stop playing the game whenever we want.

What looked like a small lead turns out to be a big expanse of water. It is now a straight shot to the island, but the shore is slow in coming. Are there really only sixty seconds in a minute? I can barely turn around now, my shoulders feel as if they have boulders embedded in them, my neck makes crepitant noises like the hinges on a rusty trunk in a haunted attic. Around three in the morning, we reach a sliver of beach and pry ourselves out of the boats. Nine hours and thirty-six minutes in transit. If we had known, we might never have started. The cliff above us produces a steady dribble of rockfall, but there is a buttress just big enough to protect our tent from all but the biggest rocks—as long as it doesn't rain. Though marginal, it is a haven compared to where we have been. We limp through the familiar routine of making camp and abandon ourselves to sleep.

Pack ice can look deceptively unchanging. In north Greenland, at first it almost always seemed impossible that we'd be able to pick a route through, but sometimes it proved easier than we thought. When it was futile to use force because there was just too much ice, we might settle in, expecting to wait for weeks—only to find that a lead had opened overnight. When we had to sit for an unknown period of time, listening to the ice melt drop by drop, my moods swung like a barometer. I loved all the unexpected sunshine; I wished for a storm. I watched, with a sense of privilege, the arrival of Canada geese, Arctic terns, snow buntings, and storm petrels; I wondered why we didn't take normal vacations. I was happy to have such a stalwart partner; I found Doug annoying. I was enjoying my book; I was sick of lying around reading. I'd decide I was wasting my life on a beach in the middle of nowhere, and then it would occur to me that this was my life and I was pretty happy with it.

By late July, we had grunted, snuck, and dragged our way through more than five hundred miles of ice. Our oars, which normally I am fastidious about, looked like they'd been chewed by beavers. Doug's boat, especially, had some mean gashes. There was still an offensive amount of garbage on the beaches. Out of range of most tourists, some of the smaller villages were like garbage dumps with gooey paths and houses plopped in the middle of them. I stood on the stairs of one house and took stock of what lay in the muck five feet around me. Besides the usual plastic containers, sanitary items, soggy cardboard, bottles, congealed seal innards, and oil cans, there were old shoes, ripped fishing nets, broken kitchen utensils, snowmachine parts, and a one-legged chair spewing its stuffing. Pretty much anything broken, used, or not needed had been heaved immediately out the door, onto a modern-day midden. A doctor later told us that in one village, almost all of the 144 residents had contracted hepatitis at the same time.

Leaving Kullorsuaq—despite a bad reputation, a relatively clean village compared to recent stops—we edged into Melville Bay. We managed to reach 75°N before being blocked by ice that clearly would not let us go any further. This was country for ice-breakers, not rowing boats. The view from the tallest hill on Red Head, the island where we were camped, was chilling—pun intended. An up-to-date ice map would have plotted the concentration at ten-tenths, a solid mash of broken pack ice studded with enormous icebergs. Give us a little water—with ice filling only seven- or eight-tenths of the available surface area—and we might have been able to bash our way through it, as we had been doing for weeks. But here there was too much glacier ice in the mix to let us even think about hauling. Some of the icebergs, more like island massifs, were four miles long and hundreds of feet high. Our predicament lent credibility to the U.S. Navy adage "Only a fool would travel north of the Arctic Circle clad in anything less than a nuclear submarine."

Though keenly aware of Melville Bay's legacy of wrecked boats and human suffering, for us there was no hardship yet. I gave Doug a lecture on staying patient—let a week or two go by, I said—then felt myself going crazy after a few hours. Waiting for conditions to change was slow, hard work. We longed for a gale to blow the ice offshore, but day after day, the weather was surrealistically placid and warm. From the tent I heard an iceberg explode, startling eider ducks into flight, their beating wings like applause. We played pretend golf with ski-pole clubs in a volcanic-red pebble field and inserted our heads into holes in wind-battered rocks. We inventoried the garbage and the graffiti carved in the slow-growing black lichen on rock ledges. Gambling was fair game—we were quick to place fifteen-minute backrub bets on when the fog was going to roll in over our tent or whether the obelisk iceberg was going to ram the one with the doughnut hole.

Our claim to a record number of ascents of the 862-foot hill on Red Head in a single season went undisputed, since there was not another soul around. One afternoon, the view from the summit looked uncharacteristically encouraging. Then we realized that what we thought was a patch of open water was a smothering layer of fog. We rowed around Red Head, changing camps every few days for sanity's sake. One evening, we heard a glacier four miles away vomit ice continuously for five minutes. The surge wave arrived after ten minutes, and even this far away, it was seven feet high. Nineteen minutes later, the surge was still sucking at the rock ramp where we had run to make sure our boats were pulled out of reach.

In a place where the mark of geologic time is everywhere, one day is nothing. A hike, a book, a nap, another hike, three meals, some snacks, lots of mosquitoes. After fifteen days, long enough for the calluses on our hands to soften and peel, the ice looked no different. I will never have the patience of geologic time.

Before my mother's cancer, I think we would have tried to muscle across Melville Bay as we'd done elsewhere. Inshore, closer to the glaciers that were so prolifically shedding ice, there was no route. We might have been able to hop between the flat, bare rock islands that lay about fifteen miles offshore and about the same distance apart. The margin of safety would have been much thinner than the ice, with great risk of us getting blown out to sea with the pack ice or finding ourselves locked in limbo, unable either to advance to the north or to retreat to the south.

But Mom's remission has been an unexpected lead of open water—not only for her but for us. It reminded us that we had a limited number of miles in our bones, and we wanted to expend them selectively. In Melville Bay, we began to talk about leaving Greenland and not returning. We had to stop hoping that it would be something it was not. Greenland is beautiful, with dramatic mountains and a landscape of power, but it is not immune to the cancer that is all around us, sickening the world at large. There are few animals and far too much shoreline trash. On Red Head, we found ourselves trying to weigh the risk and the bodily torture against the rewards of continuing. After hours of discussion, we decided to turn around.

It was not an easy decision, but once we made it, we felt as if a tumor of doubt had been removed and we were pounds lighter. As we rowed south, the ice eased, and once again the days became more than hours to count. Inevitably, I began to second-guess our decision. Maybe we should have waited longer. Maybe the ice wasn't that bad. It is easy to take open water for granted and forget how vulnerable we really are.

Why is it that turning around always seems like a failure and death takes us by surprise? Though it has been far from my favorite lesson, Nature has taught me that in my life I must accommodate aging and death. I find myself creating landmarks against the day my parents are no longer here as anything but a part of my being. I can't seem to erase their voices from our answering machine without first recording them onto another tape. Death is one of the few certainties in life. To my surprise, I'm finding that accepting it offers some degree of liberation. If I don't exhaust my energy trying to control what I cannot, I am left with more time to live as I choose.

On the jet home from Svalbard in 1996, we flew over a section of the north Greenland coast that was remarkably ice-free. With our sights already set on rowing Greenland the next summer, Doug asked the Swedish steward if he could find out the names of the tantalizing fjords below us. The steward obligingly went to check with the crew in the cockpit, but he returned after only a minute or two. He announced, with the solemnity of an undertaker, "The captain, he does not know where we are." Doug and I laughed so hard that even the staid steward eventually lost his composure. Holding hands, we laughed until we cried. Then, still holding hands, we sat back to enjoy the view.

Acknowledgments

ONE OF MY FAVORITE children's stories is Holling Clancy Holling's *Paddle-to-the-Sea*, a book I rediscovered after more than two decades, when my future husband pulled out his own cherished, tattered copy. In the book, a canoe and paddler carved by an Indian boy out of a small piece of pine are helped from the headwaters of the Great Lakes all the way to the Atlantic Ocean by a cast of unlikely characters. Since my first reading, I've undertaken my own share of long boat journeys, but none of them, including those that had me dragging boats across Arctic ice or crashing in through mountainous surf, have felt as ruggedly impossible as writing did at times. This book was brought to the moment of launch by the vital help of family and friends—both new and old.

Thanks to my agent, Julie Rubenstein of Linda Chester Agency, for finding me a safe harbor at North Point Press/Farrar,

Straus and Giroux and introducing me to my editor, Rebecca Saletan. I am grateful for Becky's extraordinary insight, frustrating talent to see through even my most clever ruses, relentlessness in making me think, and willingness to invest so much time in a rookie. Thanks as well to her assistant, Katrin Wilde, for her gentle kindness, and to all the hidden hands that have guided this manuscript to completion.

This might be the only paragraph in this book that my friend Natalie Phillips hasn't read. We've been through the three C's—childbirth, cancer, and chapter revisions—together. She worried that I might hate her for her honesty (and sometimes I did), but I remain awed by her wisdom, grace, and faith. Alaska is so far from anywhere that friends become family. In addition to Natalie, I owe huge hugs to my other Alaskan sisters—Nan Elliot, Janis Fleischman, Jennifer Johnston, and Ellen Toll. And since I never had a brother, I'll claim Mike Davidson for his contagious optimism. I am also appreciative of Lewis Schnaper's discerning eye as a reader. Throughout the process of creating this book, I turned for advice or information to many I didn't know, including Edward Burlingame and Kate Kelly Schweitzer, and always found it willingly given.

Thanks to Gunnar and Alice Knapp for providing a cabin in the woods, and to Michelle and Michael O'Leary for lending me their wildlife-rich retreat by the sea. Both were places of little distraction and great inspiration. Bodie the boat dog deserves extra treats for keeping me loyal company and swiping my hands off the keyboard, reminding me daily when it was time to go for a hike or a row.

And then there are my father and my mother, Arthur and Elinor Fredston. It is not possible for me to feel luckier in having parents who so exemplify the essence of life. I am also beholden to my sisters—Susan Fredston-Hermann and Dale Fredston—

and their families; my brother-in-law Jon Bullard did everything short of installing a hot line next to his bed to handle my computer emergencies. From the bottom of my wicked stepmother's heart, I thank Lahde, Sunna, and Turi Fesler for their enthusiasm and caring.

If I thanked everyone who has made our journeys possible, safer, or more enjoyable, these acknowledgments could easily be longer than the book itself. I take a deep bow to all of you. Special thanks are due Lars Christiansen, Robert Dearsley, Erik and Gerd Hestnes, Monica Kristensen Solås, Ole and Anne Kristiansen, and the families of John Haugen, Krister Kristensen, and Ronald Toppe in Norway; Sarah Webb in Labrador; and Earl Ramsey and the Fleischer family in Greenland. I am indebted to Anders Björck of Scandinavian Airlines Systems for huge logistical help, to Gary Piantedosi for building rowing frames that have kept us rolling smoothly, and to Mike Neckar and the late Arthur Martin for going the extra mile in designing boats that have kept us afloat.

I have saved the last acknowledgment for my husband, Doug Fesler. Without him, I cannot imagine the journeys. With him, I am often flooded by the same sensation I get rowing across a calm fjord on a sunny day, when my boat is flying and my mind is in my heart.